CHARLES F. BOWMAN

Algorithms and Data Structures

AN APPROACH IN

SAUNDERS COLLEGE PUBLISHING

Harcourt Brace College Publishers

Fort Worth Philadelphia San Diego New York Orlando Austin San Antonio Toronto Montreal London Sydney Tokyo

Text Typefaces: Caslon, Univers, Courier Bold
Compositor: Monotype Composition
Acquisitions Editor: Emily Barrosse
Managing Editor: Carol Field
Project Editor: Anne Gibby
Copy Editor: Patricia M. Daly
Manager of Art and Design: Carol Bleistine
Art Director: Jennifer Dunn
Text Designer: Tracy Baldwin
Cover Designer: Jennifer Dunn
Text Artwork: Grafcon
Director of EDP: Tim Frelick
Production Manager: Joanne Cassetti
Marketing Manager: Monica Wilson

Printed in the United States of America

Algorithms and Data Structures: An Approach in C

ISBN: 0-03-096702-3

Library of Congress Catalog Card Number: 93-086197

3456   042   987654321

For Mom

Preface

This book instructs readers on the science of developing and analyzing algorithms. It is intended for use in a one- or two-semester undergraduate course in data structures.

The text focuses on both the theoretical and practical aspects of algorithm development. It discusses problem-solving techniques and introduces the concepts of data abstraction and algorithm efficiency. More important, it does not present algorithms in a shopping-list format. Rather, the book tries to provide actual insight into the design process itself.

The book also has a practical bent. Most of the algorithms are of general use, and there is a strong emphasis placed on "real world" programming requirements. As a result of this unique approach, and the fact that all algorithms are presented in the C programming language, the book should prove useful to professional programmers as well.

ORGANIZATION

Chapter 1 introduces algorithmic analysis and discusses the motivations for its study. Although the book is not intended as a tutorial on C (see below), this chapter does provide a brief introduction to the C programming environment. Readers already familiar with this material may omit sections 1.5 and 1.6. Readers who wish a more thorough examination of the language are referred to Appendix B.

Chapter 2 discusses the various phases of algorithm design and introduces the concept of *complexity*. Static data structures are presented in Chapter 3. This is followed by a detailed explanation of *recursion* in Chapter 4. Chapter 5 follows with discussion of dynamic data structures.

Many of the algorithms presented in Chapter 3 are reimplemented using the techniques discussed in this chapter.

In Chapters 6 and 7, we discuss two of the more important abstractions found in computer science: *trees* and *graphs*. The chapters include many practical examples. In Chapter 8 we discuss searching techniques and finish with a discussion of sorting techniques in Chapter 9.

The exercises appearing at the end of each chapter are also an integral part of this text. They reinforce the concepts presented in each section and often introduce new material as well.

IMPLEMENTATION NOTES

All texts of this nature require a "host" language to serve as a vehicle for algorithm presentation. Authors of similar books have used languages ranging from assembler to *pseudo-code*. We decided that C was the best choice for this text for several reasons:

- It is an excellent vehicle for expressing algorithmic ideas.
- It is widely available. Most readers of this text will have access to a C compiler at school, work, or home.
- It has become the language of choice in many professional and academic institutions.
- Programmers familiar with other structured programming languages will readily understand the C programs presented in this book.

A note about this last item. The intent of this book is to teach algorithm design; it is not intended to serve as a tutorial introduction to the C programming language. Thus, experienced C programmers will note several instances where program segments could be expressed more succinctly using some of the more advanced features of C. In all such cases, however, cleverness gave way to clarity. The justification for this approach is two-fold:
- Syntax should not impede understanding.
- Experienced C programmers can easily re-code the algorithms with minimal effort.

Moreover, to ensure that language syntax is not an obstacle to learning, we have included the following features in the text:

- Whenever appropriate, there are thorough explanations of C-specific features.
- Chapter 1 includes an introduction to the C programming environment.
- Appendix B provides a more detailed introduction of C for programmers.

All the programs and code fragments contained herein have been compiled by the author using ANSI C compilers running under several operating systems. All program listings are—for the most part—self-contained. As a result, readers should have little difficulty transcribing them to their local environments.

ACKNOWLEDGMENTS

Although only one name appears on the cover, a project of this magnitude is by no means a solo effort. Publishing a book requires the help of many dedicated professionals, with a number of specialized talents. I would to thank all the wonderful people at Saunders College Publishing for their efforts and suggestions: Michelle Slavin, Editorial Assistant; Anne Gibby, Project Editor; and Jennifer Dunn, Art Director. They all worked tirelessly to make this project a success.

I would like to extend a special thank you to Richard Bonacci, Senior Editor, for signing the book and for his continued patience and guidance through its completion—even when it was no longer his job; and to Emily Barrosse, Executive Editor, for her ability to take on a project midstream without missing a beat. It was an honor and a pleasure to have worked with both of them.

Also, during development, a manuscript undergoes many reviews and critiques. I would like to thank Teresa Alice Hommel, Accuracy Reviewer, and all the other reviewers for their advice and suggestions:

Eric P. Bloom
Marcus Brown, University of Alabama
Michael R. Elliot, Rancho Santiago College
Peter Falley, Fairleigh Dickinson University

Robert M. Holloway, University of Wisconsin
Erich Kaltofen, Rensselaer
Danny Kopec, University of Maine
Linda Lesniak, Drew University
Tim McGuire, Texas A&M University
M. Andrew Moshier, University of California, Los Angeles
James F. Peters, Kansas State University
Arunabha Sen, Arizona State University
Bill Walker, East Central University

This text would not have been possible without their efforts.

I would also like to thank my wife Florence and my children, Charles, Michael, and Nicole, for their patience and understanding during the many long hours that I sat, seemingly transfixed, in front of my computer. Ironically, prior to having completed this manuscript, I had always thought it somewhat *pro forma* that authors always thanked their spouses for *all their help*. How wrong I was. I can honestly say that, without my wife's assistance, this book would never have been published. She chided me when I got lazy, consoled me when I got discouraged, and took upon herself many of life's mundane and thankless tasks to afford me time to write. There is no way, no words, to express my love and gratitude. The best I can offer is Thank You, Florence.

Charles Bowman
Suffern, New York
November 1993

Contents

Introduction

CHAPTER

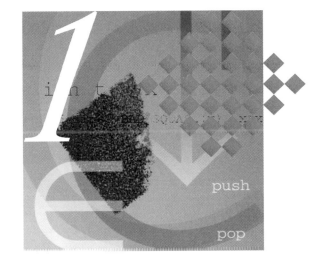

1.1 OVERVIEW

Throughout their careers, programmers are continually asked to decide whether a given problem has a computer-based solution. An affirmative answer implies that the problem is *algorithmically* solvable. That is, if we permit the program to execute long enough, and provide it with all the necessary computing resources, it will produce the desired result.

A simple yes is not sufficient, however. Decisions regarding computability must be considered in a practical perspective. For example, consider writing a computer program to play chess. We could design the program such that it would select its next move by examining every possible option for every possible board position. Is this theoretically possible? Yes. Is it practical? No. A program written in such a manner could require thousands of years to compute even a single move.

Therefore, within this framework of practicality, let's informally define an algorithm as a series of instructions that, if followed exactly, will accomplish a desired task in a finite (acceptable) amount of time. For example, refer to the **power()** function presented in Listing 1.1.

```
/*
 *  Raise X to the power Y
 */
int power( int x, int y )
{
   int i, ret;

   i = 0;
   ret = 1;
   while( i < y )
   {
        ret = ret * x;
        i = i + 1;
   }
   return( ret );
}
```

Listing 1.1
Power function.

The function **power()** accepts two arguments: a base (x) and an exponent (y), and it returns the result of raising x to the y power. It is a useful function and is provided (in some form) with most language systems. As presented here, it qualifies as an algorithm under our informal definition in that it will compute the desired value in an acceptable period of time. (This particular implementation has several shortcomings, however. Consider what would happen if we invoked the function with a y argument equal to -1. As a rule, functions and/or programs should behave intelligently when presented with erroneous data. We will be stressing this point throughout this text.)

In computer science, an algorithm is a problem-solving technique suitable for implementation as a computer program. Specifically, an algorithm is a finite set of instructions which, if followed exactly, will accomplish a particular task. Additionally, algorithms must satisfy the following criteria:

- Each instruction contained in the algorithm must be clear, concise, and sufficiently basic that we can (at least in theory) accomplish it manually.

- In all cases, the algorithm terminates after executing some finite number of instructions (the actual number may vary with each execution).
- The algorithm accomplishes at least one task and/or produces (computes) at least one value.

One last point: As stated earlier, an algorithm is a problem-solving technique *suitable* for implementation as a computer program. That is, an algorithm is not tied to its implementation. For example, consider the task of writing a program that yields the sum of the integers from 1 to *n*. One way to express this task algorithmically might be as follows:

Step 1   Initialize a counter to the value 1.

Step 2   Add to an accumulator variable the value contained in the counter; then increment the counter by 1.

Step 3   Repeat step 2 until the counter becomes greater than *n*.

Now consider the two functions presented in Listing 1.2. Both `sum1()` and `sum2()` achieve the result stipulated in the algorithm. Yet their implementations vary dramatically. Moreover, even without benefit of formal analysis, it should be clear that `sum2()` is more efficient than its counterpart. Indeed, there will be many occasions when we will be confronted with just such a choice. One of the goals of this text is to provide the insight necessary to allow the reader to make such a selection.

1.2 WHY STUDY ALGORITHMS?

Algorithms are at the heart of computer science. Much of the early work in the field was directed toward identifying the types and classes of problems that could be solved algorithmically. We refer to this subject as *computability theory*, and it is deserving of study in its own right. In contrast, this text will focus on analyzing individual algorithms designed to solve specific problems. In doing so, we will identify and discuss the key programming concepts associated with each algorithm so they may be reapplied in other programs.

Most of the algorithms presented in this text employ complex forms of data organization. These objects, called *data structures*, are central to the study of algorithms. An algorithm and its associated data struc-

```
sum1( int n)
{
    int i;
     int result;

      i = 1;
      result = 0;
      while( i <= n )
      {
          result = result + i;
              i = i + 1;
      }
      return( result );
}
sum2( int n )
{
    int result;

     result = n*(n+1)/2;

      return( result );
}
```

Listing 1.2
Two functions that
sum integers.

ture are so closely linked that a modification to one will usually precipitate a change in the other. Because of this high degree of interdependence, we will discuss both as a single unit.

Data Abstraction

It is often convenient to view an algorithm and its data structure solely in terms of the operations they support. We refer to this as an *abstract data type*. Abstract data types allow programmers to *think* in terms of the abstraction, without being concerned with implementation details. Data abstraction is more common than one might think. For example, consider the use of floating-point (real) numbers in a computer program. Programmers think in terms of adding or subtracting them. At the machine level, however, they are processed (algorithms) and stored (data structures) in a different manner.

As implied earlier, abstract data types support both a *public interface* and a *private implementation*. The public interface is the abstraction. For those programmers using an abstract data type (often referred to as *clients*), the public interface defines both the abstraction and the range of permissible operations. For example, consider once again our floating-point number example. Its public interface allows us to use real numbers in ways that seem natural to use: We can add them, subtract them, etc. In addition, the public interface does not support other operations, such as *concatenation*, that are not associated with floating numbers.

We implement abstract data types using algorithms and hidden state data (i.e., data structures). Specific details of the implementation should remain private. That is, clients should only be able to manipulate and modify an abstract data type through the proper use of its operator set (i.e., the public interface). We refer to this property as *encapsulation*. The degree to which we can enforce encapsulation is, to a large extent, based on the language we are coding in. Nonetheless, enforcement of encapsulation rules provides us with a number of benefits, including the following:

Maintainability   We can modify the implementation of an abstract data type without affecting client programs. That is, if we do not alter the public interface, then any changes we apply to the private implementation will not affect *well-behaved* client programs. A well-behaved client program is one that, either through prescription or convention, does not circumvent the public interface.

Modularity   By maintaining a private implementation, we can minimize the *ripple* effect of software modifications. That is, if the modified code remains isolated, the changes are less likely to affect other, non-related sections of the application.

Extendibility   We can construct new abstractions based on existing types. For example, we could extend the floating-point abstraction to create abstractions for *complex* and *imaginary* numbers.

Throughout this text, we will show, by example, how to write well-constructed abstract data types.

1.3 WHY C?

Every text of this nature requires the use of a host language as a
vehicle for the presentation of algorithms. Other books on this subject
employ languages ranging from assembler to *pseudo-code*. Here are
some of the reasons why we selected C for use in this text:

- C is an excellent vehicle for expressing algorithmic ideas.
- Its use is widespread, and it has become the language of choice
  in many installations.
- Because of its broad availability (from PC to mainframe), many
  readers of this text will be able to compile and execute the
  examples exactly as they appear in the listings.
- Programmers familiar with other structured languages can readily
  understand its flow-control constructs.

1.4 CODING STYLE

We made every effort to ensure that each program listing is clear and
unambiguous. Also, to avoid confusion, a consistent coding style
was maintained throughout the text.

For the most part, program listings are complete and self-
contained. In some cases, however, a later listing may assume some
declarations and/or definitions included in a previous example. All such
occurrences are noted in the accompanying text.

We could simplify some of the algorithms presented in this text—
at least in terms of the number of statements needed—by using
some of the more advanced features of C. In all such cases, however,
cleverness gave way to clarity. Nevertheless, we hope that the code presented in this book will highlight the power and grace of the C programming language.

1.5 WHAT YOU NEED TO KNOW

This book is not intended to serve as a tutorial introduction to the
C programming language (the bibliography lists several instructional
texts). As noted previously, readers familiar with other structured programming languages (e.g., PASCAL) should have little (if any) difficulty

reading the program listings contained in this text. However, C does have several unique features. Thus, to ensure that syntax does not impede understanding, we have taken the following safeguards:

1. We have deliberately avoided using some of the more advanced features of C.
2. Whenever appropriate, we provide thorough explanations of any C-specific features we use.
3. We have included a section that provides a brief introduction to the C programming environment.
4. For readers who have programming experience in other structured languages (e.g., PASCAL), Appendix B provides a more detailed introduction to C for programmers.

Readers who are unfamiliar with C should complete this chapter. Readers who are already familiar with the language should proceed directly to Chapter 2.

The C Programming Environment

A complete C program consists of one or more functions, one of which must be named **main()**. Program execution begins with the first executable statement contained in this function. The source code for a C program may be partitioned into separate source files (modules) and compiled independently. After compiling, we can combine (link-edit) all the object (machine language) files to form one executable program. For example, assume that we have stored the source code for the function **power()** (Listing 1.1) in the file **power.c**. Also, assume a second source file, **test.c**, that contains the following code:

```
#include  ⟨stdio.h⟩

main()
{
    int  x;
    x = power( 2, 4 );
    printf( "X = %d\n", x );
}
```

The command

```
cc test.c power.c
```

will compile and link the two source modules and create one executable file. (The name of the resulting executable file will vary; refer to your compiler's user manual for the actual name.) When executed, the program will generate the following output:

```
X = 16
```

Note that the statement

```
#include ⟨stdio.h⟩
```

is a preprocessor directive and is discussed in the next section.

The C Preprocessor

A complete C language implementation comes supplied with a *preprocessor*. The preprocessor is a separate program (automatically invoked by the compiler) that does just what its name implies: processes C source files before passing the modified source code on to the compiler. Two of its many features are string replacement and file inclusion.

Let's begin by describing simple string substitution. If a C program contained a definition of the form

```
#define MAX_SCORES 10
```

the preprocessor would replace all unquoted occurrences of the string **MAX_SCORES** with the string **10**. We refer to **MAX_SCORES** as a *symbolic constant*. For example, consider the following code fragment.

```
#define   MAX_SCORES        10

main()
{
    int  i;
    int  total[ MAX_SCORES ];

         .
         .
         .
```

```
        if( i >= MAX_SCORES )

                .
                .
                .

}
```

After preprocessing, the statements would be presented to the compiler as

```
main()
{
        int   i;
        int   total[ 10 ];

                .
                .
                .

        if( i >= 10 )

                .
                .
                .

}
```

This is an extremely useful facility. Not only does it make the code easier to read, but it also simplifies program maintenance. For example, if the maximum number of scores changed from 10 to 15, we would make only one change to our program and the preprocessor would take care of the rest. However, if we wrote the foregoing program without using a symbolic constant, we would have to modify the source code in at least two places. We strongly encourage the use of symbolic constants in C programs.

The preprocessor also allows symbolic constants to accept arguments. These are usually called *macros*. For example, we could create the following definition:

```
#define SQUARE(x) ((x)*(x))
```

The expansion of **SQUARE()** is now dependent on its use: The statement

```
z = SQUARE(y);
```

will be expanded to

```
z = ((y)*(y));
```

Note that **x** serves as a place holder. That is, whatever argument we place in the x position will appear wherever **x** appears in the expansion.

The parentheses surrounding the substitution string (i.e., `((x)*(x))`) are not syntactically required. Rather, they serve to ensure correct operator evaluation. For example, consider the following definition:

```
#define BAD_SQUARE(x) x*x
```

Let's say we wanted to square the sum of two variables. We might use **BAD_SQUARE()** as follows:

```
z = BAD_SQUARE(a+b);
```

The preprocessor would expand this statement into

```
z = a+b*a+b;
```

Mathematically, the compiler would evaluate this expression as

```
z = a+(b*a)+b;
```

Obviously, this is not what we had intended. However, the same call using **SQUARE()** would expand to

```
z = ((a+b)*(a+b));
```

which does yield the desired result.

The other widely used feature of the preprocessor is the file inclusion facility. Let's assume that we wanted several related program modules to use the following set of macros:

```
#define  NO    0
#define  YES   1
#define  SIZE 100
#define  SQUARE(x) ((x)*(x))
```

One solution is to type (or copy) each macro into every program source file. However, if **SIZE** were to change to, say, 200, we would be forced to apply the same edit to many source files.

A better solution is to place all the definitions in just one file and include them as needed. We can accomplish this with the following preprocessor directive:

```
#include  "defs.h"
```

This directs the preprocessor to replace the **#include** statement with the entire contents of the file **defs.h**. The **include**d file may contain any valid C statements, including nested **#include** directives. The file name itself is arbitrary—in fact, the **.h** extension (signifying 'header' file) is only a convention.

There is another form of the **#include** directive:

```
#include  ⟨filename⟩
```

The use of the angle brackets directs the preprocessor to search a predetermined location (directory) for one of several system-supplied header files. The exact location is system dependent, and the files contain definitions of a global nature. A common example is the file **stdio.h**, which contains global definitions required by the standard input/output library.

SUMMARY

Algorithms are problem-solving techniques suitable for implementation as a computer program. They are defined as a finite sequence of instructions that accomplish a particular task. Although algorithms are usually described in terms of a specific programming language, they are, by their nature, independent of any machine or environment.

Algorithms usually employ complex forms of data organization called data structures. It can be convenient to view algorithms and their associated data structures solely in terms of the operations they support. We refer to the resulting abstraction as an abstract data type. Data abstraction can improve programmer productivity and minimize the cost of software maintenance.

Algorithm Design

C H A P T E R

2.1 HOW TO DESIGN AN ALGORITHM

Algorithm design is more akin to an art than a science. Supply 100 programmers with the identical specification and, in return, you will receive 100 different solutions. The process is largely subjective, and the notion of good or bad can also be application specific (i.e., a program considered a good solution in one environment might be unsuitable in another.)

However, we are not completely on our own in this matter. There are general guidelines that we can follow and a broad notion of what is considered good programming practice. Throughout this text, our discussions of individual algorithms provide specific insights into the design process; the sections that follow serve as an introduction to the topic.

Understand the Problem

The first step in algorithm design is to understand the problem. This is called the requirements analysis phase. However obvious this might appear now, all readers of this book will, at one time or another, a program that they think solves a particular problem—only to find out later that their efforts were wasted because they solved the wrong problem. Gather data, speak to users, carefully review any written requirements. In short, try to ensure that you have all the information you need before you start to design and code an application.

Data Structures

The next step is to design the data structures. This is a critical part of the development process and the one most often overlooked by even the most experienced programmers. A correctly designed data structure will suggest the design of the definitive algorithm and yield a simple, easily maintainable program. In contrast, choosing a clumsy or inappropriate data structure will produce code that is unreadable and difficult to maintain.

Subsequent chapters of this book will introduce some very sophisticated data structures. However, you should already be familiar with the more common data types provided with most languages (e.g., integers, characters, arrays, etc.). A trivial example of an incorrect choice of a data structure is using individual variables to process the test results of a computer science class. It would be more appropriate to use an array.

After they have been designed, we need to verify the appropriateness of our data structures. One way to do this is to ask users to supply a number of questions and/or updates that they would like your program to support. You can then manually apply the questions against your design and judge how well your data structures respond to these user requirements. Modify your design as necessary.

Pseudo-Code

The next phase of the development process is to formulate or sketch the algorithm in *pseudo-code*. Each pseudo-code statement describes tasks that the programmer will implement using one or more host (real) language statements. The level of detail represented by each pseudo-code statement can vary, and programmers develop individual styles that reflect personal preference or need. The use of pseudo-code

```
while( more employee input )
    if( salaried )
        calculate tax;
        calculate fica;
    else
        determine hours;
        overtime hours;
        get hourly rate;
    print check;
```

Listing 2.1
Pseudo-code
example.

allows programmers to design and analyze algorithms without becoming entangled in syntactic detail. Listing 2.1 contains an example.

Analysis

The next phase in the development is *analysis*. We can divide this phase into three steps. First, we must determine whether our solution seems feasible with respect to memory requirements, performance constraints, ease of use, etc. Second, we should review and validate the pseudo-code description of our algorithm. Obviously, these are both manual procedures at this point because we have not, as yet, written any (compilable) code.

The third step is to perform an analysis of the *complexity* of the algorithm. Complexity in this sense does not refer to the relative difficulty of understanding the program; rather, it is a measure of the amount of work performed by the executing function. This type of analysis is especially useful when there are two or more solutions available and we wish to select only one for implementation.

In determining complexity, it would appear useful to have the actual execution times available for each function. Obviously, this is not possible because we have not, as yet, performed any actual coding. Moreover, the very point of this exercise is to eliminate the need to develop, implement, and test more than one algorithm. Furthermore, performance results can vary drastically when programs are compiled and executed on different processors, using different compilers. Therefore, the metrics that we develop for measuring complexity should allow us to rate the algorithms *independent* of their execution environment.

In summary, we want to analyze the complexity of an algorithm, without writing any code, without executing any programs, and measure the results independent of any execution environment. The question then becomes, How do we do this?

In many cases, we can identify one or more basic operations as critical to the performance of an algorithm. Once identified, we can analyze (count) these operations to yield a relative *efficiency index* or order of execution magnitude. For example, consider sorting routines. One critical operation for this class of algorithm is the *comparison*. That is, we could state that the fewer the comparisons made, the more efficient the algorithm. Thus, if we were presented with two or more different sorting functions, we would usually choose to implement the one that performed the fewest comparisons.

Now that we have suggested a method of evaluating performance, we must also develop a consistent manner in which to present it. It would seem obvious to state that the total amount of work performed by a function is proportional to the amount of data that it must process. Therefore, we will represent an algorithm's complexity as a function of the size of the input. For example, if n represents the total number of data elements, a function that requires one critical operation per input datum is an $O(n)$ (pronounced *order n*) algorithm; one that requires n^2 operations is $O(n^2)$ (pronounced *order n squared*).

We can state formally that

$$f(n) = O(g(n)) \text{ } iff \text{ there exists a } c > 0 \text{ and an } a \text{ such that for all } n \geq 0,$$
$$f(n) \leq a + cg(n)$$

This reads as follows: The complexity of a function $f(n)$ is bounded by the function $g(n)$—that is, the maximum number of basic operations executed by $f(n)$ will be no more than $g(n)$. The variable a represents the cost of any housekeeping or startup chores, and c is a constant multiplier representing the cost (in execution units) of a basic operation.

In practice, we usually ignore the effects of a, c, and any noncritical operations when comparing complexities: The overall impact of the constant a tends to become insignificant as the size of the dataset increases, and the cost of a critical operation (c) should be about the same for algorithms of a similar class. That is not to say, however, that their effect is always negligible. For some problem sizes, an $O(n)$ function, with a sufficiently large c, can be outperformed by one that has a complexity of $O(n^2)$. In addition, for some algorithms, startup costs represented by the constant a might require more than constant time (e.g., initializing arrays).

Examples of some common complexities include the following:

- $O(1)$ represents a constant complexity (e.g., a program that displays the current date and time).
- $O(n)$ is linear.
- $O(n^2)$ is quadratic.
- $O(n^3)$ is cubic.
- $O(2^n)$ is exponential.

Using these relationships, we can state that an $O(n)$ algorithm is more efficient than one that is $O(n^2)$ (for sufficiently large datasets); $O(\log n)$ is faster than $O(n \log n)$, which, in turn, is faster than $O(n^2)$.

The complexity of certain algorithms can vary not only with the size of the input, but also with its composition. Consider again algorithms that sort names. Some procedures will perform very efficiently when presented with an input stream that is already sorted; others will degrade miserably. Some operate more efficiently when the data are random; a few do not. To compensate for this phenomenon, we provide two indices of complexity behavior: worst case and average case. For sorting routines, average case behavior is the average complexity index for all input streams; worst case is function specific and represents a pathological performance degradation.

Additional Analysis Criteria

In addition to those just discussed, there are other criteria by which we can analyze and compare algorithms. These include the following:

Clarity   Clarity concerns the relative ease by which program source code can be understood by someone other than the original developer. (We usually refer to this attribute as *readability*.) A professional programmer writes programs that are clear and easy to understand. Generally speaking, if you have a choice of implementation constructs, you should opt for the one that is more readable. When you must choose a less readable construct (e.g., when performance is critical), comment your code clearly.

Maintainability The issue of maintainability focuses on how well a program can accommodate change. As discussed previously, clarity is a major consideration: You must understand code before you can modify it. However, maintenance only begins with understanding. The issue boils down to one of confidence: How confident are we that a change we might apply to one section of a program will not break some other part of the system? (This is sometimes called a *ripple* effect.)

We must design and develop programs with maintenance in mind. As a simple example, consider the following code fragment:

```
int a[ 10 ];
    .
    .
    .
while( i < 10 )
    a[i] = . . .
    .
    .
    .
while( j < 10 )
    z = a[j] . . .
    .
    .
    .
```

It might not be clear to a maintenance programmer that the literal value used in the second loop is related back to the size of **a**. Left as is, we might inadvertently introduce a bug into the program if we were to change **a**'s size.

Portability Portability can be defined simply: How easy is it for us to move a given program from one platform to another? (The term *platform* is used to describe an execution environment. Components of a platform include processor, operating system, databases, networks, etc.) Keep in mind that the two platforms (source and destination) might have

- Different hardware architectures
- Different operating systems
- Different system software.

Generally speaking, there are two levels of portability. Object code portability occurs when we can move *executable* code from one system to another. This is usually considered impractical unless the two platforms share so many common attributes that they become almost indistinguishable from each other (e.g., the systems share the same processor family).

Source code portability is the more practical alternative. We achieve this level of portability whenever we can copy source code to a new system, recompile it, and run it with no (or relatively few) modifications.

These are the advantages of portable programs:

- They are easier to move to new platforms
- They are less subject to environment changes (i.e., upgrading the operating system)
- They are easier to extend and maintain.

More and more development organizations view portability as a major factor in systems development. There are several reasons:

- The increasing costs associated with software maintenance
- The speed at which hardware improvements occur
- Increased competition and decreasing prices for application software.

Portability, however, is not without its costs. In general, portable programs are slower because we are less inclined to take advantage of machine- or operating system-specific features. In addition, portable programs usually take longer to develop: portability does not come for free, you must 'design it' into the application.

Resource usage   Generally speaking, all algorithms require some minimal amount of computing resources (e.g., memory, disk, network access, etc.). The quantity and composition of these resources will vary by algorithm and implementation. As a result, the costs associated with a given set of resources will certainly factor into your choice of algorithm.

Implementation

After the design and analysis, it is finally time to implement the algorithm. This should prove to be a fairly straightforward process if we have followed all the previous suggestions. Specifically, if we wrote a pseudo-code description of the algorithm, implementation will be little more than a line-for-line translation.

Another important consideration at this phase might be the selection of an appropriate programming language. Languages lend themselves to certain types of tasks and become difficult to use with others. If a choice is available, select one that is best suited to the needs of the application.

Testing

The last step in the development process is testing. The effort expended on this task will have a direct effect on the perceived quality of the product. There are essentially two parts to the process. In the first, we must devise a set of tests that attempt to break the function or program. This is the creative part of system testing, and it requires as much consideration and effort as any other task in the development process. It begins simply, using a few known data values for which we can manually compute a result. This establishes that the program is at least functioning to the point where we can proceed with more extensive tests.

The second and more difficult part of testing is debugging. That is, we must determine what (if anything) is wrong with the program's execution. When we determine the problem, we then develop and apply fixes to offending sections of the program. When all the problems have been corrected, we then re-execute all of our tests. This ensures that the fixes are, indeed, correct and that they have not affected (i.e., broken) other sections of the program.

When attempting to fix a program error, it is important to distinguish between symptom and cause. As an example, consider a program that displays employee salary information. The program might operate as follows:

- It prompts the user for the employee number.
- It searches a database for the appropriate employee and tax records.
- It calculates withholding taxes and other payroll deductions.
- It displays the information on the screen.

During your testing you notice that, when displayed, the net pay field is always incorrect by $1 (alas, in the company's favor). Would it be reasonable to assume that the fix is simply to add $1 to its value just before it gets displayed? No. More likely, this problem is just a symptom of another problem—such as an error in the formulas for calculating payroll deductions or incorrect values stored in the tax tables—and you must delve deeper into the program to find the real cause.

Keep in mind that testing can never demonstrate the absence of bugs—only their presence. Therefore, it is incumbent on the individual(s) conducting the tests to exercise judgment, diligence, and creativity to ensure the best possible results.

2.2   EXAMPLE 1: FIBONACCI NUMBERS

To demonstrate some of the ideas presented in this chapter, let's discuss the design and implementation of a function that computes Fibonacci numbers. The Fibonacci sequence is defined as

$$0, \ 1, \ 1, \ 2, \ 3, \ 5, \ 8, \ 13, \ \ldots$$

It begins with $F_0 = 0$ and $F_1 = 1$. We compute each subsequent term as the sum of the previous two. For example,

$$F(3) = F(2) + F(1) = 1 + 1 = 2$$
$$F(6) = F(5) + F(4) = 5 + 3 = 8$$

Formally, the series can be defined as

$$F_0 = 0$$
$$F_1 = 1$$
$$F_n = F_{n-1} + F_{n-2}, \quad \text{for } n \geq 2$$

Our task is to design and implement a function that accepts a non-negative integer argument *n* and returns the value $F(n)$.

Understand the Problem

Although it is not a formal specification, the foregoing description adequately describes the task at hand. The key points to keep in mind are as follows:

- The function's one argument corresponds to the *sequence number* of the desired Fibonacci number.
- The argument, by definition, must be non-negative; therefore, the function should do something reasonable if invoked with a negative value.

Data Structures

This algorithm does not require an extensive data structure; it will use simple integer variables to compute each Fibonacci number.

Pseudo-Code

We can use the formal definition of the Fibonacci series as the starting point for our development. Thus, the first version of our pseudo-code might appear as follows:

```
fib( n )
    if n = 0
        return( 0 );
    if n = 1
        return( 1 );
    for i = 2 to n
        fib = fmin1 + fmin2;
        update fmin1 and fmin2;

    return( fib );
```

Note that our description lacks some important details: the initial values of variables, the increments for loop variables, and a test for a valid argument.

After adding these statements, the algorithm becomes

```
fib( n )
    if n < 0
        return( -1 );
    if n = 0
        return( 0 );
    if n = 1
        return( 1 );

    fmin2 = 0;
    fmin1 = 1;
    for i = 2 to n
        fib = fmin1 + fmin2;
        fmin2 = fmin1;
        fmin1 = fib;

    return( fib );
```

Notice that we have established the convention of returning a -1 to indicate an erroneous argument. Also note how we initialize and update the two variables, **fmin1** and **fmin2**.

Analysis

If we ignore the trivial cases where $n \leq 1$, we can compute the function's complexity as follows:

- There are five housekeeping instructions executed before entering the loop.
- The loop—with its three instructions—is executed $n - 1$ times, for a total of $3(n - 1)$ or, rounding that value, $3n$.

The total number of instructions executed is $5 + 3n$. However, as mentioned earlier, we ignore the effects of the constants when analyzing algorithms; thus, the complexity of **fib()** is $O(n)$.

```
int fib( int n )
{
        int    i;
        int    fibn, fib1, fib2;

        if( n < 0 )
                return( -1 );

        if( n == 0 )
                return( 0 );
        if( n == 1 )
                return( 1 );

        fibn = 0;
        fib2 = 0;              /* F(n-2) */
        fib1 = 1;              /* F(n-1) */

        for( i = 2; i <= n; i++ ){
                fibn = fib1 + fib2;
                fib2 = fib1;
                fib1 = fibn;
        }
        return( fibn );
}
```

Listing 2.2
Fibonacci numbers.

Implementation

The pseudo-code description of this function allows for a direct conversion to C. We need only remember to adhere to C syntax, select appropriate data types, and declare all variables. Listing 2.2 contains the final C version of the algorithm.

Testing

Testing this function is a straightforward process. We want to verify that the function computes accurate values and handles errors

```
#include        <stdio.h>

#define   MAX_TEST   10

int   fib( int );

int main( void )
{
      int   i;

      for( i = -1; i <= MAX_TEST; i++ )
            printf( "\ti: %2d\tfib(%2d): %d\n", i,
            i, fib(i) );

      return( 0 );
}
```

Listing 2.3
Fibonacci test
program.

correctly. One way to do this is to write another function that repeatedly invokes **fib()** with known values. Listing 2.3 contains an example.

When compiled with the source for **fib()**, the output of the program is

```
i: -1  fib(-1): -1
i:  0  fib( 0): 0
i:  1  fib( 1): 1
i:  2  fib( 2): 1
i:  3  fib( 3): 2
i:  4  fib( 4): 3
i:  5  fib( 5): 5
i:  6  fib( 6): 8
i:  7  fib( 7): 13
i:  8  fib( 8): 21
i:  9  fib( 9): 34
i: 10  fib(10): 55
```

which we can manually inspect for errors.

━━━━━━━━ ### 2.3 EXAMPLE 2: MATRIX ADDITION

For our next example, we will design and implement a function that performs matrix addition. It must compute the sum of two matrices $(A + B)$ and store the result in a third (C).

Understand the Problem

The two matrices must be of the same dimension. We compute their sum by adding corresponding elements of A and B and storing the result in C. For example, given the matrices

$$\begin{bmatrix} 1 & 2 & 3 \\ 4 & 5 & 6 \\ 7 & 8 & 9 \end{bmatrix} + \begin{bmatrix} 8 & 7 & 6 \\ 5 & 4 & 3 \\ 2 & 1 & 0 \end{bmatrix}$$

the function would compute C as

$$\begin{bmatrix} 1+8 & 2+7 & 3+6 \\ 4+5 & 5+4 & 6+3 \\ 7+2 & 8+1 & 9+0 \end{bmatrix} = \begin{bmatrix} 9 & 9 & 9 \\ 9 & 9 & 9 \\ 9 & 9 & 9 \end{bmatrix}$$

Data Structures

We will use two-dimensional arrays to store and process the matrices. Each array entry will correspond to an element in the matrix. One word of caution: Mathematicians often reference matrix elements as

$$\begin{vmatrix} E_{11} & E_{12} & \dots & E_{1n} \\ E_{21} & E_{22} & \dots & E_{2n} \\ \dots & \dots & \dots & \dots \\ E_{m1} & E_{m2} & \dots & E_{mn} \end{vmatrix}$$

In C, however, array subscripts begin at 0. Therefore, E_{11} will correspond to array element `A[0][0]`; E_{12} will correspond to array element `A[0][1]`; and so on until E_{mn}, which corresponds to `A[m−1][n−1]`.

Pseudo-Code

To perform the addition of each corresponding matrix element, we need a way to reference every index pair (i, j) of the two arrays. We can do this using a coding construct called *nested loops*. The outer loop indexes over the rows, while the inner loop indexes over the columns. A pseudo-code description of the algorithm is as follows:

```
mat_add( m, n ) /* add m × n matrices */
    for i = 0 to m−1
        for j = 0 to n−1
            c[i, j] = a[i, j] + b[i, j];
```

Analysis

A discussion of complexity for this function is easier if we assume that $m = n$. The outer loop is executed n times. With each iteration, the inner loop is also executed n times. Thus, the total number of critical operations (additions) performed by the algorithm is n times n. This yields a complexity of $O(n^2)$.

Implementation

For the purpose of this example, we will assume that the three arrays (A, B, C) are external to the function. Listing 2.4 contains the C implementation of the function **mat_add()**.

Please note the following:

- The arrays are declared external to the function (the first three lines of the listing).
- The two macros, **NO_ROWS** and **NO_COLS**, are application dependent and must be defined.
- The function assumes that the initial values of **a[][]** and **b[][]** are established before a call is made to **mat_add()**.

    Also note the C syntax for subscripts in two-dimensional arrays. Many other languages would write subscripts something like

```
a[i, j] or a(i, j)
```

```
int     a[ NO_ROWS ][ NO_COLS ];
int     b[ NO_ROWS ][ NO_COLS ];
int     c[ NO_ROWS ][ NO_COLS ];

void mat_add( int rows, int cols )
{
   int i, j;

   for( i = 0; i < NO_ROWS; i++ )
       for( j = 0; j < NO_COLS; j++ )
           c[i][j] = a[i][j] + b[i][j];
}
```

Listing 2.4
Matrix addition.

The slightly different notation derives from the fact that in C, a two-dimensional array is defined as a one-dimensional array, where each element is another array. Its use is otherwise similar to that of other languages.

Testing

The most direct way to test this function is to write a program that generates several pairs of matrices, adds them, and then prints the results. We will leave this as an exercise for the reader.

Programmers new to C should keep in mind that there are no bounds checks on array references. In particular, because of the zero offset on array indices, the reference

    a[NO_ROWS][NO_COLS]

is out of bounds. As a result, part of your testing procedures should involve the verification of all array references.

SUMMARY
This chapter presented an overview of the software design process. We will review and expand on the ideas presented in this chapter as we continue with our discussions. For the sake of brevity, however, we will

no longer present algorithms in the expanded format used in this chapter.

This chapter is incomplete because there is one part of the development cycle that we have not discussed: documentation. Documentation is usually the first thing a user sees when working with a new application. As a result, a software product's success can be dependent on the quality of its documentation.

Documentation comes in many forms:

- Program comments
- Manual pages (a description of program usage)
- User's manual
- Programmer's manual
- Administrator's manual.

Throughout this book, we will continue to stress the need to provide well-commented source code. It is beyond the scope of this text to describe the other forms of documentation in detail. Moreover, documentation requirements vary with the installation and the application. Let it suffice to say that it is incumbent on every programmer to provide software that is well documented.

EXERCISES

1. Describe $O()$ notation.

2. Plot the curves for all the common complexities. Determine points of intersection and compare behavior.

3. Using all the described steps, design and implement a program that will count the number of characters, lines, and words contained in a text file. See if you can extend it to count unique words as well.

4. Write the complement of **fib()**: a function that takes as its sole argument a Fibonacci number and returns its ordinal position in the series. Be sure to test for arguments that are not Fibonacci numbers. How should your function process an argument of 1?

5. Write a program that tests the function **mat_add()**. Be creative. Are there any boundary conditions?

6. Design, implement, and test a function that performs matrix multiplication. What is its complexity?

7. Discuss ways in which we can modify **mat_add()** so it can work for any two arrays (i.e., pass the arrays as arguments). Implement and test your changes.

8. What is the complexity of the following pseudo-code?

```
example()
{
    for( i = 0; i < A; i++ )
        for( j = 0; j < B; j++ )
            for( k = 0; k < C; k++ )
                CRITICAL OPERATION;
}
```

Static Data Structures

3.1 OVERVIEW

Conventional languages supply the basic data types or *atoms* minimally required for programming. It is the nature of atoms that they cannot be divided into smaller components (except bit-fields). In C, they include **int**, **char**, **float**, etc. In many cases, the basic data types alone are sufficient to accomplish a given programming assignment. More often, however, the types of problems programmers are asked to solve require more complex data objects.

Fortunately, most programming languages provide facilities for combining atoms into larger aggregates. In computer science, these aggregates are called *data structures*. A data structure is an ordered collection (aggregate) of atoms combined, within the rules of the host language, to create a new, user-defined data type. Many programming languages even allow the combining of one or more user-defined aggregates into a compound aggregate. Thus, the programmer has the ability to create data structures tailored to specific needs. In this chapter, we will examine static data structures—that is, data structures that do not alter their basic memory representation during program execution. (The term *structure* is ambiguous, however. Some programming languages—most

```
main()
{
    int     i;
    int     a[10];              /* Declare 10 cells
*/
    for( i = 0; i < 10; i=i+1 )  /* Indexed 0 − 9 */
        a[i] = i;               /* Store */

    for( i = 0; i < 10; i=i+1 )  /* Retrieve */
        printf( "i: %d a[i]: %d\n", i, a[i] );

    exit( 0 );
}
```

Listing 3.1
Arrays in C.

notably C—use the term to denote a particular type of data aggregate. Its definition and use in such cases is language specific. Except
where noted, we will avoid this connotation and instead use the term to
refer to any data aggregate that is not otherwise considered atomic.)

3.2 ARRAYS

The extent to which atoms can be combined by the programmer varies
with the language—some provide more flexibility than others. However,
one data aggregate common to most languages is the *array*. In fact,
this might be the only aggregate provided with some programming
environments.

Conceptually, an array is a set of pairs: *index* and *value*. In mathematics, this is referred to as a *map* or *correspondence*. When declared in a
programming language, an array is of a specified type (e.g., **int**) and
size (range of indices). The indices or subscripts are integer quantities, though not necessarily positive. Refer to Listing 3.1 for an
example of array declaration and use in C.

The simplicity of an array's use belies its power. Consider writing

```
#define KING   'k'
#define QUEEN  'q'

main()
{
      char   chessboard[8][8];        /* Declaration */

      chessboard[2][3] = QUEEN;

      if( chessboard[4][7] == KING )
          check_mate();
}
```

Listing 3.2
Multidimensional arrays in C.

a program—without using arrays—to analyze grade scores for a computer science class. Each student's score, for each test, would have to be stored and processed in a unique variable. To go one step further, consider how difficult it would be if the number of students and test results were not known in advance.

Arrays need not be restricted to one dimension. We can create *multidimensional* arrays to handle more complex data structures. For example, we can represent a chess board as a two-dimensional (8×8) array. Refer to Listing 3.2 for an example. Note that in C, each dimension is placed in a separate set of brackets.

In addition to their more obvious uses, arrays also serve as the foundation for more complex data structures. The following sections present several examples.

3.3 ORDERED LISTS

One of the simplest forms of data aggregates is the *ordered* or *linear list*. A linear list is an ordered subset of elements from a given set S written $(E_1, E_2, E_3, \ldots, E_n)$. Examples include

$$(A, B, C, D, \ldots, Z)$$

or

(SUN, MON, TUE, WED, . . . , SAT)

An ordered list has several properties:

- The length of a list is finite and computable.
- The contents of the list can be displayed (in order).
- The ith element can be retrieved.
- The ith element can be replaced.
- New elements can be inserted into the list.
- Existing elements can be deleted from the list.

The most direct approach to implementing a list is through the use of an array. Each array element corresponds to a list member. Note that of the six properties of an ordered list, only the last two—insertion and deletion—are difficult with an array implementation. To accomplish either, we must shift elements within the array. We will return to this point in Chapter 5.

There are times when we may wish to restrict access to list elements. For example, we may want to limit the types of operations that can be performed or restrict the number of locations where insertions and deletions can occur. In short, we need not make available the full complement of operations for a given list. The sections that follow discuss some examples of restricted lists.

3.4 STACKS

A *stack* is an ordered list in which only two operations are permissible: insertion and deletion. Furthermore, these operations may occur only at one end of the list, called the *top*. The result is that items are stored and retrieved in a last-in, first-out (LIFO) manner. For example, adding the element E_5 to the list (E_1, E_2, E_3, E_4) would generate the list $(E_1, E_2, E_3, E_4, E_5)$. A subsequent deletion yields the original list.

A common example of a stack is a dish rack in a diner. A dish rack is a spring-loaded device that stores dishes in manner such that only the top dish is visible (see Fig. 3.1). After being washed, a clean dish is placed (*pushed*) on top of the stack. This forces the spring down, leaving only the new dish visible. When a clean dish is needed, the top one is removed (*popped*). This causes the spring to recoil

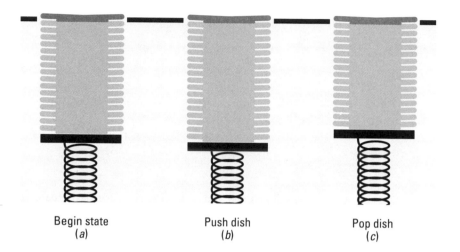

Figure 3.1
A dish rack.

Begin state	Push dish	Pop dish
(*a*)	(*b*)	(*c*)

just enough to allow what was the second plate to become visible. (The last plate cleaned is the first one reused.)

Stacks are versatile data structures and have many uses. For example, we can use stacks to reverse the order of elements in a list or serve as the basis of a software calculator. In general, we can use stacks whenever we need a LIFO structure.

As depicted in Figure 3.2, we can implement a software stack using an array. The variable **top** maintains the index of the current top-of-stack location. This is the only place where insertions and dele-

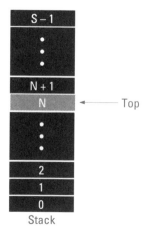

Figure 3.2
A software stack.

tions may occur. To add (push) a new element onto the stack, we increment
`top` and assign `stack[top]` the value of the new element. Note
that we should always test for a *stack full* (*overflow*) condition (i.e.,
`(top + 1) >= s`) before performing each insertion.

To delete (pop) an element from the stack, just decrement the
variable `top`. Note that we need not explicitly erase the value
stored in `stack [top]` because a subsequent push operation will
overwrite it. A *stack empty* (*underflow*) condition arises when the value of
`top` becomes negative.

The program segment in Listing 3.3 contains the example functions `push()` and `pop()`, which manipulate an integer stack declared as
`int stack[MAXSTACK];`. The function `push()` requires one argument, which it pushes onto the stack; `pop()` deletes, and returns the
value of, the topmost element. Also listed is the routine `empty()`,
which, as its name implies, tests for a stack empty condition; it returns
either `TRUE` or `FALSE`, accordingly. In this example, the function
`pop()` does not explicitly test for an underflow condition—that is, an
attempt to pop an element off an already empty stack. Therefore, you
should make a call to `empty()` before each call to `pop()`.

Note that we initialize the pointer `top` to -1. This is because,
in C, array indices range from 0 to $n - 1$ (where n is the declared
size of the array). Also note the use of the $+ +$ and the $- -$ operators.
C has two shorthand operators for incrementing and decrementing variables: $+ +$ adds 1 to its operand; $- -$ subtracts 1 from its operand.
For example, the statements `n++;` and `n--;` are equivalent to `n =
n + 1;` and `n = n - 1;`, respectively.

A unique feature of these operators is that we may place them
either before or after their associated operands. Furthermore, their
position is significant. The prefix form (e.g., $+ +n$) increments (decrements) the variable *before* it is evaluated (used); the postfix form (e.g.,
`n++`) increments (decrements) the variable *after* it is evaluated.

For example, given the assignment `n = 10;`, the statement

    ans = ++n;

sets `ans` to `11`; but the statement

    ans = n++;

sets `ans` to `10`. In both cases however, `n` is set to `11`.

```
#define    OK        0
#define    FALSE     0
#define    TRUE      1
#define    FULL      1
#define    MAXSTACK  100

int  top = -1;
int  stack[MAXSTACK];

push( int new )                 /* Add element to stack */
{
    if( top+1 >= MAXSTACK )  /* Overflow */
        return( FULL );

    stack[++top] = new;
    return( OK );
}

int pop()                   /* Delete/return top element */
{
    return( stack[top--] );
}

int empty()                 /* Test for stack empty */
{
    if( top < 0 )
        return( TRUE );

    return( FALSE );
}
```

Listing 3.3

Stack functions.

```
void reverse()        /* Function to reverse input */
{
    int  item;

    while( (item = nextinput()) != EOF )
        if( push(item) == FULL )
            error();          /* overflow */

    while( !empty() )
        putchar( pop() );
}
```

Listing 3.4
String reversal.

String Reversal

For our first example, we will use stacks to reverse a string. The problem is to read an arbitrary sequence of characters and print them out in reverse order.

With the aid of a stack, the solution for this problem is simple. We will push each character we read in from the input source onto a stack. When we have exhausted the input stream (end-of-file), we will pop all characters off the stack and print them out. Because stacks are LIFO structures, the output will naturally be reversed.

Listing 3.4 contains the code for the function **reverse()**, which reverses strings as described earlier. It uses the routines presented in Listing 3.3 to manage the stack. In addition, **reverse()** assumes two ancillary routines. The first, **nextinput()**, returns the next character from the input stream or the value **EOF** when the input has been exhausted. (**EOF** is a predefined macro supplied with standard C implementations.)

The second function, **error()**, is invoked on a stack overflow condition. It should take appropriate action such as printing an error message and terminating the program. However, this is a rather inelegant way of addressing this type of problem, and we will discuss alternative methods in Chapter 5.

Parentheses Usage

Another example using stacks involves the processing of mathematical expressions. Suppose we wanted to verify that, for some given expression, parentheses have been used correctly. That is, we want to check that

1. There are an equal number of left and right parentheses.
2. Each right parenthesis is preceded by its corresponding left parenthesis.

If you consider the problem for a moment, you will see that part 1 of the preceding definition is simple to verify. We could develop an algorithm that simply counts the number of left and right parentheses and determines if the two values are equal. However, a correct count alone does not ensure proper usage. For example, the expression

$$))a + b(+ c ($$

would have a valid count but symbol usage is nonetheless incorrect. This is the more difficult aspect of the problem as denoted in part 2 of the definition.

Let's examine a different approach to the problem. In lieu of a simple count, we could assign values to each parenthesis. For example, '(' equals 1 and ')' equals -1. This would allow us to compute a *parenthesis index* (*PI*) for each expression. We begin the computation by assigning $PI = 0$. Then, as we scan an expression, we update the *PI* by either adding or subtracting 1 from its total. For example, the partial expression $((a + b) * (c \ldots$ would have a *PI* of $1 + 1 - 1 + 1 = 2$.

This approach possesses some interesting properties. First, a final *PI* of 0 indicates that there are an equal number of open and closing parentheses. In addition, an intermediate *PI* value that is negative indicates an imbalance in the use of left and right parentheses. For example, the expression $(a + b)) \ldots$ has a *PI* of -1.

Nonetheless, this technique has one drawback. What if, in addition to parentheses, expressions may contain brackets ([]) and/or braces ({})? Using the previous approach, the expression $(\{a + b] * c)$ has a final *PI* of 0 but is obviously incorrect.

To overcome this final hurdle, we need to approach the problem from another angle. Consider that, regardless of type (i.e., (, [, or {), a left symbol opened must be closed with its corresponding right symbol. Thus, given the partial expression $(a + [b \times \{ \ldots$, we would

expect the first closing symbol to be a }, followed at some point by a
], and then a final). Upon closer inspection, you will note that the
last symbol opened is the first one closed. In other words, this problem
is well suited for a stack solution.

Listing 3.5 contains the code for the function **check_paren()**,
which verifies parentheses usage in mathematical expressions. Its one
required argument is the character array containing the expression; it
returns a status value indicating the validity of the expression.

The algorithm functions as follows. As it scans the input array,
check_paren() pushes left symbols onto a stack. When it encounters
a right object, it pops the topmost element off the stack and determines
whether the two symbols match (i.e., they form a pair). Notice
that with each pop, and again at the end of the routine, the function
tests for an empty stack condition. In addition to avoiding an underflow
condition, this processing ensures that the expression contains only
matched pairs of objects (i.e., there are no missing or extraneous symbols).

3.5   EXAMPLE CALCULATOR

The classic example demonstrating the power and use of software
stacks is a program calculator. The task is to construct a program that
computes the value of mathematical expressions. For example,

$$a + b/c - d \times e$$

Expressions are composed of operands, operators, and delimiters.
Operands are the numeric values used to evaluate the expression.
The preceding example contains five (a, b, c, d, e) that serve as place
holders for numeric literals (e.g., 16, or -13.4); but they could
also represent true variables if the calculator program contained an
assignment facility. *Operators* indicate the mathematical operations that
are to be performed on their associated operands. They also determine
the number of operands required for each type of operation. The preceding
expression contains only *binary* operators, which require two operands;
a *unary* operator requires only one operand (e.g., -3).

At first glance, the program might appear simple: Just scan the
input from left to right, evaluating the expression as we proceed.
However, the problem that quickly becomes apparent is the difficulty
of maintaining the mathematical precedence of the operations. In

```
#define OK    0
#define ERR  -1

int check_paren( char data[] )
{
    int i;

    for( i = 0; data[i] != NULL; i++ )
    {
        switch( data[i] ){
        case '{':
        case '[':
        case '(':
            push( data[i] );
            break;
        case '}':
            if( empty() || pop() != '{' )
                return( ERR );
            break;
        case ']':
            if( empty() || pop() != '[' )
                return( ERR );
            break;
        case ')':
            if( empty() || pop() != '(' )
                return( ERR );
            break;
        }
    }
    if( empty() )
        return( OK );
    return( ERR );
}
```

Listing 3.5
Function to check
parentheses.

the previous example, the implied order of evaluation is

$$(a + (b/c)) - (d \times e)$$

Obviously, the order in which the operations take place can be significant, as in the expression $6 + 4/2$. If we evaluate it as $(6 + 4)/2$, the answer is 5; if we evaluate it as $6 + (4/2)$, the answer is 8. Therefore, we must be certain that the algorithm we develop maintains proper operator precedence.

For our example calculator, we will only concern ourselves with the five basic arithmetic operations: addition ($+$), subtraction ($-$), multiplication ($\times$), division ($/$), and exponentiation ($\uparrow$). The precedence of these operators, from highest to lowest, is

Operator	Value
$\uparrow$	3
$\times$, $/$	2
$+$, $-$	1

Parentheses can be used to change the order of evaluation for a given expression, but in their absence operations of highest precedence must be performed first. When an expression contains operators of equal priority, they are evaluated left to right (e.g., interpret $a/b \times c$ as $(a/b) \times c$). The sole exception (at least for our example) is exponentiation, which is evaluated from right to left (i.e., $a \uparrow b \uparrow c$ is evaluated as $a \uparrow (b \uparrow c)$).

Prefix and Postfix Notation

All the preceding expressions have been presented in their *infix* form. Infix notation places operators between their operands. As we have seen, this notation—although commonly used by humans—is not convenient for our calculator program. There are, however, two alternative ways of representing expressions:

$$+ \, a \, b \quad \text{(prefix)}$$

$$a \, b \, + \quad \text{(postfix)}$$

The first, where the operator precedes its operands, is termed *prefix* notation. The second, which positions the operator after its operands, is referred to as *postfix* notation. Both forms are not as strange as they might first appear. For example, consider computing the value of $2 \uparrow 4$ in a C program. We cannot use a statement of the form

```
x = 2 ↑ 4;
```

because C has no exponentiation operator. Instead, we must use a statement such as

```
x = power( 2, 4 );
```

in which the operator (`power()`) precedes its two operands.

Using the rules of operator precedence, we can convert infix expressions to their corresponding postfix form. The steps required are as follows:

- Fully parenthesize the infix expression.
- Reposition (i.e., move) operators—one at a time and in order of precedence—to their final postfix position (to the right of their operands).
- Remove the parentheses.

For example, let's convert the expression $a + b \times c$ into its postfix form. The first step is to add parentheses:

$$a + (b \times c)$$

Next, in order of precedence, we must reposition the operators. Thus, the first operator we must move is $\times$, and the resulting expression appears as

$$a + (bc \times)$$

Clearly, the two operands of the $\times$ operator are b and c, and, consequently, its postfix position is simple to determine. But what are the two operands for the $+$ operator? The answer is a and the result of the subexpression $(b \times c)$. Therefore, we do not position the $+$ operator after the operand b (as might appear obvious at first glance), but instead we place it after the right parenthesis:

$$a\,(b\,c\,\times)\,+$$

The final step is to remove the parentheses:

$$a\,b\,c\,\times\,+$$

Now, using parentheses, let's change the evaluation order of the operators and convert the expression $(a + b) \times c$ to its postfix form:

$(a + b) \times c$ infix expression

$(a + b) \times c$ add parentheses (no change)

$(ab +) \times c$ convert +

$(ab +) c \times$ convert $\times$

$a\, b + c \times$ remove parentheses

Notice the resulting position of the + operator in this example. This is a direct result of using parentheses to alter the evaluation order of the operators.

We can convert infix expressions into their prefix form in the same manner. The only difference is that we place the operators before their operands rather than after. You should take a moment to convert the two previous examples into their prefix forms.

Returning now to our calculator program, the problem we had encountered was that the program could not correctly scan an infix expression and maintain proper operator precedence. However, if we take a closer look at postfix notation, we notice that a left-to-right scan will process both operands and operators in the correct order. That is, the order of the operators in a postfix expression determines the order of the operations. Therefore, to implement our calculator program, we need only develop two major functions: The first will convert infix expressions into their corresponding postfix forms; the second will compute the result of a postfix expression.

Automating Infix-to-Postfix Conversion

Before we begin discussing how to automate an infix-to-postfix conversion, consider the following point. Regardless of the form (prefix, infix, or postfix), the order of the operands remains unchanged. For example, the expression $a + b \times c$ has a postfix form of $a\, b\, c \times +$. The operators have moved but the relative position of the operands remains constant. Our conversion algorithm will take full advantage of this fact.

Just like the manual operation described earlier, our infix-to-postfix conversion algorithm must reposition operators within the expression string. Unfortunately, the function cannot just duplicate the manual operation. As a result, we need to modify our approach. As an alternative, consider a function that serves as a *gate* device. That is, as it scans its input (an infix expression), it outputs some symbols immediately (operands); others it holds until a more appropriate time (operators).

Specifically, our conversion routine will function as follows:

- Read the input stream (the infix expression) one symbol at a time.
- Output all operands immediately.
- Delay writing operators to the output stream until they will be positioned correctly in the postfix position.

Thus, the resulting output is the correct postfix form of the infix expression.

Our algorithm will need a stack to serve as the temporary repository for delayed operators. However, before we discuss its implementation, let's trace the function's execution while converting the expression $a + b \times c$ to its postfix form:

Input	Type	Stack	Operation	Output
a	Operand	Empty	Pass a directly to output	a
$+$	Operator	$+$	Stack (delay) operator	a
b	Operand	$+$	Pass b directly to output	ab
$\times$	Operator	$+ \times$	Stack (delay) operator	ab
c	Operand	$+ \times$	Pass c directly to output	abc
Empty	Empty	$+$	Empty stack	$abc +$
Empty	Empty	Empty	Empty stack	$abc \times +$

When read, the first operand is passed directly to the output stream. The first operator $(+)$ is then read and pushed (delayed) on the stack. Then, like its predecessor, the second operator is scanned and passed directly to the output stream.

However, why isn't the first operator $(+)$ popped off the stack and written out? The reason is that the second operator $(\times)$ has a higher precedence than the operator currently on the stack $(+)$. That is, because a stack is a LIFO structure, the $(\times)$ operator will appear before $(+)$ in the output stream when we ultimately empty the stack.

The operation continues with the processing of the final operand, followed by the repeated popping of the stack until the last operator is written to the output stream.

Now let's switch the order of the operators and see how the function should handle the expression $a \times b + c$.

Input	Type	Stack	Operation	Output
a	Operand	Empty	Pass a directly to output	a
$\times$	Operator	$\times$	Stack (delay) operator	a
b	Operand	$\times$	Pass b directly to output	ab
$+$	Operator	Empty	Pop stack and output	$ab \times$
		$+$	Push (delay) operator	$ab \times$
c	Operand	$+$	Pass c directly to output	$ab \times c$
Empty	Empty	Empty	Empty stack	$ab \times c +$

This time, after the second operator ($+$) was read, the first ($\times$) was popped and placed on the output stream. This is because ($\times$) has a higher precedence than that of the incoming operator ($+$).

Now let's look at an example that contains parentheses:

$$a/(b + c).$$

The operation of the algorithm is as follows:

Input	Type	Stack	Operation	Output
a	Operand	Empty	Pass a directly to output	a
$/$	Operator	$/$	Stack (delay) operator	a
$($	L-Paren	$/($	Stack L-Paren	a
b	Operand	$/($	Pass b directly to output	ab
$+$	Operator	$/(+$	Stack (delay) operator	ab
c	Operand	$/(+$	Pass c directly to output	abc
$)$	R-Paren	$/$	Unstack down to L-Paren	$abc +$
Empty	Empty	Empty	Empty stack	$abc +/$

In this example, the parentheses change the evaluation order of the operators. To produce an equivalent postfix representation, the algorithm must stack the left parenthesis and then, after scanning the corresponding right parenthesis, unstack all enclosed operators. Note that we never need to push the right parenthesis onto the stack; it serves only as a flag signaling that unstacking should begin.

Operator	Incoming	Instack
↑	4	3
×, /	2	2
+, −	1	1
(	4	0
)	−	−

Figure 3.3
Operator priorities.

Based on these examples it appears that, when processing an operator, the function should output all previously stacked operators having a priority greater than, or equal to, the priority of the incoming one. There is one exception, however. The expression $a \uparrow b \uparrow c$ has a postfix form of $abc \uparrow \uparrow$ (remember, this operator has right-to-left grouping). As it stands now, our algorithm would incorrectly generate $ab \uparrow c \uparrow$ as the postfix form of this expression.

To overcome this problem, we can make the following modifications:

- Assign two priorities to each operator, *incoming* (ICP) and *instack* (ISP).
- Modify the algorithm so that it will unstack operators that have an *instack* priority greater than, or equal to, the *incoming* priority of the new operator.
- Establish a (↑) entry in the priority table such that its ICP is greater than its ISP.

Now, when processing the expression $a \uparrow b \uparrow c$, our algorithm will push the second (↑) operator without popping the first one off the stack.

Figure 3.3 lists ISP and ICP priorities suitable for our calculator program. Note that the values selected are arbitrary; what is important is the relationships they define. We can also expand the table —as is done routinely in compiler design—to address all types of operators; boolean, relational, assignment, etc.

Listing 3.6 contains the function **itop()**, which converts infix expressions to their postfix form. The function uses the operator priorities listed in Figure 3.3 and the stack functions of Listing 3.3. It also assumes the function **nextinput()**, which returns the next available input symbol; if none remain, it returns the value **EOF** to signify end-of-file.

As for complexity, note that this algorithm only makes one pass over the input. That is, if the infix expression has n symbols, the total number of operations is some constant value (the cost of the basic operation) times n. This yields a complexity of $O(n)$.

Postfix Evaluation

To complete our calculator program, we now need to develop a function that evaluates postfix expressions. As noted earlier, a postfix expression can be evaluated in a single left-to-right scan. The only data requirement is a temporary location for storing operands until they are needed. Again, we will use a stack.

Here is an outline of the function's operation:

1. It will push operands onto the stack until it scans an operator.
2. When it scans an operator, it will pop an appropriate number of operands off the stack (1 for unary, 2 for binary).
3. It will perform the indicated mathematical operation.
4. It will push the result back onto the stack (so the result, itself, can become an operand for a subsequent operation).

When the expression string is exhausted, the one element remaining on the stack is the final result. We can display this value as the answer.

Input	Operation	Stack
123 × +	BEGIN	EMPTY
23 × +	PUSH	1
3 × +	PUSH	12
× +	PUSH	123
+	POP	12
+	POP	1
+	2 × 3	1
+	PUSH	16
EMPTY	POP	1
EMPTY	POP	EMPTY
EMPTY	1 + 6	EMPTY
EMPTY	PUSH	7
EMPTY	POP	EMPTY
EMPTY	PRINT 7	EMPTY

```
void itop()
{

    int     item;
    int     temp;

    while( (item = nextinput()) != EOF )
    {
        switch( item ){
        case '/\':
        case '*':
        case '/':
        case '+':
        case '-':
        case '(':
            /*  Pop operators */
            while( !empty() && isp(top_of_stk()) >= icp(item) )
                    putchar( pop() );

            /*  Push new operator onto stack */
            push( item );
            break;
        case ')':
            /*  Unstack until matching '(' */
            while( (temp = pop()) != '(' )
                    putchar( temp );
            break;
        default:
            /*  Operand  */
            putchar( item );
            break;
        }
    }
    while( !empty() )        /* Empty the rest of Stack */
            putchar( pop() );
}
```

Listing 3.6

Infix-to-postfix conversion.

Let's trace this function's execution for one of our previous examples: $a\,b\,c\,\times\,+$. However, to make the discussion clearer, we will substitute the values 1, 2, and 3 for a, b, and c, respectively.

There are several important points to consider here. First, note that all the operations are performed in the correct order (e.g., multiplication before the addition). Also, operators only pop the appropriate number of operands required to perform their individual operation. (Both are binary operators in this example and, as such, require two operands.) Finally, when the input is exhausted, the only operand remaining on the stack is the result of the expression.

Listing 3.7 contains the function **eval()**, which evaluates postfix expressions in the aforementioned manner. It assumes the **push()** and **pop()** functions from earlier in the chapter and the function **power()** from Chapter 1. It also assumes the function **nextitem()**. This routine returns either the next available symbol from the input stream, or the value **EOF** if none remain.

As it processes each input symbol, **eval()** automatically pushes each operand onto the stack (**default:**). When it encounters an operator, it pops the appropriate number of operands off the stack, performs the operation, and pushes the intermediate result back onto the stack. Note the care taken to ensure that operands are evaluated in the correct order. Also note the comment associated with the division operator. A production version of this algorithm should include an explicit test for division by zero and take appropriate action. The function returns the only remaining value on the stack; this is the result of the expression. The complexity analysis for this function is similar to that of **itop()**, yielding an $O(n)$ algorithm.

3.6 QUEUES

Another special form of a list is the *queue*. A queue is an ordered list in which insertions occur at one end (the *rear*) and deletions occur at the other (the *front*). For example, the result of adding the element E_5 to the queue (E_4, E_3, E_2, E_1) would be $(E_5, E_4, E_3, E_2, E_1)$. Deleting an element now would yield the queue (E_5, E_4, E_3, E_2). Because its operation preserves the entry order of the elements, a queue is a first-in, first-out (FIFO) list.

```
int eval()
{
    int  temp, item;

    while( (item = nextitem()) != EOF )
    {
        switch( item ){
        case '+':
            /* Watch order of operands */
            temp = pop();
            push( pop() + temp );
            break;
        case '-':
            temp = pop();
            push( pop() - temp );
            break;
        case '*':
            temp = pop();
            push( pop() * temp );
            break;
        case '/':
            /* Division by Zero? */
            temp = pop();
            push( pop() / temp );
            break;
        case '^':
            temp = pop();
            push( power(pop(),temp) );
            break;
        default:           /* Operand */
            push( item );
            break;
        }
    }
    return( pop() );            /* Answer */
}
```

Listing 3.7
Postfix evaluation
function.

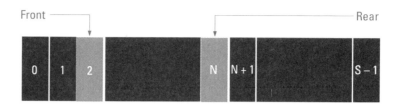

Figure 3.4
A queue array.

Like stacks, queues are also versatile data structures. One of the more common examples of their use is in job scheduling, such as that found in print spoolers. Users enter their print requests in the job queue (this is typically accomplished through the use of a utility program); when a printer completes its current job, the scheduler selects the next request from the queue and routes it to the printer. To add more flexibility, multiple queues can be used to establish priorities. Print requests placed on the high-priority queue take precedence over jobs placed on the low-priority queue.

We can also use arrays to implement queues. Two pointers (**front** and **rear**) maintain the FIFO order (see Fig. 3.4); both are initialized to **−1**. To add (*enqueue*) an element, we increment the pointer **rear** and store the new value in **queue[rear]**. To remove (*dequeue*) an element, we increment the variable **front** and return the value contained in **queue[front]**.

Listing 3.8 contains the source code for routines that manage a simple queue. The function **addqueue()** requires one argument, which it adds to the queue (space permitting); it returns the value **OUT_OF_SPACE** to indicate a queue full condition.

The function **delqueue()** returns the next available element (if any) off the queue. Note that a queue empty condition occurs whenever both pointers are equal (i.e., **front == rear**). Because **delqueue()** does not make an explicit test for this condition, you should call **queue_empty()** before each deletion. The function **queuesize()** is trivial and returns the total number of elements currently enqueued.

The test for queue full is interesting. Regardless of the number of elements currently enqueued, the queue becomes full when the pointer **rear** reaches the end of the array. This is obvious in cases where elements are continually added to the queue without any intervening deletions. However, the queue will become full just as quickly for

```
#define   OK              0
#define   QUEUE_EMPTY    -1
#define   OUT_OF_SPACE   -2
#define   MAXQUEUE       100

int       queue[ MAXQUEUE ];
int       rear = -1, front = -1;

int addqueue( int element )
{
    if( front+1 >= MAXQUEUE )
        return( OUT_OF_SPACE );
    queue[ ++front ] = element;
    return( OK );
}

int delqueue()
{
    if( front == rear )   /* Queue is empty */
        error();
    return( queue[++rear] );
}

int q_empty()
{
    if( front == rear )
            return( QUEUE_EMPTY );
        return( OK );
}

int queuesize()
{
    return( front - rear );
}
```

Listing 3.8
Queue functions.

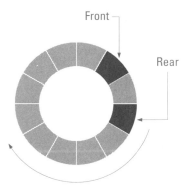

Front

Rear

Figure 3.5
Circular list.

programs that repeatedly add and delete elements because the body of the queue continually moves toward the right (i.e., the high-order indices) with each insertion.

One solution to this problem is to include code in the function **addqueue()** that would shift the queue back to the left whenever **rear** reached the end of the array. That is, the function would copy all the elements—preserving their order—beginning back at **queue[0]**; then modify the index variables, **front** and **rear**, to reflect the new position of the queue within the array. However, this is an extremely inefficient solution because we must move all elements in the queue individually.

A more efficient solution is to represent the queue as a *circular list* (see Fig. 3.5). As with our previous implementation, we still need two index variables to maintain the front and rear of the queue. This time, however, instead of moving from *left to right*, they progress in a *clockwise* manner. That is, when they reach the end of the array, both variables *wrap around* to the beginning. In other words, both pointers chase each other around a circular track: The **rear** pointer moves ahead as elements are added to the queue; the **front** pointer catches up as elements are removed.

This model ensures that we can continue to insert new elements into the queue—regardless of the values contained in the index variables— provided that the number of currently enqueued elements is less than the total size of the array. Figure 3.6 depicts the operation of a circular queue during several insertions and deletions.

We can modify the queue functions of Listing 3.8 to support a

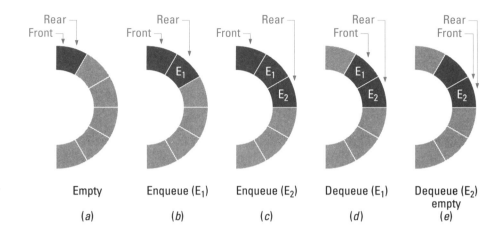

Empty	Enqueue (E$_1$)	Enqueue (E$_2$)	Dequeue (E$_1$)	Dequeue (E$_2$) empty
(a)	(b)	(c)	(d)	(e)

Figure 3.6
Circular list operation.

circular queue. Listing 3.9 contains the modified source code. First, both pointers must now be able to wrap around. This is accomplished with the macro **NEXT(x)**, which uses modulo arithmetic to calculate the next array position.

The queue empty test remains the same (e.g., **rear == front**). However, we can no longer detect a queue full condition by just testing for the end of the array. As depicted in Figure 3.7, if another element is added to the queue, **rear** would become equal to **front**—thus rendering it impossible to distinguish queue full from queue empty. Therefore, it is convenient to define queue full as **NEXT(rear) == front**. Thus, a maximum of **MAXQUEUE-1** elements can be enqueued because **queue[front]** must always remain empty.

Arbitrary-Length Arithmetic

As an example of the application of queues, let's discuss how we might implement functions to perform arbitrary-length arithmetic. To begin, consider that regardless of their power, most computers impose a limit on the size of integers. For example, many machines restrict integers to only 4 bytes; some even smaller. We are going to overcome this restriction by writing functions that deal with numbers represented as character strings.

Suppose that we had two queues of characters, and that each

```
#define   MAXQUEUE        100
#define   NEXT(x)         ((x + 1) % MAXQUEUE)

#define   OK              0
#define   QUEUE_FULL     -1
#define   QUEUE_EMPTY    -2

int       queue[ MAXQUEUE ];
int       rear = 0, front = 0;

int cir_addq( int element )
{
        if( NEXT(rear) == front )
                return( QUEUE_FULL );
        rear = NEXT( rear );
        queue[ rear ] = element;
        return( OK );
}

int cir_delq()
{
        if( front == rear )    /* Error! */
            cir_error();
        rear = NEXT( front );
        return( queue[front] );
}

int cir_empty()
{
        if( front == rear )
            return( QUEUE_EMPTY );
            return( OK );
}

int cir_sizeq()
{
        return( ((front-rear) + MAXQUEUE) % MAXQUEUE );
}
```

Listing 3.9

Circular list functions.

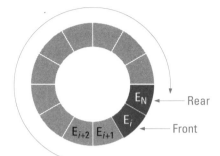

Figure 3.7
Queue full condition.

represented a positive number stored as individual digits. We could add those two numbers in much the same way as a grammar school student would:

1. Remove the top two elements from each queue.
2. Add them together, along with any carry value.
3. Determine the result digit and the new carry value.
4. Repeat until all digits are processed.

For the most part, we can convert this outline directly to an algorithm. There are, however, several points we need to consider. First, when we add numbers, we work from the low-order to the high-order digits of the addends. Thus, the digits must be enqueued such that, when they are dequeued, they are processed in the correct order.

We also need to display digits in the reverse order of processing. Consider the following example:

$$\begin{array}{r} 1234 \\ +\,4444 \\ \hline 5678 \end{array}$$

Even though we compute the value 8 first, 5 is the first digit we would print.

Finally, we need to address the problem of summing addends of different lengths. For example, $123 + 23 = 146$.

Listing 3.10 contains the code for the function **addnums()**. It begins processing by loading its queues. Obviously, this function requires two queues, one for each addend. However, as written, our queue routines handle only a single queue. For the purposes of this

```
void addnums()
{
    char i;
    int  n1, n2, carry, digit;

    while( (i=nextinput()) != EOF )   /* 1st addend */
        addq1( i );

    while( (i=nextinput()) != EOF )   /* 2nd addend */
        addq2( i );

    /*
     *    Loop until both queues are empty
     */
    carry = 0;
    while( !emptyq1() && !emptyq2() )
    {
        n1 = delq1() - '0';
        n2 = delq2() - '0';
        digit = n1 + n2 + carry;
        push( digit % 10 );
        carry = digit / 10;
    }

    if( carry > 0 )
        push( carry );

    while( !empty() )
        printf( "%d", pop() );

    printf( "\n" );
}
```

Listing 3.10
Adding arbitrary-length integers.

example, we simply duplicated the routines of Listing 3.8 to provide support for an additional queue. A better solution is to write a set of general routines that can process any queue passed as an argument. This is discussed further in the exercises at the end of this chapter and again in Chapter 5. **addnums()** assumes that the addend digits are read in the correct order (i.e., low digits first). If they came in reverse order, we would simply use stacks in lieu of queues.

The third **while** loop performs the addition operation described previously. However, note that the conditional test will only terminate the loop when *both* queues are empty. So how do we handle the situation in which addends are not the same length? Specifically, how do we handle the case in which one queue is empty and the other is not? We simply add the following code to the **delq1()** and **delq2()** routines:

```
if( front2 == rear2 )  /* Queue is empty */
    return( 0 );
```

This statement ensures that each time we try to remove an element from an empty queue, the deletion function returns the value 0 (rather than a queue empty indication). Thus, we can continue processing the non-empty queue (adding a harmless 0 to each digit) until it, too, is exhausted.

The body of the **while** loop also contains some interesting processing. The first two statements convert each digit from its character value to its numeric value. This is accomplished by subtracting the character value of the digit '0' from each addend digit as it is removed from the queue. That is, the result of this subtraction will yield the numeric equivalent of the digit. For example, the numeric value for the character '2' is 50; the numeric value for the character '0' is 48. If '2' were the digit just removed from the queue, the result of the expression would yield 50 − 48 = 2.

The next three lines of code compute and store the new digit and the carry value. Finally, note that the function uses a stack to store the digits so that they can be displayed in the correct order.

SUMMARY

In this chapter we discussed static data structures. Static data structures do not alter their basic memory configuration during program execution. These structures are typically constructed by combining atoms into larger data aggregates.

One of the more common types of aggregates is the array. Although simple in concept, arrays can serve as the basis for complex data structures, such as:

Ordered lists   An ordered set of elements.

Stack   A LIFO list that permits insertions and deletions at only one end, called the *top*.

Queue   A FIFO list that allows insertions at one end (called the *rear*) and deletions at the other end (called the *front*).

Circular list   An extension to the basic queue. It can be likened to a track wherein the front and rear pointers chase each other in a circular manner. Circular queues allow you to continue to add elements as long as there are slots available in the array.

The data structures discussed in this chapter can serve as a foundation for solving complex problems.

EXERCISES

1. What type of data structure would you use to model the following?
   a. Customers entering and leaving a bank
   b. Piles of lunch trays in a school cafeteria
   c. Cars waiting in line to pay a toll

2. Implement the calculator program of Section 3.5. See if you can include support for floating-point operands and an assignment facility for variables. Also, modify the functions `itop()` and `eval()` so they will write/read postfix expressions to/from a queue. How should your program handle errors such as $A + B) \times C$?

3. Write a set of general-purpose stack routines, similar to those in Listing 3.3, that will operate on any array supplied as an argument to the functions.

4. Do the same for the queue routines of Listing 3.8.

5. Implement a set of stack routines that allow two stacks to share the same data array. (*Hint:* Let one stack grow from right to left; the other from left to right.)

6. Write a function to reverse the order of elements in an array. Can this be done in place?

7. Trace the growth and decay of the stack managed by the function **itop()** when converting the following infix expressions:

$$3 \uparrow 2 \times 4 \uparrow 3$$

$$3 \uparrow ((2 \times 4) \uparrow 3)$$

$$4 \uparrow 3 \uparrow 2 \uparrow 1$$

8. Trace the growth and decay of the stack managed by the function **eval()** when evaluating the postfix forms of the expressions presented in question 7.

9. Trace the behavior of a circular queue during the following sequence of events:

```
cir_addq(1)

cir_addq(2)

cir_delq()

cir_addq(3)

cir_delq()
```

Assume an array size of 5 and that the sequence of function calls is repeated five times.

10. Add the necessary code to the function **addqueue()** to allow it to shift queue elements left—if there is room—when **rear** reaches the end of the array.

11. A *deque*, or double-ended queue, is a linear list that permits insertions and deletions at either end. Write a set of routines to implement a deque using an array. (*Hint:* Use a circular representation.)

12. Complement the **addnums()** function (Listing 3.10) by developing routines that perform subtraction, multiplication, and division.

13. Extend the functions you wrote for exercise 12 to handle negative numbers.

14. Discuss how you would extend the functions of exercise 12 to handle floating-point numbers.

Recursion

CHAPTER

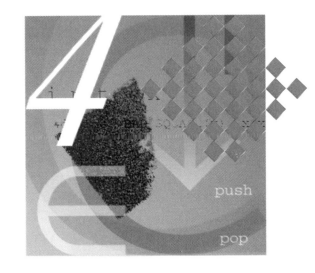

push

pop

4.1 INTRODUCTION

A procedure that calls itself, either directly or indirectly, is termed *recursive*. Direct recursion occurs when function A makes another call to function A; indirect recursion occurs when function A calls function B, which, in turn, calls function A. It is important to understand that each *instantiation* (active copy) of a recursive procedure is entirely unique and has its own arguments, local variables, return address, etc. Further, each instantiation returns to the procedure that directly invoked it. Thus, if C calls A, then A calls B, and then B calls A, the second instantiation of A is completely independent of the first and returns to its caller B, not C.

Most beginning computer science students shudder at the mention of the term *recursion*, or believe the technique is reserved solely for the most sophisticated programmers writing the most arcane programs. On the contrary, recursion is a powerful tool that every programmer should understand and use.

```
int fact_iter( int n )
{
    int  i, ans;

    if( n == 0 )                    /* By definition */
        return( 1 );

    ans = 1;
    for( i = 1; i <= n; i++ )
        ans = ans * i;

    return( ans );
}
```

Listing 4.1
Factorial numbers—
iterative solution.

4.2   FACTORIAL NUMBERS

The best way to introduce recursion as a programming technique is by way of example. The notation $n!$ reads "n factorial" and denotes the product of the positive integers from 1 to n, inclusive. For example,

$$3! = 1 \times 2 \times 3$$
$$4! = 1 \times 2 \times 3 \times 4$$
$$5! = 1 \times 2 \times 3 \times 4 \times 5$$
$$n! = 1 \times 2 \times 3 \times \cdots \times n-2 \times n-1 \times n$$

We also define $1! = 1$, and $0! = 1$. If asked to develop a function that would compute factorial numbers, how would you do it? Based on the previous definition, an iterative solution is suggested and might look similar to the function provided in Listing 4.1.

However, we can reverse the definition of the formula:

$$n! = n \times (n - 1) \times (n - 2) \times \cdots \times 3 \times 2 \times 1$$

Thus, $4! = 4 \times 3 \times 2 \times 1$. Note that $3 \times 2 \times 1$ is 3!; therefore, we can define 4! recursively as

$$4! = 4 \times 3!$$

In general, we can define $n!$ as

$$n! = n \times (n - 1)!$$

$$(n - 1)! = (n - 1) \times (n - 2)!$$

$$(n - 2)! = (n - 2) \times (n - 3)!$$

$$\vdots$$

Having established a recursive definition for factorial numbers, we can begin to formulate a recursive algorithm. Consider the following pseudo-code:

```
fact( n )
     x = n - 1;
     compute x!;          /* (n-1)! */
     return( n*x! );      /* n! = n * (n-1)! */
```

The function **fact()** computes the value of $n!$ by calculating the value of $(n - 1)!$ and then multiplying the result by n. However, as you may have noted, statement two is not adequately defined: We must find a way to compute the value of **x!**. But if you think about it, we already have one: **fact()**. The function **fact()** computes factorial numbers. Let's use that knowledge and rewrite the routine as

```
fact( n )
     x = fact( n-1 );    /* (n-1)! */
     return( n*x );       /* n! = n * (n-1)! */
```

Now, when computing the value of $n!$, the function will recursively call itself to compute the value of $(n - 1)!$.

Is the function complete? Let's take a closer look and trace its execution when computing 2!. Processing begins when the function is invoked with an argument of 2. It computes 2! by recursively calling itself with an argument of 1; to compute 1!, it again calls itself with an argument of 0. The third copy of the function will call itself with an argument of -1, the next -2, and so on. The problem is now becoming clear: The function is infinitely recursive.

All recursive procedures need some way of stopping the recursion. We call this the *terminating condition* or the *out*. It is usually placed at the top of a recursive function and contains the statements that eventually put an end to the recursion and begin the unstacking of all the nested invocations. If it is omitted or incorrect—as we have just seen—functions can become infinitely recursive.

Returning to our example, let's identify a terminating condition for the function **fact()**. By definition, we know that 0! = 1 and 1! = 1. We can therefore add tests for these values at the top of the procedure as follows

```
fact( n )
    if( n == 0 OR n == 1 )
        return( 1 );


    return( n * fact(n-1) );
```

Now, when invoked with an argument of 0 or 1, the function will return an explicit value rather than making another recursive call. (Note that we have also removed the unneeded temporary variable **x** from our algorithm.)

We have one more problem, however. The function can be initially called with a negative argument. We should therefore add one more test to ensure that the function has been invoked properly:

```
fact( n )
    if( n < 0 )            /* Bad argument */
        return( -1 );


    if( n == 0 OR n == 1 )
        return( 1 );


    return( n * fact(n-1) );
```

The final C version of the function appears in Listing 4.2. It depends on your point of view, but **fact_recr()** is slightly more readable than **fact_iter()** (Listing 4.1), if for no other reason than that it has no loop to consider. Take the time here to review both functions and convince yourself—if you are doubtful—that the two implementations are equivalent.

```
int fact_recr( int n )
{
        if( n < 0 )  /* Check for bad argument */
            return( -1 );

        if( n == 0 || n == 1 )
            return( 1 );

        return( n * fact_recr(n-1) );
}
```

Listing 4.2
Factorial numbers—
recursive solution.

4.3 FIBONACCI NUMBERS

Let's return to our discussion of Fibonacci numbers. As you may recall from Chapter 2, the Fibonacci sequence is defined as

$$F_0 = 0$$
$$F_1 = 1$$
$$F_n = F_{n-1} + F_{n-2} \qquad \text{for } n \geq 2$$

The solution we presented previously (Listing 2.2) computed a given Fibonacci number iteratively. Upon closer inspection, however, we see that the series is also defined recursively. That is, we can compute a given F_n by summing the values F_{n-1} and F_{n-2}. Therefore, we can begin to construct a recursive solution as follows

```
fib_recr( n )
        return( fib_recr(n-1) + fib_recr(n-2) );
```

We must again consider a terminating condition. In this case, we can use the two initial values, F_0 and F_1, and insert tests into our algorithm:

```
fib_recr( n )
    if( n == 0 )
            return( 0 );

    if( n == 1 )
            return( 1 );

    return( fib_recr(n-1) + fib_recr(n-2) );
```

```
int fib_recr( int n )
{
    if( n < 0 )          /* Bad argument */
        return( -1 );

    if( n == 0 )         /* By definition */
        return( 0 );

    if( n == 1 )         /* By definition */
        return( 1 );

    return( fib_recr(n-1) + fib_recr(n-2) );
}
```

Listing 4.3
Fibonacci numbers—
recursive solution.

The algorithm is just about complete, but notice that **fib_recr()** also can be incorrectly invoked with a negative argument. We will therefore add one more test at the beginning of the routine. Listing 4.3 contains the final C version of the function.

As a programming note, both **fib_recr()** and **fact_recr()** perform tests for invalid arguments during each recursive call. However, the test is really needed only during the initial call to ensure that invoking functions have passed valid arguments. After that, every additional comparison (testing for **n < 0**) is unnecessary. It would be to our advantage if we could somehow prevent the test from executing after the first call.

We can accomplish this by splitting the algorithm into two functions. The first, called from other routines, will test for valid arguments; it will then invoke the second function, which will actually do the work. As an example of this technique, **fib_recr()** has been rewritten and appears in Listing 4.4.

4.4   WRITING RECURSIVE FUNCTIONS

Thus far, we have used recursion to solve problems that we have been able to define recursively. Now let's begin to explore the use of this

```
int fib_recr2( int n )
{
    if( n < 0 )              /* Bad argument */
        return( -1 );

    return( fibx(n) );       /* Compute F(n) */
}
                             /* The work routine */
                             int fibx( int n )

{
    if( n == 0 )
        return( 0 );

    if( n == 1 )
        return( 1 );

    return( fibx(n-1) + fibx(n-2) );
}
```

Listing 4.4
Split functions.

technique for problems in which a recursive solution may not be
readily apparent.

Towers of Hanoi

One of the classic examples demonstrating the power of recursion is
the ancient puzzle, The Towers of Hanoi:

There are three pegs A, B, and C, and a set of five rings, all of
different sizes. The puzzle begins with all rings positioned on peg A
in a manner such that no ring is resting on a smaller one. That
is, they are stacked one atop the other, beginning with the
largest, followed by the next largest, and so on (see Fig. 4.1 for
an example). The object of the puzzle is to stack all five rings in the
same order on peg C. At any time during the solution, you may

Figure 4.1
Towers of Hanoi
puzzle.

place rings on any of the three pegs. However, you must adhere to the following conditions:

- You can only move the topmost ring on any peg.
- At no time may a larger ring rest on a smaller one.

Try to solve the puzzle manually, for a small number of rings (say four or five), before proceeding to the algorithmic solution.

The problem confronting us is to write a program that will solve the puzzle for any number of rings. Let's begin by considering a general solution for n rings. If we had a solution for $n - 1$ rings, it would seem obvious that we could solve the puzzle for n rings: Solve the puzzle for $n - 1$ rings, then move the remaining ring to peg C. Similarly, if we could solve $n - 2$ rings, the $n - 1$ case would also be simple. We could continue in this manner until the trivial case in which $n = 1$: Simply move the ring from peg A to peg C. Although it may not be obvious, what we have just described is a recursive solution to the problem. That is, we solved the problem for a given n in terms of $n - 1$.

Let's examine a more concrete example and solve the puzzle for five rings. Suppose we know how to solve the puzzle for four rings, moving them from peg A to peg C. Obviously, we could just as easily move the four rings from peg A to peg B instead (using C as the auxiliary peg). Then, to complete the solution, we need only move the largest ring from peg A to peg C and move the four rings on peg B to peg C (using A as auxiliary).

We can summarize the solution more precisely as follows:

1. If $n = 1$, move the ring from A to C and halt.
2. Move $n - 1$ rings from A to B using C as auxiliary.
3. Move the nth ring from A to C.
4. Move $n - 1$ rings from B to C using A as auxiliary.

```
void towers( int n, char a, char b, char c )
    /* n: Number of Rings       */
    /* a: The 'From' Peg        */
    /* b: The 'Auxiliary' Peg   */
    /* c: The 'Destination' Peg */
{
    if( n == 1){
        printf("Move ring %d from peg %c to peg %c\n",n,a,c);
        return;
    }

    /*
     * Move n-1 rings from peg A to peg B (C is aux)
     */
    towers( n-1, a, c, b );

    /*
     * Move remaining ring from peg A to peg C
     */
    printf("Move ring %d from peg %c to peg %c\n",n,a,c);

    /*
     * Move the n-1 rings from peg B to peg C (A is aux)
     */
    towers( n-1, b, a, c );
    return;
}
```

Listing 4.5
Towers function.

Note that steps 2 and 4 are recursive in that they suggest that we repeat the solution for $n - 1$ rings. Also note that the pegs change roles as the solution progresses.

Now that we understand the solution, we must convert these rules

```
Move ring 1 from peg A to peg B
Move ring 2 from peg A to peg C
Move ring 1 from peg B to peg C
Move ring 3 from peg A to peg B
Move ring 1 from peg C to peg A
Move ring 2 from peg C to peg B
Move ring 1 from peg A to peg B
Move ring 4 from peg A to peg C
Move ring 1 from peg B to peg C
Move ring 2 from peg B to peg A
Move ring 1 from peg C to peg A
Move ring 3 from peg B to peg C
Move ring 1 from peg A to peg B
Move ring 2 from peg A to peg C
Move ring 1 from peg B to peg C
```

Listing 4.6

Sample output:
Towers function.

into an algorithm. We will design a function, called `towers()`, that will display all the moves required to solve the puzzle for a given number of rings. Its output will be commands of the form

`Move ring X from peg Y to peg Z`

The function `towers()` will require four arguments. The first will indicate the number of rings to use. The other three will determine the role of each of the three pegs: source, destination, or auxiliary. Listing 4.5 contains the code.

The code is almost a line-for-line transcription of our verbal solution. Note how the routine changes the function of each peg with each recursive call. A sample of the output produced by the function, invoked with $n = 4$, appears in Listing 4.6. However, as written, the function lacks one important detail: It does not check for bad argument values. We will leave this as an exercise for the reader.

Eight Queens Puzzle

Another classic example of recursive programming is the Eight Queens Puzzle. The problem is to place eight queens on a chess board such that no two queens are attacking each other. In chess, a queen can capture another piece by moving any number of squares along its row, column, or diagonals (see Fig. 4.2). Thus, the problem is to place eight queens on an 8 × 8 board such that no two queens share the same row, column, or diagonal. Try to solve the puzzle manually before reading on.

To begin our solution, suppose we were to develop a procedure, **nextqueen()**, that would attempt to place a queen in the row indicated by its one argument. That is, the function would scan all the squares of the specified row and, upon locating one that was not under attack, would place a queen on it; it would then recursively call itself to place a queen in the next row. If all eight queens can be placed on the board, the function returns the value **SOLVED**. If all the squares of a given row should be under attack, **nextqueen()** will return a status of **FAIL**.

Let's begin to sketch the algorithm. (Note that for programming convenience, rows and columns will be indexed from 0 to 7.)

```
nextqueen( row )
   for( i = 0; i < 8; i++ )  /* Try each column         */
      if( safe(row, i) )      /* Is square under attack */
         if( nextqueen(row+1) == SOLVED )
            return( SOLVED );

   return( FAIL );           /* All squares under attack */
```

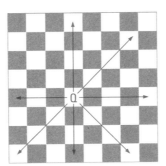

Figure 4.2
Attacking queens.

Clearly, the description is far from complete. First, we need a terminating condition for the recursion. Let's think about that for a moment. We know that, by definition, there is a maximum of eight queens in the puzzle. Therefore, we can test for **row > 7** at the beginning of the function. But consider for a moment the significance of the value contained in the argument **row**. If a recursive call is made to **nextqueen()** with **row** equal to some value n, it means that rows 0 to n − 1 have been solved. Thus, if **nextqueen()** should be called with **row = 8**, it means that all the queens (rows 0 to 7) have been placed and the function should return the value **SOLVED**.

Next, we need a way to track the placement of the queens as the function proceeds. To do this, we will use an 8×8 character array to represent the board. In each position, we will store (for display purposes) one of the following characters: − to denote an empty square; or * to represent a square containing a queen.

Finally, we need to define the function **safe()**, which determines whether a given square is under attack. However, let's postpone our discussion of **safe()** until we have completed the definition of **nextqueen()**.

Let's incorporate the changes we suggested and see how our function is taking shape:

```
nextqueen( row )
  if( row > 7)                       /* The 'out'*/
      return( SOLVED );

  for( i = 0; i < 8; i++ )           /* Try each column 0-7    */
      if( safe(row, i) ){            /* Is square under attack */
          board[row][i] = QUEEN;     /* Place queen on board   */
          if( nextqueen(row+1) == SOLVED )      /* Next row */
              return( SOLVED );
          else
              board[row][i] = EMPTY;   /* Restore board pos */
      }
  return( FAIL );                    /* All squares under attack */
```

Notice that we have added the statement

```
board[row][i] = EMPTY;
```

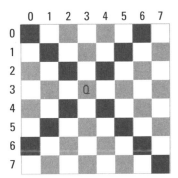

Figure 4.3
Diagonal attacks.

because if a recursive call to **nextqueen()** should fail to find a solution (with a queen located at that position), this statement will restore the board to its previous state; the function is then free to try the next available square.

Our algorithm is beginning to take shape, and we now need to discuss the implementation of the function **safe()**. The problem we must address is how the function will determine whether a given square is under attack from previously placed queens. First, note that there is really no need to check for attacks along rows. By virtue of our implementation, we can be certain that the only queen that could reside on a given row is the one we are attempting to place. Also, checking for attacks along columns could be accomplished directly, if crudely, by indexing through the board along the column in question.

Diagonal attacks will prove to be the most difficult to discern. As depicted in Figure 4.3, a queen positioned on any one of the shaded squares would be attacking the queen placed on the [3,3] slot. How can we easily determine whether a square is under attack along either of its two diagonals?

If you take a closer look at the board in Figure 4.3, you will notice that each diagonal can be uniquely identified as a function of its indices. For example, consider Figure 4.4a. The sum of the indices (row + column) of each square in the forward-tilting diagonal is equal to 6. Therefore, any queen that has been previously placed on a square whose indices sum to 6 will have the [3,3] slot under attack. Similarly, we can derive a unique value for the backward-slanting diagonals (Fig. 4.4b) by subtracting (column − row) the indices. Note that each of the

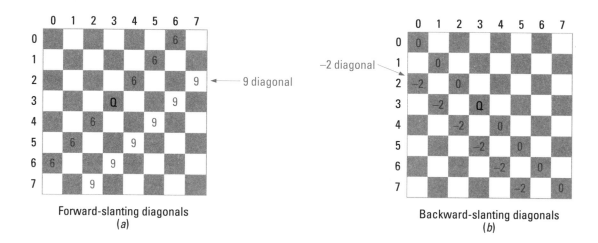

Figure 4.4
Diagonal values.

15 forward-slanting diagonals range in value from 0 to 14, and the backward-slanting diagonals range in value from -7 to $+7$.

We can incorporate this concept into our **safe()** function. The idea is that as each queen is placed onto the board, we will update two arrays: one to track the forward diagonal and one to track the backward diagonal. The index into each array will be the index value of each diagonal. (As a programming convenience, we will add 7 to the index value of the backward diagonal.) Thus, **safe()** need only check the appropriate array slots to determine whether a given square is under attack along one of its diagonals. We will extend this idea to track attacks along columns. In this case, we use only the column value as the index into a third array.

The complete solution to the puzzle appears in Listing 4.7. The function **eightqueens()** is the driving routine. It initializes the board and flag arrays and calls **nextqueen()** to solve the puzzle. If **nextqueen()** returns **SOLVED**, **eightqueens()** also invokes **disp_board()** to print the solution.

The routine **set_flags()** calculates the column and diagonal values and sets the appropriate array flags; it is called whenever a queen is placed onto the board. The procedure **reset_flags()** resets the column and diagonal flags whenever we remove a queen from the board (i.e., after a **FAIL**). The function **safe()** tests the flags associ-

```
#define    FAIL       0
#define    SOLVED     1
#define    EMPTY      '-'
#define    QUEEN      '*'

char colmk[8]; /* Flags for testing rows & diags */
char tiltf[15];
char tiltb[15];
char board[8][8];

void eightqueens()
{
    int  i, j;

    /*
     *    Initialize board & flags
     */
    for( i = 0; i < 8; i++ )
        for (j = 0; j < 8; j++ )
            board[i][j] = EMPTY;

    for( i = 0; i < 15; i++ ){
        tiltf[i] = EMPTY;
        tiltb[i] = EMPTY;
    }

    for( i = 0; i < 8; i++ )
        colmk[i] = EMPTY;

        /*
         *    Attempt to solve puzzle
         */
    if( nextqueen(0) == SOLVED )
        disp_board();
    else
        printf( "No solution found!\n" );

}
```

continued on p. 76

```
int nextqueen( int row )                              continued from p. 75
{
      int  i;

      if( row > 7 )
            return( SOLVED );

      for( i = 0; i < 8; i++ )            /* Try each col */
            if( safe(row, i) == 1 ){
                  board[row][i] = QUEEN;
                  set_flags( row, i );
                  if( nextqueen(row+1) == SOLVED )
                        return( SOLVED );
                  else {
                        /*
                         * Restore board & try next slot
                         */
                        board[row][i] = EMPTY;
                        reset_flags( row, i );
                  }
            }

      return( FAIL );      /* No safe slots - backtrack */
}

void
set_flags( int row, int col ) /* Set col & diag flags */
{
      colmk[ col ] = QUEEN;
      tiltf[ row+col ] = QUEEN;
      tiltb[ (row-col)+7 ] = QUEEN;
}

void
reset_flags( int row, int col )    /* Reset col & diag flags */
{
      colmk[ col ] = EMPTY;
      tiltf[ row+col ] = EMPTY;
      tiltb[ (row-col)+7 ] = EMPTY;

}
```
continued on p. 77

```
int safe( int row, int col )                    continued from p. 76
{
    int  i;

    if( colmk[col]  ==  QUEEN
     || tiltf[row+col]  ==  QUEEN
     || tiltb[(row-col)+7]  ==  QUEEN )
        return( 0 );

    return( 1 );            /* Safe */
}

void disp_board()
{
    int  i,j;

    putchar( '\n' );
    for( i = 0; i < 8; i++ ){
        for(j = 0; j < 8; j++ )
            putchar( board[i][j] );
        putchar( '\n' );
    }
}
```

Listing 4.7
Eight Queens solution.

ated with a given board position; if it returns 1, the square is not under attack.

Backtracking

In the previous example, we described a programming methodology wherein many alternate solution paths are examined. This is a form of *backtracking*. Backtracking is a programming technique in which you proceed along a given path in search of a goal. At each *fork* in the road, you *guess* which path you should follow. If any choice should prove unsuccessful, you backtrack; that is, you back up to the previous fork and try another path. Execution continues in this manner until you either reach a solution or exhaust all possibilities. The latter condition signifies that no solution exists and the program should exit with an indicative status.

Non-Deterministic Programming

Backtracking is a coding technique belonging to a more general class called Non-Deterministic Programming (NDP). In conventional software design, we program all the steps required to attain a desired result. This implies that a definitive, a priori understanding of the solution is available and that the problem itself is algorithmically solvable. Thus, as each successive statement is executed, the program draws progressively closer to the desired result.

NDP is somewhat different in that we do not code a solution. Instead, we program the *method* by which we attain a solution—if one exists. In fact, we do not assume that a solution does exist. The program literally makes guesses until it either finds a solution or exhausts all available alternatives. Moreover, there can be zero, one, or multiple solutions for a given problem. This method of programming has obvious benefits in artificial intelligence applications and expert systems development.

Chronological Backtracking

There are two types of backtracking: Chronological Backtracking (CBT) and Dependency-Directed Backtracking (DDB). CBT is effectively an exhaustive search, similar to the earlier discussion. Each solution path is exhaustively searched until one of the two outcomes is determined. For example, consider the following pseudo-code:

```
 1: bktk_exe( node )
 2: {
 3:  if( node = SUCCESS )
 4:  then
 5:      return( I_FOUND_IT)
 6:  endif
 7:  for( each_choice_at_this_node )
 8:  do
 9:      ret_stat = bktk_exe( child_node )
10:      if( ret_stat = SUCCESS )
```

```
11:         then
12:             return( ret_stat )
13:         endif
14:   done
15:   return( FAIL )
16: }
```

If at any time a solution is found (lines 3–6, 9–13), the function returns a value indicative of success. If not, it must try an alternate choice (lines 7–14). If all the alternatives have been exhausted (line 7), a value indicating failure is returned, forcing the previous invocation of the function to back up to a previous path (line 15) before continuing the search.

There are two important points to consider. First, whenever we perform a backup, we must restore the environment to its previous state before trying the next path. Saving and restoring state data can become very expensive. Second, backtracking typically yields an algorithm that is exponential in order of execution magnitude. The following sections discuss methods of improving the performance of this technique.

Dependency-Directed Backtracking

Dependency-Directed Backtracking functions essentially as described earlier, but attempts to eliminate some unnecessary searching (and therefore unnecessary backups). This is accomplished in two ways. First, as the name DDB implies, we can backtrack to choices that are dependent on the dead end. That is, we back up until we reach a point where a dependency was created and continue searching from there.

As an example of this technique, consider a case in which we are searching for a solution that requires that four conditions (A, B, C, and D) be satisfied for our program to return a successful status. Let us further assume that we have reached a state in our processing in which conditions A and B are satisfied but C and D are not. In lieu of just automatically backtracking to the closest fork, continue backtracking to a point where A and B are still true and resume the search from there. We can skip all the intervening paths.

The second method of eliminating unnecessary searching is called *pruning*. If we reach a point in the search where it becomes obvious that any further effort along a given path is fruitless, we can eliminate all subsequent paths from that point onward (i.e., force a backtrack to occur). Pruning is a straightforward approach and is often implemented in game-playing simulations. For example, we could write a chess program that could determine its next move by assigning a quantum value to each board position it examines. At any given point, it would select the move that yields the most advantageous (highest) value. If the algorithm were to traverse a path representing the moves queen takes pawn, pawn takes queen, it could elect to eliminate any further searching along that trail.

For the sake of completeness, we should also mention a third method of improving a backtracking procedure: managing an explicit stack. Recursive procedures are costly. This is attributable to the considerable amount of overhead processing required for each successive call. The execution environment must save registers, store a return address, allocate local storage, etc., in preparation for the return. Most of this information is not directly related to the problem at hand and, therefore, having to save and restore it only wastes CPU cycles. We could save time and space if we were to code the stack explicitly. This can be accomplished by transforming the algorithm from recursive to iterative and maintaining the to-do list in an application-controlled stack.

Acrostic Example

As an example of the backtracking technique, we will design a program that solves acrostic puzzles. An acrostic puzzle is simply a crossword puzzle without the clues: You are supplied the words and the diagram and, through trial and error, you must enter all the words into their appropriate slots (see Fig. 4.5).

The overall operation of the program is as follows: Read the puzzle and word list into internal data structures; search for a solution; if there is one, print it. The actual backtracking logic can be found in the function **solve()**, which is what we will focus on here. A complete discussion of the program appears in Appendix A.

The function **solve()** is a recursive procedure that works as follows:

1. It chooses, and determines the size of, the next puzzle slot to fill (horizontal or vertical).

TO
ERA
BEST
TAMP
TOPS

Figure 4.5
Sample acrostic
puzzle.

2. It selects, at random (i.e., sequentially), an appropriately sized word from the available list. It calls the function **itfits()** to determine whether a given word fits into the slot (in typical crossword puzzle fashion).

3. If the word fits, **solve()** enters it into the puzzle. At this point, with the aid of the function **enter()**, a snapshot of the current state (puzzle) is saved.

4. It then recursively calls itself to continue toward a solution.

5. If at any point a solution is found (i.e., there are no more slots to fill), the function returns the value **SOLVED**.

6. If a given recursive call fails to find a solution, the puzzle is restored to its previous state (with the help of the function **restore()**); the word that had been tried at that point is returned to the free list and the next available word is selected; if none remain, the function returns the value **FAIL** to its caller.

Let's trace the execution of the function as it begins to solve the sample puzzle depicted in Figure 4.6. Note that the line numbers in the following discussion refer to Listing 4.8; also, the "random" selection of the words will be the order in which they appear in Figure 4.6.

First, we need a four-letter word for the *1 across* position. The function randomly selects *best* (line 14), marks it as **USED** (line 16), and inserts it into the puzzle (line 17). It then calls itself recursively to continue the processing (line 19). Next, for the *2 down* position, a three-letter word is needed and *era* is similarly inserted into the puzzle.

The function now attempts to fill the *3 down* position. It selects the next available four-letter word, *tamp* (line 13); checks to see that it fits (line 14); and inserts it into the puzzle (line 17).

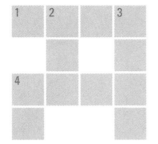

TO
ERA
BEST
TAMP
TOPS

Figure 4.6
Acrostic puzzle.

The next slot to fill is *4 across*, and the function selects the next available four-letter word—in this case, *tops*. This time, however, the **itfits()** test (line 15) fails. Recognizing that the last four-letter word has been used (line 13), the function performs a backtrack (line 27).

After backtracking, the function resumes processing at the point where it, again, needs to fill the *3 down* position. It discards what was its first choice, *tamp* (lines 22 and 23) and selects the next available word, *tops* (line 14). (Just as a reminder, *tops* was put back on the available list just prior to the backtrack.) From this point on, the function solves the puzzle without any additional difficulties.

4.5 USE OF RECURSION

Once the technique of recursion is understood, the question most often asked is when to employ it. Let's begin by discussing when not to use it. By definition, all recursive functions have a corresponding iterative solution. With few exceptions, iterative solutions are more efficient than their recursive counterparts. Therefore, you should not use recursion when run-time performance is critical.

However, this does not tell the whole story. Properly used recursion can be no less efficient than using procedure calls where appropriate. For example, tests have shown that for some sorting algorithms (see Chapter 9) a recursive solution is no more than 2% slower than its iterative counterparts. This is a negligible difference, especially considering the speed of today's processors.

Nonetheless, there are two cases in which the use of recursion can lead to significant performance degradation:

```
 1: solve( length, width )
 2: int     length, width;
 3: {
 4:         int     l, w, i, len, tmp, type;
 5:         char    old[ WORDLEN - MINWORD + 1 ];
 6:
 7:         w = width;
 8:         l = length;
 9:         len = next( &l, &w, &type );
10:         if( len == 0 )
11:                 return( SOLVED );
12:
13:         for( i = 0; i<MAXWORD && WORD(len,i)[0]!=NULL; i++ ){
14:                 if( FLAG(len, i) == FREE
15:                 && itfits(l, w, WORD(len, i), type) ){
16:                         FLAG(len, i) = USED;
17:                         enter(old, l, w, WORD(len,i), type);
18:                         prev = type;
19:                         tmp = solve( l, w );
20:                         if( tmp == SOLVED )
21:                                 return( SOLVED );
22:                         restore( old, l, w, type );
23:                         FLAG(len, i) = FREE;
24:                 }
25:         }
26:
27:         return( FAIL );
28: }
```

Listing 4.8
Acrostic solution.

1. The algorithm performs redundant computations. The recursive implementation of the Fibonacci algorithm is a clear example of this problem. When you invoke **fact_recr()** to compute F_n, it computes the value of F_{n-2} twice: once during the initial call, and once when it make a recursive call to compute F_{n-1}. In a similar manner, it computes F_{n-3} three times, F_{n-4} four times, and so on. As a result of all the redundant computations, the complexity of

`fact_recr()` becomes $O(\phi^n)$, where ϕ is the golden ratio $(1 + \sqrt{5}/2 \simeq 1.618)$. (The actual analysis is beyond the scope of this text.)

2. The recursion becomes deeply nested. This problem is clearly highlighted in the function `fact_recr()` (the recursive version of the factorial algorithm). Note that in computing $n!$, the depth of the recursion (i.e., the number of nested invocations) the function attains is $O(n)$. For large values of n, this can place excessive demands on the run-time machine environment. In fact, even if we discount all other problems (e.g., integer overflow), for a large enough n, the function might not have access to enough resources (e.g., memory and stack) to compute a solution on some systems. Contrast this behavior with that of the function `eight-queens()`. Its depth of recursion never exceeds 9.

In addition to any performance considerations, you should not use recursion when each successive invocation would result in a larger task. Each recursive call should receive a *smaller* portion of the work.

Do use recursion, however, when the problem is, itself, defined recursively. This is common in mathematical formulas (e.g., recurrence relations). Use it also when processing a recursively defined data structure (e.g., binary trees) or when a problem can be solved with a divide-and-conquer approach. Keep in mind that a recursive implementation of an algorithm is usually smaller and therefore it is usually less expensive to develop and less costly to maintain.

SUMMARY   Recursion is a powerful programming technique. Proper use of recursion results in simple, maintainable algorithms. One of the most important aspects of a recursive algorithm is the *out*. All recursive functions must have a terminating condition to stop the recursion and unwind the stack.

A powerful programming technique that employs recursion is called backtracking. You can improve the performance of backtracking algorithms using several techniques, including pruning and explicit stack management.

1. Define recursion.

2. Describe the programming technique called backtracking.

3. Write a recursive function that counts from 1 to n, where n is a positive integer argument passed to the function.

4. Write a recursive function to sum the numbers from 1 to n, where n is a positive integer argument passed to the function.

5. Trace the execution of the function **fact_recr()** when invoked with an argument of 10.

6. Trace the execution of the function **fib_recr()** when invoked with an argument of 8.

7. Implement the function **towers()** and manually verify its output when solving for five rings.

8. Rewrite the function **towers()** as an iterative algorithm.

9. Implement, and trace the exucution of, the Eight Queens program.

10. How many different solutions exist for the Eight Queens Puzzle? Modify the program of the previous question so it will generate all of them.

11. Convert the function **nextqueen()** to an iterative solution. Which version is easier to maintain? Which version executes faster? Explain your answers.

12. Implement and test a program that solves acrostic puzzles (see Appendix A).

13. Write a backtracking program that will compute a knight's tour of a chessboard. A knight moves by jumping two squares in one direction (either vertically or horizontally) and one square in a perpendicular direction. A knight's tour is a sequence of moves, starting at any square, that visits each square exactly once. Try to implement some of the improvements discussed in this chapter.

Dynamic Data Structures

C H A P T E R

5.1 INTRODUCTION

In the preceding chapters, we used static data structures to implement our example algorithms. That is, storage was pre-allocated and of a fixed size. One advantage of this type of allocation is that it provides direct access to individual elements. For example, if we needed to change the ith element of a list, we could code **a[i] = new value;**.

Nevertheless, static data structures have several disadvantages. The first becomes evident when attempting to insert or delete elements in the middle of a list. For example, consider maintaining a list of names in alphabetical order. To insert a new element, a program must do the following (see Fig. 5.1):

- Determine the location for the new name.
- Allocate space by shifting existing elements one slot to the right.
- Enter the new name into the list.

For a list of size n, we would need to shift, on average, $n/2$ elements to complete each insertion. To delete an element, the program must remove the designated element from the list and then shift all succeeding members one position to the left to fill the vacant slot.

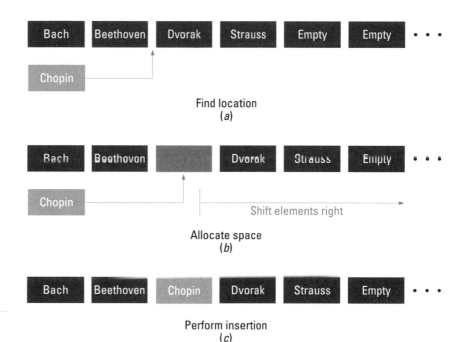

Find location
(*a*)

Shift elements right

Allocate space
(*b*)

Perform insertion
(*c*)

Figure 5.1
Array insertion.

A second disadvantage of static storage structures is that they are unable to respond to increasing or unanticipated demand. If we allocate space for ten elements, the arrival of the eleventh will likely present a problem. If, on the other hand, we decided to overcompensate, the program might become too large for the target execution environment. The following sections discuss methods by which we can overcome these difficulties.

5.2 LINKED LISTS

One solution to the first problem mentioned—that of difficult insertions and deletions—is to use a second array to implement a *linked list*. A linked list is a data structure wherein each element contains both a data value and a pointer to the next element in the list. That is, each element contains information that allows us to locate the next element in the list: The first node points to the second, the second to the third, and so on. This type of structure usually

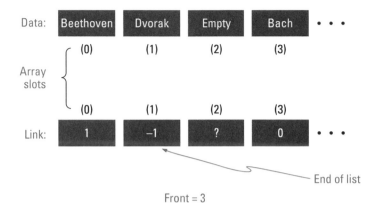

Figure 5.2

A linked list.

requires a so-called *head pointer* to indicate the beginning of the list, as well as some convention to signify its end.

For example, consider the list presented in Figure 5.2. The order of the elements is not determined by their position in the data array (**data[]**), but rather by the entries contained in the link array (**link[]**.) The variable **front**, serving as our head pointer, identifies the beginning of the list (slot 3 in this example). To access the data value of the first element (BACH), we index into the data array at **data[front]**. The location of the next element (BEETHOVEN) is determined by the value stored in the link array at **link[front]**, in this case **0**; likewise, its corresponding data value is accessed as **data[0]**. The traversal continues in this manner until we encounter a link value of −**1** (by convention, we will use this value to signify the end of the list).

This form of *indirection* allows us to store list elements in any available slot of the data array. Further, free slots (holes) no longer present a problem—just mark them as available for reuse.

The second and more significant advantage of this method is that it simplifies insertions and deletions. To demonstrate this, let's insert the element CHOPIN into the list depicted in Figure 5.2. The first step is to determine the logical position of the new element. Specifically, we must identify the node that will become the direct *predecessor* of the new element (i.e., the node that will ultimately point to CHOPIN, in this example BEETHOVEN).

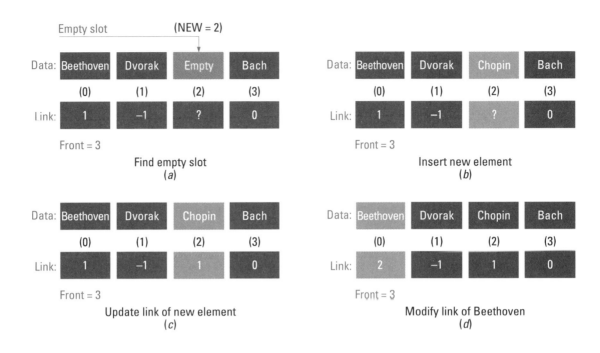

Figure 5.3
Linked-list insertion.

After determining the location, the steps required to perform the actual insertion are as follows (see Fig. 5.3):

- Find an empty slot in the data array (**data[2]**).
- Store (copy) the new element (CHOPIN) into the free slot.
- Update the link for the new element (**link[2] = 1;**).
- Insert the new element into the list (**link[0] = 2;**).

Deleting list elements is essentially a two-step procedure (see Fig. 5.4). First, remove the deleted element from the list by setting the link value of its predecessor to point to its successor. Then mark the deleted element's data slot as available.

Listing 5.1 contains two example procedures, **insert()** and **delete()**, that perform insertions and deletions on a linked list. There are several points worth noting about the implementation. First, both functions require an argument indicating the logical position for the operation. Specifically, this argument must be the index of the

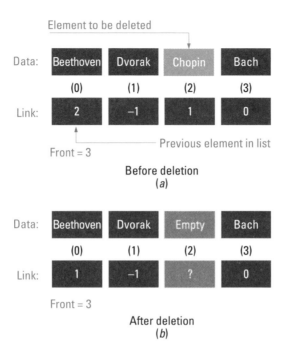

Figure 5.4
Linked-list deletion.

target element's predecessor. (We will return to this point later in this chapter when we discuss doubly linked lists.) In line with this, note the first **if** condition in the function **delete()**. It tests whether its **prev** argument refers to the last element in the list. If that is the case, the function cannot delete any elements from the list because, by definition, the last element of the list cannot be a predecessor node. In all such cases, **delete()** returns the value **END** to indicate to the calling function that the list has not changed.

Next, both routines handle the special cases involving the first element of the list. The reason is that when the first element is either deleted, or has another element inserted in front of it, there is no predecessor node. (The variable **front** is not part of the list proper.) As a result, both functions use a special value (**BEG**) to indicate an operation on the list's first element.

In closing, keep in mind that the benefits provided by this implementation are not without their costs: Additional memory is required for the link array and we no longer have the ability to access

```
#define    OK          0
#define    NO_SPACE   -1

#define    BEG        -2
#define    END        -3

#define    MAXLEN       20
#define    MAXENTRIES   100

int  front = END;
int  link[ MAXENTRIES ];
char data[ MAXENTRIES ][ MAXLEN ];

int
insert( int where, char item[] )   /* Ins item after 'where' */
{
    int  i;

    /*
     *    Find free slot in data array
     */
    for(i = 0; i  <  MAXENTRIES && data[i][0] != NULL; i++)
        /* NULL BODY */;

    if( i >= MAXENTRIES )
        return ( NO_SPACE );

    strncpy( data[i], item, MAXLEN ); /* Store entry */

    if( where == BEG ){      /* Insert at beginning */
        link[ i ] = front;
        front = i;
    } else {
        link[ i ] = link[ where ];
        link[ where ] = i;
    }

    return( OK );

}
```

continued on p. 92

continued from p. 91

```
int delete( int prev )          /* Delete member after 'prev' */
{
     int  t;

     if( link[ prev ] == END )  /* Nothing to Do! */
          return( END );

     if( prev == BEG ){
          /*
           *    Delete first element
           */
          t = front;
          front = link[ front ];
     } else {
          /*
           *    Delete element after 'prev'
           */
          t = link[ prev ];
          link[ prev ] = link[ t ];
     }
     data[t][0] = NULL;  /* Free data slot */

     return( OK );
}
```

Listing 5.1
Linked-list insertion and deletion functions.

individual list elements directly. The sections that follow will discuss ways that we can improve on the ideas developed in this section.

5.3 LINKED LISTS USING POINTERS

We will now address the second problem mentioned previously, that of space limitation. Although it has several advantages, the double array implementation of the previous section does not overcome the disadvantages associated with pre-allocated memory aggregates. Indeed, the problem is compounded because we need a second (link) array.

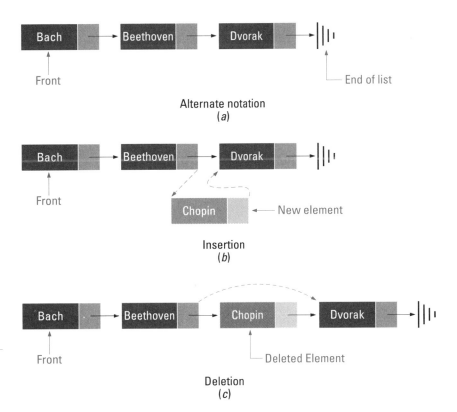

Figure 5.5

Linked lists: Preferred representation.

Figure 5.5a presents another way that we can represent lists in memory. As depicted, each list member can be viewed as a self-contained unit (referred to as a *node*), with both a data field and a pointer to the next element (successor).

In previous examples, the pointer (link) field was strictly an index into another array. We will now expand this capability and permit link fields to reference any node residing at any valid memory location (address). As a result, programs can now construct and process lists of arbitrary sizes. In addition, as we will see, we can create nodes 'on the fly'; this allows us to overcome the limitations associated with pre-allocated storage.

Figures 5.5b and 5.5c briefly illustrate how we perform list insertions and deletions using this representation; the sections that follow discuss the implementation in detail.

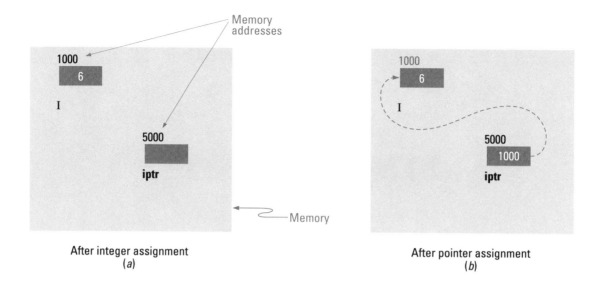

After integer assignment
(*a*)

After pointer assignment
(*b*)

Figure 5.6
Pointer assignment.

Pointers

Before we can continue the preceding discussion on linked lists, we must determine how link fields can reference any node positioned anywhere in memory (not just in another array). To understand how this is accomplished, this section introduces and describes a new type of variable called a *pointer*.

Regardless of data type, all variables possess several generic *attributes*. These include name, size, type, and address (location in memory). When writing programs, developers reference variables by name. However, after a program is compiled and loaded into memory (executed), variables are referenced solely by their addresses. For example, consider an integer variable **i**, loaded at memory location **1000**. The assignment **i = 6;** will cause the *contents* at memory location **1000** to be overwritten with the value **6** (see Fig. 5.6a).

As mentioned earlier, programmers usually reference variables by name. However, there are times when it more convenient to reference variables by their addresses. For example, consider a program that processes employee records. (Typically, employee records are quite large;

for our example, we'll assume that they are 2048 (2K) bytes in size.) Let's assume we had to write a payroll function that processes these records and prints checks. One way to provide our function with data is to pass each employee record as an argument. However, that means we would have to copy 2K bytes worth of data with each call to the function.

A better approach is to tell the function *where* records reside in memory. In effect, each time we invoke the function, we tell it to process the employee record that resides over *there* (wherever *there* happens to be for each record). Using this technique, we only need to pass the address of a record (typically only 4 to 8 bytes worth of information) rather than its entire contents.

Pointers in C

In C, we store and process address information in variables called *pointers*. A pointer is a variable that uses an address to reference, indirectly, another data object. Put simply, a pointer is a variable that contains the address of another variable.

The C declaration for a pointer has the general form

*data_type   *ptr_name;*

where *data_type* determines the type of object at which *ptr_name* can point. This can range from one of the basic data types to a user-defined aggregate (as we will see shortly).

For example, we can define a pointer to integer as

```
int *iptr;
```

(The trick to understanding C declarations is to read them from right to left. Also, pronounce * as "pointer to." Thus, *iptr is a *pointer to* int.)

The preceding pointer declaration creates storage for a variable that has all the attributes of any other data object: name, type, size, address, and so on. The sole difference is the type of data that we can store in it. Specifically, iptr does not hold an integer value; rather, it holds the address of another integer variable.

After declaring a pointer, our next concern is to determine where it is pointing. As we have been stressing, pointers are just like any other variable. As a result, they, too, must be *initialized*. Assuming the preceding declaration for `iptr` and the declaration `int  i;`, the C statement

```
iptr = &i;
```

assigns the address of **i** to **iptr** (see Fig. 5.6b). That is, we say that **iptr** points at **i** and that we can access the contents of **i** indirectly through **iptr**. Note that the symbol **&** is a unary operator (i.e., requires only one operand) that yields the address of its operand. Also note that the preceding assignment modifies the contents of **iptr**.

Typically we are not interested in the exact values of addresses; that is a concern best left to the compiler and the memory management subsystem of the host operating environment. However, if we wanted to, we could print addresses as follows:

```
printf( "The address of i is: %d\n", &i );
```

or

```
printf( "The address of i is: %d\n", iptr );
```

Once assigned, we can use a pointer to modify the contents of the memory cell at which it points. Assuming all of the preceding declarations and assignments, the statement

```
*iptr = 6;
```

is equivalent to the assignment

```
i = 6;
```

The ***** operator *dereferences* the pointer **iptr**; thus, we access **i** indirectly via the pointer.

Listing 5.2 contains some additional examples of pointer manipulation in C.

Pointer dereferencing is dynamic. That is, the cell at which a pointer is pointing at the time of dereferencing is the one that is modified. For example, consider the following code fragment:

```
int i, j, *ptr;

ptr = &i;
*ptr = 10;     /* assign 10 to i */

ptr = &j;
*ptr = 10;     /* assign 10 to j */
```

```
void ptr_ex()
{
    int  i, j;    /* Declare integer variables  */
    int  *p;      /* Declare a pointer variable */

    p = &i;       /* 'p' now points to 'i'    */
    *p = 6;       /* equivalent to 'i = 6;'   */
    i = 7;        /* equivalent to '*p = 7;'  */
    j = *p;       /* equivalent to 'j = i;'   */
}
```

Listing 5.2
Examples of pointer manipulation in C.

The first time we assign **10** to the cell at which **ptr** points, we modify **i**; the second time we modify **j**.

As with any variable, type checking also applies to pointers. Specifically, pointers should only point at objects consistent with their declaration. For example, a pointer, declared as pointing to an **int**, should not be assigned the address of a variable declared as a **double**.

As a final note, programmers new to C are sometimes confused by what appears to be conflicting uses of the * operator. In a declaration statement, * adds levels of indirection; in an executable statement, it removes levels of indirection. (Keep in mind that * is also the binary multiplication operator!) Obviously, its meaning depends on its use. This idea, however, is certainly not a new one. For example, consider the English word *read*. The only way we can tell whether it should be pronounced "reed" or "red" is by context. In computer languages, *operator overloading* occurs when symbols have more than one meaning. Operator overloading is not unique to C. For example, most computer languages (including C) overload the (−) operator. It can mean subtraction (as in **a − b**) or it can mean negation (as in **x = −y**), depending on usage. Keep operator overloading in mind when working the * operator in C.

Pointer Example

As an example of the use of pointers, let's write a function that swaps the value in two variables. As a first cut, you might write a function similar to the following:

```
void bad_swap( int x, int y )
{
    int temp;

    temp = x;
    x = y;
    y = temp;
}
```

However, in C, function arguments are passed by *value*. That means, when we call a function such as

```
bad_swap( a, b );
```

the value of each *actual* parameter (e.g., **a** and **b**) is copied into the corresponding *formal* parameter (e.g., **x** and **y**, respectively). The variables **x** and **y** are local to their function. Thus, any changes we make to **x** and **y** will have no effect on their corresponding actual parameters. As a result, **bad_swap()** will not accomplish the desired task. (Languages that permit formal parameters to modify actual parameters support a calling convention referred to as *call by reference*. Take on the role of compiler writer for a moment and consider how you would deal with a function call such as **swap(a+b, c+d)** in a call-by-reference environment.)

One way to overcome this problem is to pass the address of the actual parameters, as in

```
void good_swap( int *x, int *y )
{
    int temp;

    temp = *x;
    *x = *y;
    *y = temp;
}
```

This allows us to swap the value of any two integers with a call such as

```
good_swap( &a, &b );
```

At first glance, it might seem that we are now calling by reference.

On the contrary, we are still calling by value; it's just that the values we are passing are addresses.

C Structures

Before we can resume our discussion of linked lists, we must also decide how we will organize the complex data structures we will need. We have already seen one way that programming languages (C in particular) allow us to organize data: the array. Arrays allow us to aggregate multiple elements of the same type. But to implement linked lists, we need a way to group elements of dissimilar types. In C, we can accomplish this through the use of *structures*.

A C structure is a collection of one or more variables (called *members*) that we can manipulate as a single unit. They are akin to the notion of *record* in other languages. For example, consider an employee record. Companies must maintain a diverse set of attributes for their employees: *name* (**string**), *social security number* (**long integer**), *salary* (**float**), and *job code* (**char**), to name a few.

To demonstrate the definition and use of structures in C, let's construct a simple employee record. Before we begin, consider the following point. When we declare a variable (in any language), the compiler must know what that variable looks like before it can construct it for us. For example, if we code

```
int i;
```

the compiler must know how to build an integer cell in memory. The same holds true for structures in that we must provide the compiler with a description of the object before it can reserve storage. In C, we can define a structure as follows:

```
struct employee {
       char    name[ 25 ];
       long    ssnumb;
       float   salary;
       char    job_code;
};
```

The reserved word **struct** introduces the declaration. **employee** is a user-defined name for the structure, called a *structure tag*. The

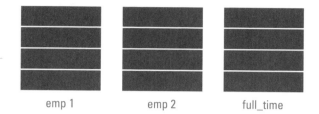

emp 1   emp 2   full_time

Figure 5.7
Structure memory
allocation.

structure tag is analogous to a data type (e.g., **int**) and provides us (and the compiler) a name by which we can reference objects of this type. Note that the compiler does not reserve storage as a result of this statement. Rather, the declaration serves only to describe this new data type to the compiler.

We can define **struct** variables using declarations such as

```
struct employee emp1, emp2, full_time;
```

This declaration reserves storage for three variables of type **struct employee**. Figure 5.7 depicts what memory might look like as a result of this declaration.

We reference individual structure members as

variable . member

where *variable* is a structure variable and *member* is a valid member of that type of structure. Thus, to reference the **salary** member of structure **emp1**, we code

```
emp1.salary
```

Note that when we reference a member, the data type of the resultant expression is based on the data type of the member:

Expression	Data type
emp1	struct employee
&emp1	address of (pointer to) a struct employee
emp1.salary	float
&emp1.salary	address of (pointer to) a float

As with any data type, we can also declare pointers to structure objects:

```
struct employee *ptr;
```

This statement declares storage for a variable that can point at objects of type **struct employee**. As usual, we must initialize the pointer:

```
ptr = &emp1;
```

We can reference structure members via pointers using the following syntax:

$$pointer \rightarrow member$$

For example, the expression

```
ptr->salary
```

references the salary member of **emp1**. Remember, pointer references are dynamic. Thus, if we were to assign **ptr = &emp2**, the preceding expression would reference the **salary** member of **emp2**.

The data type of structure references involving pointers is also based on the data type of the member:

Expression	Data type
ptr	address of (pointer to) a struct employee
ptr->salary	float
&ptr->salary	address of (pointer to) a float

Structures may contain members of any data type. For example, we can modify our employee structure as follows:

```
struct emp_name {
      char    first_name[ 30 ];
      char    last_name[ 30 ];
      char    middle_init;
};

struct employee {
      struct    emp_name name;
      long      ssnumb;
      float     salary;
      char      job_code;
};
```

Given the following declarations and assignment:

```
struct employee emp1, *ptr;
ptr = &emp1;
```

we could reference **middle_init** as

```
emp1.name.middle_init
```

or

```
ptr—>name.middle_init
```

The only restriction placed on structures is that they cannot contain instances of themselves. For example,

```
struct bad_decl {
    char    a;
    float   b;
    struct bad_decl c;     /* Wrong! */
};
```

If permitted, the declaration would be infinitely recursive.

However, structures can contain instances of pointers to themselves. These are sometimes referred to as *self-referential* structures.

```
struct list_node {
    /*
     *    data elements here
     */
    struct list_node *next; /* ok */
};
```

This allows structures to point to other instances of objects of the same type. We will use this feature in the next section to implement dynamic linked lists.

This has been but a brief overview of pointer and structure usage in C. The bibliography lists several excellent references that provide more thorough discussions of the topics.

Linked Lists and Pointers

As noted earlier, pointers can be used to process data efficiently, especially large objects: Instead of copying enormous chunks of data from location to location, we need only pass an address.

Figure 5.8

Linked list using pointers.

We can also use pointers to implement lists of the type depicted in Figure 5.5. We begin by defining a C structure that will serve as our node:

```
struct    node {
    int     data;
    struct  node    *next;
};
```

This structure contains two members. The first field, **data**, stores data values for individual nodes. The second field, **next**, is a pointer to objects of type **struct node**. In other words, it can point to the next node in a list. The following code fragment demonstrates one way to construct a list:

```
void a_list()
{
    struct    node *head, n1, n2, n3;

    head = &n1;
    n1.next = &n2;
    n2.next = &n3;
    n3.next = NULL;
}
```

The function begins by assigning the address of **n1** to the pointer **head**; this establishes the beginning of the list. Then, using the variables **n1**, **n2**, and **n3**, it constructs the body of the list: The **next** field of each node is assigned the address of its successor. By convention, we use the value **NULL** to indicate end-of-list. Figure 5.8 depicts the internal representation of the preceding list.

List Insertion and Deletion with Pointers

We can now process lists using simple pointer manipulation (refer back to Fig. 5.5). For an insertion, assign to the link field of the new node the value contained in the link field of its intended predecessor; then set the predecessor's link field to point the new node.

```
struct      node *head  =  NULL;

/*
 *    Insert "new" after "pre"
 */
void insert2( struct node *pre, struct node *new )
{
    if( pre  ==  NULL ){
        /*
         *    Insert in front of first node
         */
        new->next  =  head;
        head  =  new;
    } else {
        new->next  =  pre->next;
        pre->next  =  new;
    }
}


/*
 *    Delete the node after pre
 */
void delete2( struct node *pre )
{
    if( pre  ==  NULL )              /* delete first node */
        head  =  head->next;
    else
        pre->next  =  pre->next->next;
}
```

Listing 5.3
List processing using pointers.

A list deletion is even simpler. Store the address contained in the link field of the deleted element into the link field of its predecessor. We can then reuse the deleted node (i.e., place it on an *available* list).

As an example of this processing, Listing 5.3 contains the list manipulation routines **insert2()** and **delete2()**. They func-

```
void iter_trav( struct node *ptr )
{
      while( ptr != NULL ){
            print_node( ptr );
            ptr = ptr->next;
      }
}
```

Listing 5.4
List traversal: Iterative.

tion in a manner similar to that of their counterparts, **insert()** and **delete()** (Listing 5.1), but use pointers instead of array indices.

The variable **head**, which points to the beginning of the list, is initialized to **NULL**; this signifies an empty list. Both functions begin their processing by testing for the special case in which the first element of the list is to be updated. However, note that the test performed is **pre == NULL**. Why not test for **pre === head**? In answering this question, keep in mind that we always need to have access to an element's predecessor to perform an insertion or deletion. Thus, to insert a new element in front of the third element, we pass **insert2()** a pointer to the second element; to insert a new element in front of the second element, we pass a pointer to the first. As you can see, there is no way to indicate that an insertion should take place in front of the first element. To overcome this problem, we have established the convention that a null pointer indicates a first element operation.

5.4 LIST PROCESSING

List Traversal

Of the many operations that we can perform on lists, the most common is the traversal. A list traversal requires that we "visit" each node in succession, processing the data field(s) as required. For example, after constructing our list of composers, we might need to generate a printed listing of the names.

Listings 5.4 and 5.5 contain examples of list traversal routines.

```
void recv_trav( struct node *ptr )
{
        if( ptr != NULL ){                /* The 'out' */
                print_node( ptr );
                recv_trav( ptr->next );
        }
}
```

Listing 5.5
List traversal: Recursive.

The first, **iter_trav()**, uses a loop (iterative) construct to step through the list and print out each data element. In contrast, **recv_trav()** employs a recursive algorithm to process each node. Both functions assume a routine called **print_node()** to display data elements in some predetermined manner.

List Reversal

There are occasions when we need to reverse the order of list elements. For example, we might need to print our list of composers in reverse alphabetical order. Listing 5.6 contains the function **reverse()**, which reverses the order of elements in a linked list. Its one required argument is a pointer to the list it will process. When invoked, the function steps through the list, reversing pointers on the fly. It returns the address of the new first element (formerly the last) and therefore should be invoked as

```
head = reverse( head );
```

This ensures that we can still reference the list after the routine completes.

Notice that reversing does not make a copy of the original list. That is, by using three pointers, we can reverse the list *in place*. Thus, for any list of size $n \geq 1$, the **while** loop is executed exactly once, yielding a complexity of $O(n)$.

```
struct     node *
reverse( struct node *headptr )
{
     struct     node *tmp, *curr, *prev;

     /*
      *    Set-up pointers
      */
     prev = NULL;
     curr = headptr;

     while( curr != NULL ){
          tmp = prev;
          prev = curr;
          curr = curr->next;
          prev->next = tmp;
     }

     return( prev );
}
```

Listing 5.6
Reversing a linked list.

List Concatenation

Another useful function for list processing is a routine that concatenates two lists. The function `lconcat1()` (Listing 5.7) appends its second argument to the end of its first, creating one large list. To accomplish this, it locates the last element of list `list1` and assigns to it the address of the first node of `list2`. The first `if` statement is a "sanity check" to ensure that `list1` points to a non-empty list. The `while` loop is executed only for each element of `list1`; this yields a complexity of $O(n)$.

There is one problem with this implementation of `lconcat1()`. As it stands, it will fail whenever `list1` is `NULL`. That is, the pointer to the first list in the calling function will remain `NULL`. Although it appears that `lconcat1()` addresses this problem with the first `if` statement, this is not the case. Keep in mind that the parameter

```
void
lconcat1( struct node *list1, struct node *list2 )
{
    if( list1 == NULL ){
        list1 = list2;
        return;
    }

    /*
     *    Locate end of list
     */
    while( list1->next != NULL )
        list1 = list1->next;

    list1->next = list2;        /* Concatenate */
}


struct node *
lconcat2( struct node *l1, struct node *l2 )
{
    if( l1 == NULL ){
        return( l2 );
    }

    /*
     *    Locate end of list
     */
    while( l1->next != NULL )
        l1 = l1->next;
    l1->next = l2;                  /* Concatenate */

    return( l2 );
}
```

Listing 5.7

Two versions of list concatenation.

calling convention in C is by value. Thus, when we assign to **list1** in **concat1()**, we only modify the formal parameter (a local variable), not the actual parameter passed by the calling function.

As illustrated in **lconcat2()**, we can easily rectify this problem with a simple change to the procedure. In this version, the function returns a pointer to the concatenated lists. Thus, if we call the function in this manner:

```
list1 = lconcat2( list1, list2 );
```

we are assured of a correct result regardless of the value in the first parameter.

5.5 STACKS REVISITED

Let's take another look at implementing a stack, this time using pointers. As in our first implementation, we will use one pointer (**top**) to maintain the top of stack. In this case, however, it will be a pointer to a list of structures of type **node** (see Fig. 5.9).

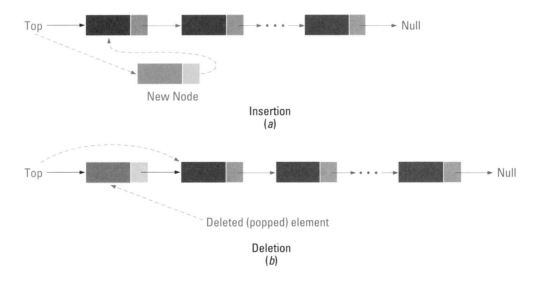

Figure 5.9
Stack: Pointer
implementation.

Listing 5.8 contains the functions **ppush()** and **ppop()**, which implement a pointer stack. Note that **ppush()** requires a node, not a value, as its one argument.

```
struct    node {
    char data;
    struct    node *next;
};

struct    node    *ppop( void );

void ppush( struct node * );

struct   node    *top = NULL;

void ppush( struct node *new )
{
    new->next = top;
    top = new;
}

struct   node *ppop()
{
    struct    node *tmp;

    if( top == NULL )
        return( NULL );

        tmp = top;
        top = top->next;
        return( tmp );
}
```

Listing 5.8
Stack: Pointer implementation.

5.6 QUEUES REVISITED

We can also convert our queue functions in a similar manner. As depicted in Figure 5.10a, we need two node pointers to maintain the FIFO order of the elements. Figures 5.10b and 5.10c demonstrate how to accomplish queue insertions and deletions. Listing 5.9 contains the code.

```c
struct node {
        char data;
        struct node *next;
};

struct node *head = NULL,
            *tail = NULL;

void ptr_insq( struct node *new )
{
        new->next = NULL;
        if( tail == NULL )   /* Empty List */
                head = new;
        else
                tail->next = new;
        tail = new;
}

struct node *ptr_delq()
{
        struct node *tmp;

        if( head == NULL )   /* List Empty */
                return( NULL );

        tmp = head;
        if( head == tail )  /* Last Node in List */
                head = tail = NULL;    continued on p. 112
```

```
        else                          continued from p. 111
             head = head->next;

        return( tmp );
}
```

Listing 5.9
Linked-list functions.

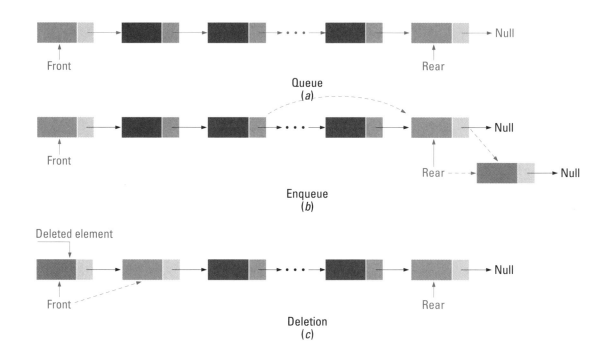

Figure 5.10
Queues: Pointer
implementation.

5.7   DYNAMIC MEMORY ALLOCATION

Through the use of pointers, we have seen how programs can create linked lists of virtually unlimited size. The only practical restriction is the amount of memory available to a process at execution time. Nevertheless, all the previous examples have used variables explicitly declared at compile time (e.g., **struct node n1;**); this still limits a program's ability to respond to varying demand. It would be helpful if a program could allocate memory (nodes) as needed.

Many languages and operating systems support dynamic memory allocation. Using this capability, an executing process can request additional memory on the fly. The specifics of such a facility vary from system to system, and the details are beyond the scope of this text. However, for purposes of demonstration, we will assume that two functions are supplied as part of our compilation environment: **malloc()** and **free()**. (These routines are part of the ANSI C standard.)

The function **malloc()** allocates chunks of memory. It takes one argument—the size (in bytes) of the requested memory segment—and returns either a pointer to (i.e., the address of) the new segment or the value **NULL** if a segment of that size is unavailable. The function **free()** returns a previously allocated memory segment to the system, making it available for reuse. Its one argument is the address of the segment to be returned.

As an example of how we can use these routines, let's incorporate these two functions into the stack routines of the previous section. Specifically, the function **ppush()** will now automatically allocate a new node with each push request; and **ppop()** will free each popped node.

The code for the new routines, **ppush2()** and **ppop2()**, appears in Listing 5.10. Note that the argument to **ppush2()** is now a data value, not a node. If the call to **malloc()** should fail, **ppush2()** returns **OUT_OF_SPACE**. Also note that we have modified **ppop2()**. The function returns status in the usual manner. However, we have added a pointer argument so that it can also return a data value. A call to **ppop2()** is made as follows:

```
stat = ppop2( &data );
```

If **stat** is **OK**, **data** contains the value of the popped element.

```c
struct    node {
     char data;
     struct  node  *next;
};

#define   OK                0
#define   EMPTY            -1
#define   OUT_OF_SPACE     -2

struct    node *head = NULL;

int ppush2( int data )
{
     struct    node *new;

     if((new=(struct node *)malloc(sizeof (struct node))) == NULL)
          return( OUT_OF_SPACE );

     new->data = data;
     new->next = head;
     head = new;

     return( OK );
}

int ppop2( int *data )
{
     struct    node *old;

     if( head == NULL )  /* Stack empty */
          return( EMPTY );

     *data = head->data;
     old = head;
     head = head->next;
     free( old );

     return( OK );
}
```

Listing 5.10
Stack functions with dynamic memory allocation.

If **ppop2()** returns **EMPTY,** the value contained in **data** remains unchanged.

5.8 SIMULATION EXAMPLE

As with computer systems, it is not desirable to deploy physical systems until they are thoroughly tested. For example, an automobile manufacturer would not want to begin construction of a new manufacturing plant unless it was certain that the design of the new facility was operationally sound. Obviously, it would be much too costly to build the new plant only to discover later that it produces fewer cars than did the old one.

As typified by this example, there are many cases in which it is too expensive or too impractical to test a physical system directly. However, in many cases, we can create a computer *simulation* that imitates the behavior of a physical system. Designers and engineers can then use the data generated from the simulation to modify and adjust the operational design of physical systems before they are built. This reduces the risk and expense of large-scale development. We will now make use of the data structures we have been discussing to develop a simulation program.

Problem Overview

The system we are going to simulate is one currently under consideration by the manager of a branch of the First National Databank. The Databank now uses multiple queues for each teller (Fig. 5.11a). That is, upon arrival, each customer selects one of several lines (one per teller) in which to wait. The branch manager believes this method is inefficient and is considering adopting a single line operation. Under the new system, all arriving customers would enter the same queue (Fig. 5.11b).

The manager's concern is that in order to support the new system, the branch office will need extensive remodeling. More important, there is a possibility that customers may experience some interruption of service while the branch undergoes alterations. Given the costs and the risk of losing business, the manager would like some assurance that the new system will better serve Databank's customers before committing to the conversion.

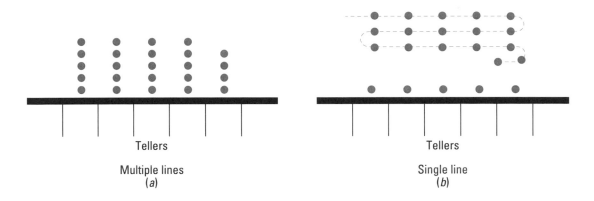

Figure 5.11
Bank lines.

Our job, as members of Databank's data processing department, is to develop a simulation of the new system to determine how it will compare with the old. To do this, the program we develop must simulate customer traffic for a typical business day (based on historical data) and generate a summary report containing the number of customers served, the number of transactions completed, and the average wait time incurred by each customer. The latter is of primary concern and will determine the fate of the new system. To aid our simulation, Databank has accumulated historical data reflecting the performance of the existing system (e.g., number of customers per day, types of transactions, average duration of transactions, etc.).

Implementation

There are several events our program will need to track:

- Bank open
- Customer arrival
- Teller/customer transaction
- Customer departure
- Bank close

The program must also generate—based on the historical data—random customer arrivals and transaction types.

We will need two structures to track these events and accumulate statistics for both customers and tellers. The first will be a simple structure array to count the number of transactions performed by each teller and to indicate when a teller becomes available to serve the next customer.

The second is a linked list that will simulate the customer queue. The structure definitions appear in Listing 5.11.

The driving routine of the program will be a function called **simulate()**. It will require three arguments: the closing time (as expressed in clock ticks, which, for our example, will be minutes), the number of tellers on hand, and the number of expected customers.

Let's begin to sketch the algorithm:

```
simulate( close, no_tellers, no_customers )
    clock = 0;
    while(1) {                      /* Forever */

        /*
         *    New customer?
         */
        if( arrive() ){
            if( add_cust_q() != OK ){
                /*
                 *    LOST SALE!
                 */
            }
        }

        /*
         *    Process tellers & customers
         */
        for( i = 0; i < no_tellers; i++ ){
```

```
struct    tellers    {
    int custs;              /* No. of custs served */
    int trans;              /* Trans complete time */
};

struct    cust {
    int time_in;            /* Arrival time        */
    int time_out;           /* Departure time      */
    int time_trans;         /* Duration of trans   */
    struct cust *next;      /* Ptr to next struct  */
};
```

Listing 5.11

Data structures for simulation program.

```
        /*
         *    Is teller done with transaction?
         *
        if( clock >= teller[i].trans )
            teller[i].trans = 0; /* Available */

        /*
         *    Next Please?
         */
        if( teller[i].trans==0 AND Queue NOT Empty )
            del_cust_q();   /* Get cust from Q */
            teller[i].custs += 1;
            teller[i].trans=clock+trans_duration;
            accum(); /* Accumulate tots */
    }

if( clock > close ){
    print execution summary;
    return;
}
clock += CLK_INCR;
    }
}
```

We seem to have accounted for all events except bank open and
close. Clearly, invoking the function is equivalent to opening the
bank for business. Simulating the bank close event, however, is not
that simple. Specifically, we cannot just stop processing at closing
time because, although we will no longer permit customers to enter,
there may still be some customers awaiting assistance inside the
bank. Therefore, **simulate()** must continue to process customers
until the queue is empty.

The code segment commented **'LOST SALE'** is also interesting.
We could place a limit on the size of the customer queue that represents
the maximum physical capacity of the branch. Processing in this section
of the program would then represent an unsuccessful attempt by a customer to enter the bank. The effect of this event varies with the type
of business. For a bank, this may represent only an irate client
that, although sent away grumbling, will return later to complete his

or her transaction. However, if this simulation were for a fast-food empo-
rium, such an event would most likely represent a lost sale.

Let's add the processing for bank close and see how our algorithm
is progressing:

```
simulate( close, no_tellers, no_customers )
     open = 1;
     clock = 0;
     while(1){
          if( clock >= close )        /* Time to close */
              open = 0;
          /*
           *    New customer?
           */
          if( open AND arrive() )
              if( add_cust_q() != OK ){
                  /*
                   *    LOST SALE!
                   */
              }
          /*
           *    Process tellers & customers
           */
          for( i = 0; i < no_tellers; i++ ){
              /*
               *    Is teller done with transaction?
               */
              if( clock >= teller[i].trans )
                  teller[i].trans = 0; /* Available */
              /*
               *    Next Please?
               */
              if( teller[i].trans==0 AND Queue NOT Empty ){
                  del_cust_q();   /* Get cust from Q */
                  teller[i].custs += 1;
                  teller[i].trans=clock+trans_duration;
                  accum();   /* Accumulate tots */
              }
          }
```

```
if( open == 0 AND Queue Empty ){
    print execution summary;
    return;
}
clock += CLK_INCR;
    }
}
```

The basic algorithm is taking shape; now let's take a closer look at some of the supporting functions.

arrive()   This function determines customer arrivals. It will take two arguments: the close time and the number of expected customers. Using a pseudo-random number generator, it will compute customer arrivals. For our example, we will use a simple percentage calculation. Note, however, that this does not reflect reality because customer traffic is typically not proportionally spaced throughout the entire business day.

add_cust_q()   This routine adds an arriving customer to the queue. It notes the time of arrival and calls **duration()** to determine the transaction type.

duration()   This function will use a pseudo-random number generator to determine transaction type and duration. For our example, we will assume four transaction types (numbered 1 through 4) with a historical occurrence rate of 30%, 50%, 15%, and 5%, respectively. The function returns the duration of the transaction in clock ticks.

accum()   This routine accumulates event data for summary and display.

We will not discuss the implementation of each of the aforementioned functions. However, the complete C version of our simulation appears in Listing 5.12.

This simple example is by no means representative of the detail that we can incorporate into a simulation program. Here are some ways we can extend this model:

- Allow the number of tellers to vary, simulating lunch breaks, personal time, and so on.
- Vary customer arrivals based on day of week, time of day, weather conditions, etc.

```
#define    CLK_INCR        1  /* # Minutes in each loop */
#define    MAX_TELLERS     10 /* Max # of tellers          */

#define    OK              0
#define    QUEUE_FULL      -1
#define    QUEUE_EMPTY     -2

struct    tellers    {
     int   custs;                  /* No. of custs served */
     int   trans;                  /* Trans complete time */
} teller[ MAX_TELLERS ];

struct    cust {
     int   time_in;                /* Arrival time        */
     int   time_out;               /* Departure time      */
     int   time_trans;             /* Duration of trans   */
     struct    cust *next;         /* Ptr to next struct  */
};

int  open = 1;
int  clock = 0;

simulate( int close, int no_tellers, int no_customers )
/* close:        what time to close?      */
/* no_tellers:   no of tellers for run    */
/* no_customers: no of customers for run  */
{
     int  i;
     struct    cust tmp;

     while( 1 ){
          if( clock >= close )      /* Time to close */
               open = 0;

          if( open==1 && arrive(close, no_customers) ){
               /*
                *    New Cust
                */
               if( add_cust_q(clock) == QUEUE_FULL ){
                    /*
                     *    Lost Sale
                     */
               }

          }
```

continued on p. 122

```
              /*                          continued from p. 121
               *    Process tellers & customers
               */
              for( i = 0; i < no_tellers; i++ ){
                  /*
                   *    Is teller's current trans done
                   */
                  if( clock >= teller[i].trans ){
                      teller[i].trans = 0;
                  }
                  /*
                   *    Next Please?
                   */
                  if(teller[i].trans==0 && !queue_empty()){
                      del_cust_q( &tmp );
                      teller[i].custs += 1;
                      teller[i].trans=clock+tmp.time_trans;
                      accum( clock, tmp.time_in );
                  }

              }

              if(queue_empty() && (open==0)){
                  print_totals();
                  return( OK );
              }

              clock += CLK_INCR;
        }
}

struct    cust *head = NULL;
struct    cust *tail = NULL;

int add_cust_q( int time_in ) /* Add new cust to queue */
{
      struct    cust *new;

      if( (new = get_cust()) == NULL )
          return( QUEUE_FULL );              continued on p. 123
```
continued from p. 121
continued on p. 123

```
        new->next  =  NULL;                          continued from p. 122
        new->time_in  =  time_in;
        new->time_trans  =  duration();

        if( tail  ==  NULL ){       /* First element */
             tail  =  new;
             head  =  tail;
        } else {
             tail->next  =  new;
             tail  =  new;
        }

        return( OK );
}

int del_cust_q( struct cust *dest )
{
        struct      cust *tmp;

        tmp  =  head;
        if( head  ==  tail )   /* removed last node */
             head  =  tail  =  NULL;
        else
             head  =  head->next;

        dest->time_in  =  tmp->time_in;
        dest->time_trans  =  tmp->time_trans;
        free( tmp );

        return( OK );
}

int queue_empty()
{
        if( head  ==  NULL )
             return( QUEUE_EMPTY );
        return( OK );
}

struct      cust *
get_cust()
{
        return( (struct cust *)malloc(sizeof(struct cust)) );

}
```
continued on p. 124

```
int duration()                                    continued from p. 123
{
    float       p;

    p = (float)rand()/32767.0;

    if( p <= .30 )                           /* 30% chance-type 1 */
        return( 6 );
    else if( p > .30 && p <= .80 )       /* 50% chance-type 2 */
        return( 9 );
    else if( p > .80 && p <= .95 )       /* 15% chance-type 3 */
        return( 11 );
    else                    /*  5% chance-type 4 */
        return( 16 );
}

int arrive( int min, int cus )
{
    if( (float)cus/(float)min > ((float)rand()/32767.0) )
        return( 1 );

    return( 0 );
}

float       tot_cust;
float       tot_wait;

void accum( int now, int arrive )
{
    tot_cust += 1.0;
    tot_wait += ((float)now - (float)arrive);
}

void print_totals()
{
    print("%f customer%swaited an average of %.2f mins\n",
        tot_cust, tot_cust > 1 ? "s " : " ",
        tot_wait/tot_cust );
}
```

Listing 5.12

Databank simulation.

- Add more transaction types and vary their durations.
- Permit multiple transactions by a customer.
- Make the program more efficient by placing all events in an event queue. Currently, many iterations of the **for** loop in the function **simulate()** may be wasted. That is, there may be many clock ticks for which no event occurs. We could, instead, place all events (arrivals, departures, open, close, transaction complete, etc.) on a queue (sorted by time); then, during each iteration of the **for** loop, the function would simply dequeue the next event and adjust (advance) the clock accordingly.

There are several specialized languages specifically designed to simplify the development of system simulations. The bibliography lists several good texts on the subject.

5.9 DOUBLY LINKED LISTS

Thus far, we have been working with singly linked lists: Each node contains only one pointer. Although an improvement over the two-array implementation, singly linked lists—for some applications—can be too restrictive. First, they can be traversed in only one direction. Second, inserting or deleting a node requires access to the node's predecessor. (Note that this problem does not arise when using a restricted form of a list—such as a stack or a queue—because nodes are referenced by external pointers.)

We can overcome both of these problems through the use of *doubly linked* lists. Each node in a doubly linked list has link fields that point to both predecessor and successor elements. Along with simplifying insertions and deletions, this enables a program to traverse a list in either direction. Examples of doubly linked lists appear in Figure 5.12.

To simplify implementation, we will use a *head node* to maintain the beginning of the list. Initially, both of its links will point to itself, signifying an empty list (see Fig. 5.12a).

As depicted in Figure 5.13a, a list insertion now requires the modification of four links:

- the *next* pointer of the predecessor
- the *prev* pointer of the successor
- both the *next* and *prev* pointers of the new node.

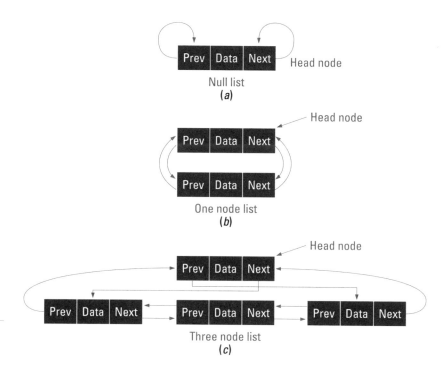

Figure 5.12
Doubly linked lists.

In a list deletion (Fig. 5.13b), predecessor and successor nodes are made to point to each other.

Functions that demonstrate insertions and deletions in a doubly linked list appear in Listing 5.13. The decision to insert a new element to the right of a given node was arbitrary; we could easily modify **dbl_insert()** so that it inserts nodes on the left. In addition, the deletion function, **dbl_delete()**, no longer requires the address of a predecessor node (this can be determined from **ptr −>prev**); its one argument is a pointer to the node it will delete.

Note that there are incremental costs associated with the increased flexibility provided by doubly linked lists. First, there is the additional space required by the second link pointer. Second, each list operation requires additional CPU time to complete. This is attributable to the time required to manipulate the additional pointers.

```
struct     dbl_node {
     int       data;
     struct    dbl_node *next;
     struct    dbl_node *prev;
};

/*
 *   Insert 'new' to the right of 'ptr'
 */
void dbl_insert( struct dbl_node *ptr, struct dbl_node *new )
{
     struct    dbl_node *nxt;

     nxt = ptr->next;
     new->next = nxt;
     new->prev = ptr;
     ptr->next = new;
     nxt->prev = new;
}

/*
 *   Delete 'ptr'
 */
void dbl_delete( struct dbl_node *ptr )
{
     struct    dbl_node    *prev, *succ;

     prev = ptr->prev;
     succ = ptr->next;
     prev->next = ptr->next;
     succ->prev = ptr->prev;
}
```

Listing 5.13
Doubly linked list functions.

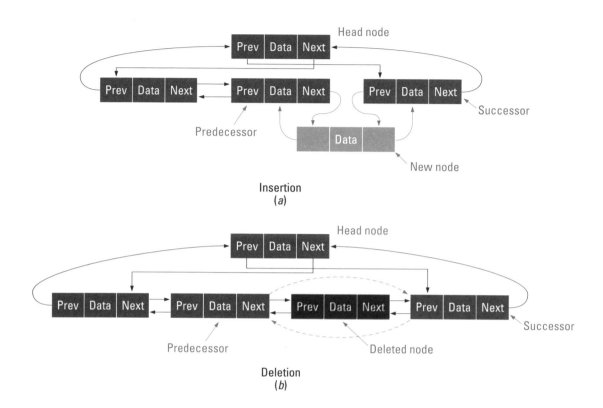

Insertion
(a)

Deletion
(b)

Figure 5.13
Doubly linked lists:
Insertion and deletion.

5.10 GENERALIZED LISTS

The lists in all the previous examples were composed of only atomic elements. The only attribute associated with a given node, $\in_n$, was its location in the list: $\in_{n-1} < \in_n < \in_{n+1}$. We will now extend our definition of a list to include *non-atomic* elements. That is, individual list elements may now be other lists. These are referred to as *generalized lists*. For example, the third element of the list

$$L = (A, B, (C, D), E)$$

is the list (C, D).

More formally, we can define a generalized list as

A = ()	The NULL (empty) list; it has a length of 0.
B = (a, b, c)	A linear list of length three.
C = (e, (f, g), h)	A list of length three. Elements 1 and 3 are atomic; the second element is a sublist.
D = (i, B, C)	A list of length three containing previously declared lists. This is an example of list *sharing*. (More on this later.)
F = (j, k, (), l)	A list of length four that has the NULL list as its third element.
G = (m, G)	A recursive list of length two that generates the list (m, (m, (m, ...

Figure 5.14

Examples of generalized lists.

a finite sequence of elements $\in_1, \in_2, \ldots, \in_n$, for $n \geq 0$, that are either atoms or lists. If a given element is not an atom, it is a list and is referred to as a *sublist*.

The list is written as before: $L = \in_1, \ldots, \in_n$, with sublists contained within enclosing parentheses. (By convention, we will use uppercase letters to denote lists and sublists and use lowercase letters to represent atomic elements.) The length of the list is n regardless of the number of elements contained in any sublists. As you may have noted, the previous definition is recursive and, as such, allows for lists that contain sublists, which contain sublists, etc. This permits the construction of lists of arbitrary size and complexity. Figure 5.14 provides some examples.

Implementation

The node structure we have used throughout this chapter requires two modifications to support generalized lists. First, because elements are now expected to perform double duty, we need a **type** field to classify a node as either an atom or a sublist. Thus, we will establish the convention that a value of **1** in the type field indicates an atom, **0** denotes a sublist. Second, if the node is non-atomic, we will need a second pointer, **list**, to point to the sublist. The new definitions are as follows:

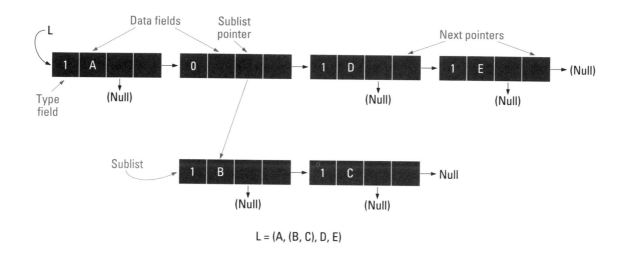

L = (A, (B, C), D, E)

Figure 5.15
Generalized list:
(*A*, (*B*, *C*), *D*, *E*).

```
#define    TRUE        1
#define    FALSE       0

#define    T_LIST      0
#define    T_ATOM      1

struct     list {
       short     type;
       char      data;
       struct    list  *next;
       struct    list  *list;
};
```

Figure 5.15 depicts the implementation of the list

$$L = (A, (B, C), D, E)$$

using the new structure definition.

Note that the length of list L is 4 and that each element is linked via its **next** field. The second element of L is a sublist—as indicated by the value zero in the **type** field—and its **list** field points to the

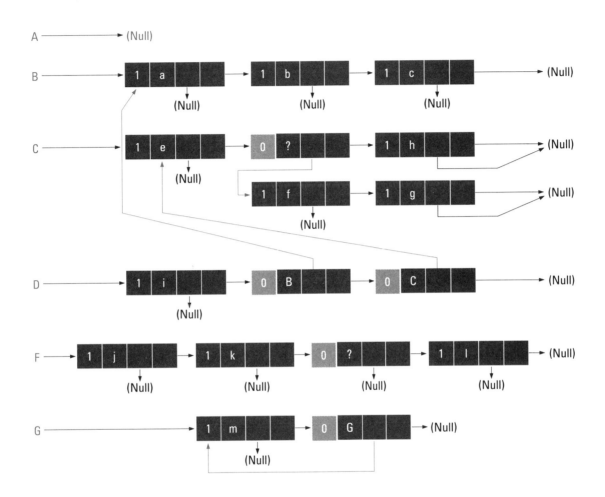

Figure 5.16
Internal list
representation.

sublist (**B, C**). Additional examples of generalized lists appear in Figure 5.16, which depicts the internal representation for all the lists contained in Figure 5.14.

At this point, we should make a few comments regarding the definition and use of the **list** structure. The **data** field of a sublist node remains unused, and this may seem wasteful. This will change, however, when we discuss reference counts later in this chapter. Also, having an explicit **type** field might be viewed as redundant: If a given node's **list** pointer is non-null, we could assume that the node is non-atomic (i.e., a sublist). Nevertheless, we decided to sacrifice space for the sake of pedagogical clarity.

Generalized List Functions

There are a number of utility functions that are useful when working with generalized lists. The first, **gencopy()**, creates a copy of a generalized list. For example, assuming the list **oldlist**, the statement

```
newlist = gencopy( oldlist );
```

will create an exact copy of **oldlist** and assign the address of the newly created list to **newlist**.

Although the address fields will necessarily be unique, the list created by **gencopy()** will posses the same structure and contain the same data values as that of the original list. As presented in Listing 5.14, the function accomplishes this by

- Creating a duplicate node for each node in the original list
- Inserting each new node into the new list
- Processing the next element of the old list (via a recursive call using the **next** pointer)
- If the node is of type **T_LIST**, calling itself recursively to process the sublist.

As you may have noted, **gencopy()** cannot copy recursive lists (such as example G in Figure 5.14). It will repeatedly process the recursive portion until it is terminated by the operating system. Because **gencopy()** processes each node exactly once, its complexity is $O(n)$.

Another useful utility function, **list_equal()**, compares two lists for equality. It assumes that its two arguments point to non-recursive lists. As in the case of **gencopy()**, the term *equal* will be interpreted as functionally equal, meaning that both lists have the same overall structure and identical data elements. **list_equal()** traverses lists in much the same manner as **gencopy()**, comparing elements as it proceeds. Its complexity is therefore equivalent to that of **gencopy()**. Listing 5.15 contains the code.

Two other useful functions are **first()** and **rest()**, which return the first and all but the first elements of a generalized list. For example, given the list L = ((A, B), C, D), the call

    first(L);

would return the list

    ((A, B));

and the call

    root(L);

would return the list

    (C, D)

These functions—which are equivalent to the LISP functions

```
struct    list *
gencopy( struct list *ptr )
{
     struct    list *new;

     if( ptr == NULL )
          return( NULL );

     if( (new = getnode()) == NULL )
          return( NULL );

     new->data = ptr->data;
     new->type = ptr->type;
     if( new->type == T_LIST )
          new->list = gencopy( ptr->list );
     new->next = gencopy( ptr->next );


return( new );

}
```

Listing 5.14
Copying a generalized list.

```
int list_equal( struct list *l1, struct list *l2 )
{
    int   tmp;

    if( l1 == NULL && l2 == NULL )
        return( TRUE );
    if( l1 == NULL || l2 == NULL )
        return( FALSE );

    if( l1->type == l2->type ){
        tmp = FALSE;
        if( l1->type == T_ATOM ){
            if( l1->data == l2->data )
                tmp = TRUE;
        } else
            tmp = list_equal( l1->list, l2->list );

        if( tmp == TRUE )
            return( list_equal(l1->next, l2->next) );
    }

    return( FALSE );
}
```

Listing 5.15
Determining list equality.

car() and cdr()—can be used to step through all elements of a list, as in

```
r = worklist;
while( (f = first(r)) != NULL ){
        .
        .
    /* Process 'f' */
        .
        .
    r = rest( r );
}
```

Note that the functions, as presented in Listing 5.16, are non-destructive to their original lists. That is, the functions make a copy (using `gencopy()`) of the portion of the list they will return. For some applications, it might be desirable for the functions to operate directly on the original lists.

Shared Lists and Reference Counts

In the previous sections, we saw several examples of shared sublists (refer to Fig. 5.13). This is a case in which two or more list members point to the same sublist. For many applications, this could result in a significant savings in memory.

Implementing this feature presents us with two problems, however. First, if two or more list elements are pointing to the same sublist, insertions become difficult. For example, consider Figure 5.17. If we wanted to insert an element before node n_1 of list S, we would be forced to modify the pointers E_1 and E_2. Unless the program maintains backward references, the task of keeping all pointers current is tantamount to impossible.

The second problem arises during a list deletion. Without additional reference information, it is impossible for us to determine whether we can place a deleted node back on the available list. Specifically, there might be other elements still pointing at it.

We can solve the first problem by establishing a convention that all lists must use *head nodes*, and that all referencing elements must point at them, not at any individual nodes of a sublist. Thus, insertions and deletions within a given sublist will not affect any referencing elements. The additional memory requirement to implement this feature is minimal: one additional node per list.

We can solve the second problem through the use of reference counts. Specifically, each time a new list element points to a sublist, we increment the sublist's reference count. Conversely, we decrement

Figure 5.17
Multiple references.

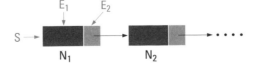

```
struct    list *
first( struct list *lp )
{
    struct    list *new;

    new = getnode();
    new->next = NULL;
    new->data = lp->data;
    new->type = lp->type;
    if( new->type == T_LIST )
        new->list = gencopy( lp->list );
    if( new->type == T_LIST && lp->next == NULL )
        return( new->list );

    return( new );
}

struct    list *
rest( struct list *lp )
{
    struct    list *new;

    lp = lp->next;      /* Point to rest of list */
    new = getnode();
    new->data = lp->data;
    new->type = lp->type;
    new->list = gencopy( lp->list );
    new->next = gencopy( lp->next );

    return( new );
}
```

Listing 5.16
Functions first() and rest().

```
void gen_delete(struct list *ptr )
{
    struct    list *tmp;

    if( ptr->type != T_LIST )   /* Must be a list ptr */
        return;

    ptr->data -= 1;              /* Decrement count */

    if( ptr->data == 0 ){        /* Delete entire list */
        for(tmp=ptr->next; tmp != NULL; tmp=tmp->next)
        {
            /*
             *    Step through each node
             */
            if( tmp->type == T_LIST )
                /* Delete a sublist */
                gen_delete( tmp );
            else
                /* Return node to free list */
                gen_free( tmp );
        }
        gen_free( ptr );
    }
}
```

Listing 5.17

Generalized list deletion function.

the count each time we remove a reference. Thus, during a deletion, if the reference count for some sublist becomes zero, we can
place all of its nodes back on the available list. Note that this is a recursive
process in that a deleted list might point to other lists. Also observe
that there is no way to determine when a self-referencing list (example
G, Fig. 5.14) may be deleted; it will always have a reference count of
at least 1.

Listing 5.17 presents the recursive function **gen_delete()**,
which deletes multiply referenced lists. It assumes the function
gen_free(), which places a deleted node back on the available list.
The function begins by ensuring that its one argument is of type
T_LIST. If it is, **gen_delete()** decrements the reference count. If

the count falls to zero, the entire list is subject to deletion. To accomplish this, **gen_free** scans every element of the list. It places each node of type **T_ATOM** back on the free list, and calls itself recursively for each node node of type **T_LIST**.

SUMMARY

Dynamic data structures simplify some of the problems associated with static storage allocation: difficult insertions and deletions in lists, and the inability to respond to unanticipated demand.

We can use pointers to reference data objects efficiently. Pointers have all the attributes that we normally associate with any variable; the sole exception is that the values pointers contain are addresses. Pointers also help us overcome the call-by-value restrictions associated with C function calls.

Using pointers, we can simplify insertions and deletions in lists. We accomplish this by adding link fields into our data structures (nodes). The cost for this added capability is the additional storage and processing required for the link fields.

This technique has another benefit: We can allocate storage for nodes dynamically. That is, we can create new storage on the fly. In C, the routines that manage dynamic memory management are **malloc()** and **free()**.

EXERCISES

1. Implement a stack using pointers.

2. Implement a queue using pointers.

3. Implement a circular queue using pointers. Is this practical? Explain your answer.

4. Write a program that sorts a random list of names contained in a file. (*Hint:* Use a linked list with a character array as your data field.)

5. Discuss the positive and negative aspects of both static and dynamic data structures.

6. Extend the functions **insert2()** and **delete2()** to allow them to process list nodes of different types.

7. Explain why holes in lists (array implementation) are problematic. Design a method to overcome the problem.

8. Rewrite the calculator program of Chapter 2 using linked lists.

9. What would be the result of moving the call to **print_node()** after the recursive call in the function **recv_trav()** of Listing 5.5?

10. Suggest other ways in which the functions **insert2()** and **delete2()** (Listing 5.3) can determine that operations are to be performed on the first element of the list. Implement your suggestions.

11. Implement the simulation program of Section 5.8. Add as many of the suggested extensions as you can.

12. As you may recall from Chapter 3, a *deque*, or double-ended queue, is a linear list that permits insertions and deletions at either end. Write a set of routines to implement a deque using a linked list and dynamic memory allocation.

13. Given the following code:

```
struct    node {
    int   data;
    struct    node *next;
};


void zaptest()
{
    struct node *head, a1, a2, a3, a4;

    head = &a1;
    a1.data = 1;
    a2.data = 2;
    a3.data = 3;
    a4.data = 4;
    (void)zap( &head, head );
}
```

determine the result after the function call:

```
(void)zap( &head, head );
```

where `zap()` is defined as

```
struct node *zap( struct node **head,
                  struct node *ptr )
{
    struct    node *tmp;

    if( ptr->next == NULL )
        *head = ptr;
    else {
        tmp = zap( head, ptr->next );
        tmp->next = ptr;
        ptr->next = NULL;
    }

    return( ptr );
}
```

Trees

C H A P T E R

6.1   BASIC PRINCIPLES

In this chapter, we focus our attention on an important data structure
found in computer science: the tree. Conceptually, a tree is an object that
begins with a trunk (or root) and extends into several branches (edges),
each of which may extend into other branches until finally terminating at a leaf.

Trees are common structures, and examples can be found in everyday life. Most people, for example, refer to their lineage as their
family tree. As another example, Figure 6.1 shows an organization
chart for a typical corporation. Note that for convenience, we draw
the root of the tree at the top of the diagram and the leaves at the
bottom.

In computer science, we define a tree as a set of *nodes* and *edges*.
A node is an item of information that resides in the tree. An edge
is an ordered pair of nodes $\langle u, v \rangle$, and sequence of edges is called a *path*.

In addition, trees have the following properties:

- There is one node designated as the *root* of the tree.

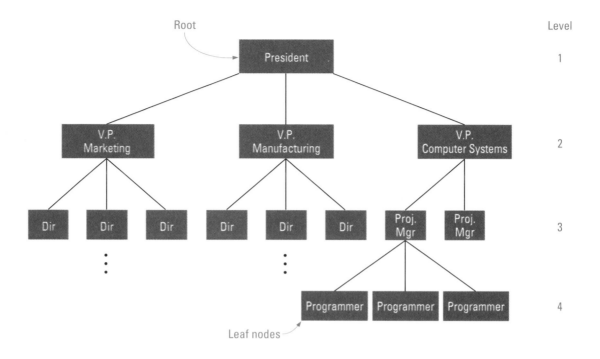

Figure 6.1
Organization chart.

- All nodes—except for the root—have only *one* entering edge (the root node has none).
- There exists a unique path from the root node to all other nodes in the tree.
- If there exists a path ⟨*a*, *b*⟩, then *b* is called a *child* of *a* and is the root node of a *subtree*.

Refer to Figure 6.1 where the element labeled President is the root node of the tree. The entries labeled Vice President are root nodes of subtrees, and the boxes labeled Programmer are examples of leaf nodes. Note that because each node has only one entering edge, cross references within the tree cannot occur.

We can cite many examples in which data found in the real world is tree structured. Because they can serve as a basis for modeling many types of problems, trees have become an important topic for

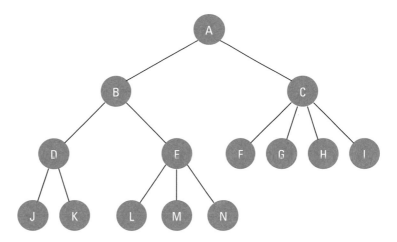

Figure 6.2
Example tree.

study in computer science. As we shall see, we can use trees to search, sort, and prioritize data.

Definitions

Before we can continue with our discussion of trees, we must define a number of basic terms. (All examples refer to Fig. 6.2.)

The term *node*—used in previous chapters—will continue to denote an item of information. *Terminal* nodes are the leaf nodes of a tree (*J, K, L, M, N*). We refer to all other (internal) nodes (*A, B, C, D, E*) as *non-terminal*.

For a given node (e.g., *B*), the root nodes of its subtrees (*D, E*) are its *children*. Extending the analogy, *B* is considered the *parent*, and the children—with respect to each other—are *siblings*. Generally speaking, a node may have an infinite number of children; in practice, however, we usually limit their number (more on this later).

We define the *degree* of a node as the number of subtrees (children) it has. For example, node *A* has a degree of 2, node *C* a degree of 4, and node *J* a degree of 0. All nodes with a degree of 0 are terminal; nodes with a degree greater than zero are non-terminal.

The tier on which a node resides is its *level*. By definition, the root node (*A*) is on level 1. Its children, nodes *B* and *C*, are on level 2, nodes *D* through *I* are on level 3, and so on.

The *height* of a tree is defined as the number of edges in a path originating at the root and terminating at the most distant leaf node; the height of a tree with only one node (the root) is 0. By extension, the height of any node in a tree is the length of the longest path from that node to a leaf node. The *depth* of a node is the number of edges on the path from the root to that node.

A *forest* is a set of zero or more disjoint trees. For example, if we were to remove the root node from a tree, the result would be a forest.

We can view a tree as a special form of a list. For example, refer to the tree depicted in Figure 6.2. We could use list notation to represent the tree as follows:

$$(A, (B, C, (D, (J, K), E, (L, M, N)), C, (F, G, H, I)))$$

We represent each subtree as a sublist. We begin with the list (*A*) that represents the root node of the tree. When we add a sublist for *A*'s two children, the list becomes (*A* (*B, C*)). We then add another sublist for nodes *D* and *E* to yield the list (*A* (*B*, (*D, E*), *C*)). Adding the children of *D*, we get (*A*, (*B, D*, (*J, K*), *E*), *C*)). We continue in this manner until we have added all tree nodes into the list. This type of representation is flexible in that it allows us to maintain varying numbers of children for each parent. However, it does have one drawback: Children are not directly accessible from their parents. That is, we must perform a linear search through a sublist. For most computer applications, the additional search time is undesirable. However, if we restrict the number of children nodes may have, we can implement trees more efficiently. The next section introduces the first of these types of trees, called the *binary tree*.

6.2 BINARY TREES

Binary trees are a restricted form of a tree. Each node—including the root—may have a maximum of two children. Figure 6.3 provides an example.

Formally, we define a binary tree as

a finite—possibly empty—set of nodes, one of which is designated as the *root*. The root node may have at most two *subtrees*, each of which is also a binary tree. The two subtrees of a given node are ordered and we refer to them as the *left child* and the *right child*, respectively.

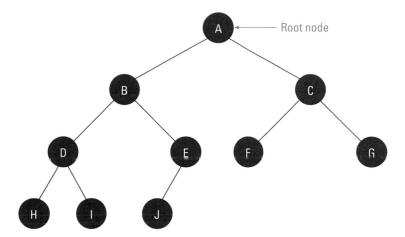

Figure 6.3
Binary tree.

Based on the preceding definition, nodes in a binary tree may have zero, one, or two children. For nodes with only one subtree, the definition does not specify which of the two subtrees (i.e., left or right) must be used. As a result, the list depicted in Figure 6.4a is, in fact, a binary tree; we refer to it as a *skewed* tree. Binary trees may be skewed either left or right, making them unique. For example, the two trees presented in Figure 6.4b are not equal.

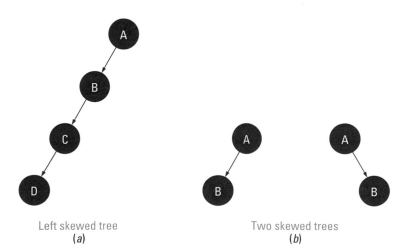

Figure 6.4
Skewed binary trees.

Left skewed tree
(*a*)

Two skewed trees
(*b*)

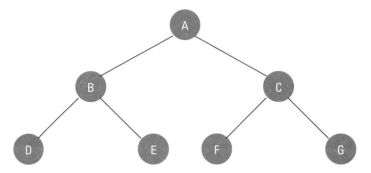

Binary Tree Definitions

Restricting the number of children in a binary tree permits us to define several formulas. The maximum number of nodes on a given level i is 2^{i-1}, for $i \geq 1$. (The root node, as you may recall, is on level 1.) The maximum number of nodes for an entire binary tree of depth k is $2^k - 1$, for $k \geq 1$. We can compute the depth of a binary tree with n nodes as

$$\lfloor \log_2 n \rfloor + 1$$

A *full* binary tree (of depth k) is a binary tree with $2^k - 1$ nodes. As suggested earlier, this is the maximum number of nodes a binary tree may contain. Figure 6.5 presents an example of a full binary tree.

Although we did not mention it at the time, the tree presented in Figure 6.3 is also a special form of a binary tree. We can sequentially number the nodes of this tree from left to right, level 1 to n, to produce the tree depicted in Figure 6.6. The result is called a *complete* binary tree. A binary tree with n nodes and k levels is complete if, and only if, its nodes correspond to all the nodes numbered in the same manner for a full binary tree of equal depth. However, as illustrated in this example, a complete tree is not necessarily a full tree; the last level may remain incomplete.

Binary Tree Implementation

Keeping in mind the preceding definition of a complete tree, the most direct approach to implementing a binary tree is using an array. Each numbered node would correspond to an array index. Figure 6.7

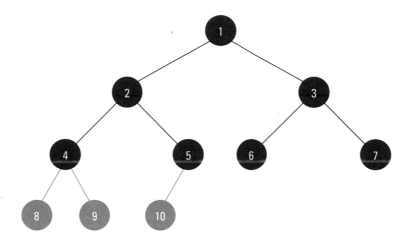

Figure 6.6
Complete binary tree.

Figure 6.7
Array implementation
of a binary tree.

depicts such an implementation for the tree contained in Figure
6.5.

An array implementation allows us to move through the tree using
simple calculations. For a given node i, its left child is located in slot $2i$,
for $2i \leq n$; its right child is located in slot $2i + 1$, for $2i \leq n$. A
computation that yields a value $>n$ means that i has no child in that
position. The parent of i can be found at $\lfloor i \div 2 \rfloor$, for $i > 1$. (Obviously,
when $i = 1$, we are positioned at the root node and there is no parent.)

For a full or complete binary tree, this implementation might
seem ideal because little, if any, space is wasted. However, consider
the tree presented in Figure 6.8a, and its corresponding array representation in Figure 6.8b. Notice that with a skewed or sparse tree, a
large percentage of the array remains unused. Moreover, this implementation suffers from the same deficiencies as a sequential list representation: We might need to move a large number of nodes in order to
insert or delete elements within the body of the tree.

In a similar manner to lists, these limitations can be overcome
using a linked representation. We can represent each node of a
binary tree using a C structure as follows:

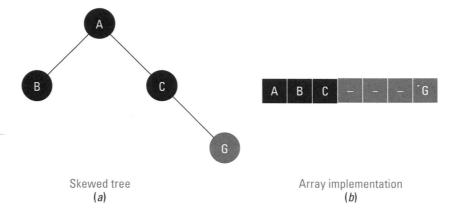

Figure 6.8
Array representation
of a skewed binary
tree.

Skewed tree
(*a*)

Array implementation
(*b*)

```
struct   bt_node {
         int      data;
         struct   bt_node *lchild;
         struct   bt_node *rchild;
};

struct    bt_node   *root = NULL;
```

A simple integer variable (**data**) will serve as our data field. The members, **lchild** and **rchild**, point to the two subtrees. (We will assume that the value **NULL** indicates the absence of a subtree.) The variable, **root**, points at the root node of the tree. Initially, its value is set to **NULL** to signify an empty tree. We will use these definitions throughout the following discussions.

Binary Tree Traversal

The versatility of the binary tree may be best demonstrated by way of an example. Suppose that after having constructed a tree similar to the one in Figure 6.6., we wish to process (e.g., print) the data values stored within it. That is, we wish to move through the tree, *visiting* each node exactly once. We classify this type of algorithm as a *traversal*.

As it stands, however, this notion is too general and must be

further defined. Consider that when positioned at any given node,
a traversal function may

- Continue down the left subtree, or
- Continue down the right subtree, or
- Process (i.e., visit) the datum.

To simplify matters, we will adopt the convention that we always
traverse the left subtree before the right subtree. However, that
still leaves open the question of when we should process the data
item. Our choices are as follows:

- Visit the node before moving down the left subtree.
- Visit the node after traversing the left subtree but before traversing
  the right subtree.
- Visit the node after traversing both subtrees.

All three of these traversal methods are equally important, and
we refer to them by the names *preorder*, *inorder*, and *postorder*, respectively.

Inorder Traversal

Let's begin by describing inorder traversal (sometimes referred to as
symmetric order). Informally, an inorder traversal requires that we

1. Move down the tree as far left as possible.
2. Visit the current node.
3. Back up one node in the tree and visit it.
4. Move down the right subtree of the node visited in step 3 if it
   has one and it has not been visited previously; otherwise, back up
   one node.
5. Repeat steps 1 through 4 until all nodes have been processed.

This is illustrated by the procedure **inorder()** presented in
Listing 6.1.

The function works as follows: It recursively moves down the left
subtree until it finds itself positioned on a leaf node; it prints the
value of that node and then attempts to move down the right subtree;
it then returns to the previous level and repeats the process. If called to
process the tree depicted in Figure 6.6, **inorder()** would generate
the following output:

```
void inorder( struct bt_node *node )
{
    if( node != NULL ){
        inorder( node->lchild );
        print_node( node->data ); /* The Visit */
        inorder( node->rchild );
    }
}
```

Listing 6.1
Inorder traversal.

8, 4, 9, 2, 10, 5, 1, 6, 3, 7

Take the time to convince yourself that the output is, indeed, correct.

Preorder Traversal

In a preorder traversal, we visit the data item before traversing the left subtree. The function **preorder()**, presented in Listing 6.2, provides an example. Note that the function calls **print_node()** before it invokes either of its recursive calls. Again, assuming the tree in Figure 6.6 as input, the output produced by **preorder()** is

1, 2, 4, 8, 9, 5, 10, 3, 6, 7

```
void preorder( struct bt_node *node )
{
    if( node != NULL ){
        print_node( node->data ); /* The Visit */
        preorder( node->lchild );
        preorder( node->rchild );
    }
}
```

Listing 6.2
Preorder traversal.

```
void postorder( struct bt_node *node )
{
    if( node != NULL ){
        postorder( node->lchild );
        postorder( node->rchild );
        print_node( node->data ); /* The Visit */
    }
}
```

Listing 6.3
Postorder traversal.

Postorder Traversal

A postorder traversal positions the visit after the two recursive calls. The code for the function, **postorder()**, appears in Listing 6.3. A postorder traversal of the tree in Figure 6.6 produces the following output:

8, 9, 4, 10, 5, 2, 6, 7, 3, 1

Breadth First Traversals

The three traversal methods we just discussed are similar in that they process all of a node's descendents before processing any of its siblings. As a result, they are classified as *depth first* searches. Another class of tree traversal is a *breadth first* search. In a breadth first search, we processes nodes by levels, left to right within a level. For example, consider the function **bt_bfs()** as it appears in Listing 6.4. It uses a queue to ensure that nodes are processed in the correct order.

   bt_bfs() begins by placing the root node on the queue. During each iteration of its **while** loop, the function removes the next node from the queue, processes it, and then enqueues the node's children (if any). Processing terminates when the queue becomes empty. The function assumes the routines **addq()** and **delq()** to manage the queue (please refer back to Chapter 5).

   When processing the tree depicted in Figure 6.6, **bt_bfs()** produces the following output:

```
void bt_bfs( struct bt_node *tree )
{
      struct      bt_node     *t;

      addq( tree );
      while( (t = delq()) != NULL )
      {
            print_node( t ->data );        /* The visit */
            if( t ->lchild != NULL )
                  addq( t ->lchild );
            if( t ->rchild != NULL )
                  addq( t ->rchild );
      }
}
```

Listing 6.4
Breadth first traversal.

```
1, 2, 3, 4, 5, 6, 7, 8, 9, 10
```

Binary Tree Insertion

Most programs that employ binary trees usually proceed in two phases: Phase one constructs the tree; phase two traverses it. We have already described several traversal methods. Now we need to discuss the construction of binary trees. Specifically, we need to develop an *insertion* algorithm.

Generally speaking, there are two places where binary tree insertions may occur: at terminal (leaf) or non-terminal nodes. To add a non-terminal node, the insertion function requires three pieces of information: a pointer to the new node, a pointer to the node that will become the parent of the new node, and a flag variable indicating whether the new node should be inserted as the left or right child of its parent. Figure 6.9 provides an example.

Tree insertions more commonly occur at leaf nodes. For example, consider the problem of reading a list of numbers and printing them out in ascending order. There are many ways to construct a solution for this problem. One of the simplest uses a special form

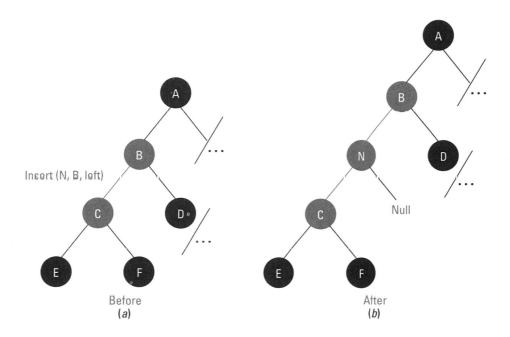

Figure 6.9
Binary tree insertion.

of binary tree called an *ordered binary tree* (OBT). The driving section of the program can be described by the following pseudo-code:

```
set_up_chores();
while( more input )
do
    bt_insert( new_item );  /* Insert new node */
done
print_ascending();
```

As its name implies, an ordered binary tree places restrictions on insertions. Specifically, an OBT has the property that, for any given node *n*, the data values contained in the left subtree of *n* are less than *n*, and the data values contained in the right subtree of *n* are greater than *n*.

Thus, all OBT insertions must begin with a traversal. With the arrival of each new data element, the insertion routine compares the new

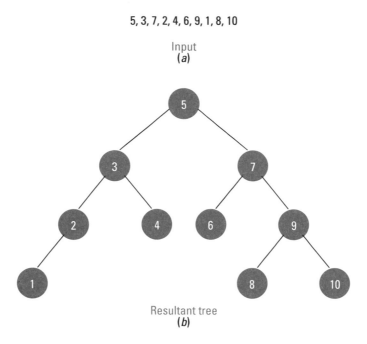

5, 3, 7, 2, 4, 6, 9, 1, 8, 10

Input
(*a*)

Resultant tree
(*b*)

Figure 6.10
Ordered binary tree
insertion.

data value with that of existing nodes. It continues to move down
either the left or right subtree of each successive node predicated
on the results of each comparison. When it finally encounters a node
that is either a leaf or a non-terminal node that has no subtree in
the indicated direction, the function inserts the new element as a child
of that node. Figure 6.10 contains an example of this processing.
It shows a sample input stream and its resultant OBT.

The function **bt_insert()**, presented in Listing 6.5, performs
binary tree insertions as just described. The initial **if** statement
checks for an empty tree and inserts the first node. Otherwise, the
function iteratively steps through the tree, moving either left or right based
on the results of each comparison. When it encounters a leaf node,
bt_insert() allocates and inserts a new node. The last **if** statement
determines which of the parent's pointers is assigned the new
node. The ancillary function, **get_new_bt()**, allocates memory for
each new element.

The question that now arises is, How should we process duplicate
data values? As you may have noticed, **bt_insert()** currently handles

```
struct    bt_node *root = NULL;

void bt_insert( int new )
{
     struct    bt_node    *p, *q;

     if( root == NULL ){              /* NULL Tree */
          root = get_new_bt();
          root->data = new;
          return;
     }

     p = root;
     while( p != NULL ){              /* Location for insertion */
          q = p;
          if( new < p->data )
               p = p->lchild;
          else
               p = p->rchild;
     }

     /*
      *    'q' points to parent of new node
      */
     p = get_new_bt();
     p->data = new;
     if( new < q->data )
          q->lchild = p;
     else
          q->rchild = p;
}

struct    bt_node *get_new_bt()
{
     struct    bt_node *newnode;

     newnode=(struct bt_node *)malloc(sizeof(struct bt_node));
     newnode->lchild = NULL;
     newnode->rchild = NULL;

     return( newnode );
}
```

Listing 6.5
Binary tree insertion.

the problem by default. That is, the function uses a less-than test to initiate a move down the left subtree; consequently, it inserts duplicate nodes along the right subtree.

For applications that anticipate only a small number of duplicate values, this is an acceptable solution. However, this implementation is wasteful for applications that expect many duplicate records. A better solution is to add a count field to the node structure. Upon recognizing a duplicate value, the insertion routine can then just increment the counter rather than adding a node to the tree.

Adding a count field to the node structure implies two coding modifications. First, the insertion algorithm must include an explicit test for equality. Second (and this can only be stated in general terms), traversal routines must take this additional field into account when processing the completed tree. For example, assume that after constructing a tree, a program must print all nodes in ascending order. If *all* elements must appear in the output, the display function must emit the proper number of duplicate elements based on the values contained in the count fields.

Concluding Remarks

If you consider the structure of an ordered binary tree you will observe that, in general, we can locate a particular value (node) more quickly than we can with a linked (linear) list. This is because with each comparison, we eliminate the need to search half of the remaining subtree. We lose this advantage if the tree should become skewed.

You should also note that the OTB insertion function is input sensitive. That is, the order in which input is presented to the routine will affect the resultant tree's shape. Specifically, a sorted input stream will create a tree that resembles a linear list. Obviously, this will directly affect the performance of searching algorithms. Chapters 8 and 9 will elaborate on this discussion.

Binary Tree Deletion

Most applications using binary trees do not require a deletion function. It is more often the case that trees continue to grow rather than shrink. (The typical scenario is that programs construct trees and then process

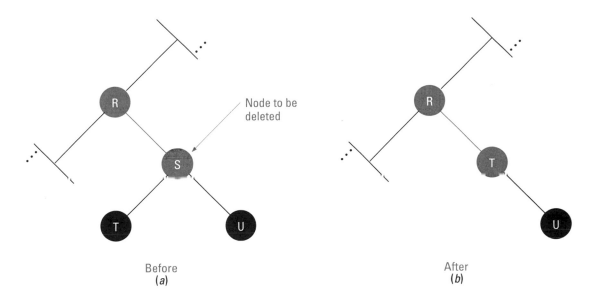

Node to be deleted

Before
(*a*)

After
(*b*)

Figure 6.11
Binary tree deletion.

the data contained within them.) Nevertheless, there are some applications that require a deletion capability.

Broadly speaking, we can divide node deletion in a binary tree into two types: the removal of terminal nodes and the removal of non-terminal nodes. Deleting a leaf node is simple and is analogous to a list deletion: Assign the value **NULL** to the appropriate pointer in the parent node and return the deleted node to the available list.

However, as depicted in Figure 6.11a, deleting a non-terminal node is more problematic. If we remove node *S* from the tree, we will need to reattach two nodes (*T* and *U*). However, there is only one pointer available (the right child of *R*). Therefore, one of node *S*'s children must become the parent of the other (see Fig. 6.11b). Even if the left child of *R* was available, we could not just mechanically assign to it one of the unattached nodes. As with the case of an ordered tree, there might be an explicit relationship between a parent and its subtrees. For example, consider that if all right subtrees are to hold data values greater than that of their parents, inserting either *T* or *U* as the left child of *R* would invalidate that relationship.

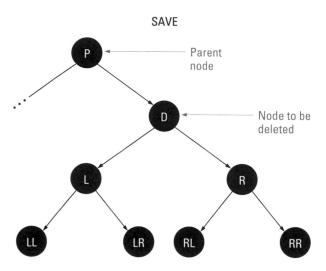

Figure 6.12
Deletion example.

Using Figure 6.12 as a model, we can divide binary tree deletion into several distinct cases, as follows. Figure 6.13 depicts the results of each example.

1. If D is a leaf node, then **P—>rchild = NULL**.
2. If the left child of D is **NULL**, then **P—>rchild** = R.
3. If the right child of D is **NULL**, then **P—>rchild** = L.
4. If the right child of node L is **NULL** (node LR in the example), then L can become the right child of P, and R can become the right child of L. It is important to note that this processing maintains the ordered property of the tree.
5. If the left child of node R is **NULL** (node RL in the example), then R can become the right child of P, and L can become the left child of R. As in case 4, this maintains the ordered relationship.
6. If none of the previous cases exist, set the right child of P to either L or R, and then reinsert the other subtree.
7. The root node of the tree is to be deleted. Perform the same processing as in case 6 but modify the **root** pointer accordingly.

The code for the function **bt_delete()** appears in Listing 6.6. The function deletes nodes, case by case, as just described. It requires three arguments: pointers to both the node that will be deleted and

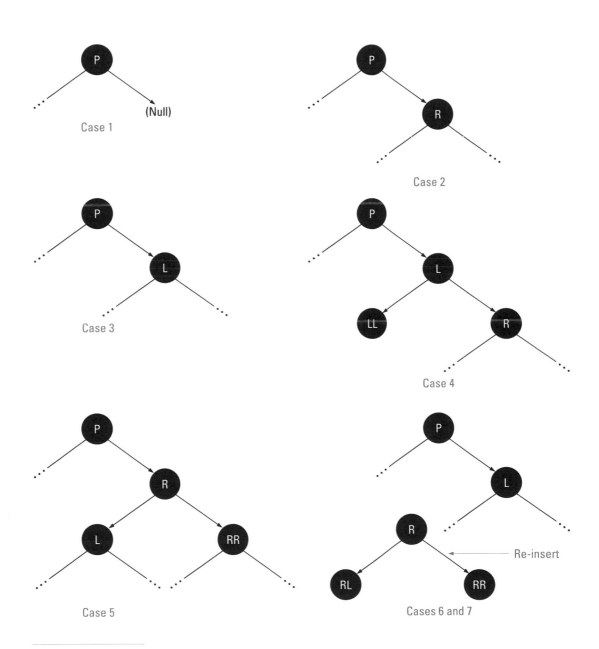

Figure 6.13
Deletion results.

```
#define   OK        0
#define   ERROR    -1
#define   LCHILD    1
#define   RCHILD    2

int bt_delete( struct bt_node *pred,
               struct bt_node *node, int stat )
{
    struct    bt_node   *child;

    if( node == NULL )
        return( ERROR );

    if( pred == NULL ){                                      /* 7 */
        root = node->rchild;
        child = node->lchild;
        bt_freenode( node );
        return( bt_insert2(child) );
    }

    if( node->lchild == NULL && node->rchild == NULL ) /* 1 */
        child = NULL;
    else if( node->lchild == NULL )                          /* 2 */
        child = node->rchild;
    else if( node->rchild == NULL )                          /* 3 */
        child = node->lchild;
    else if( node->lchild->rchild == NULL ){                 /* 4 */
        child = node->lchild;
        node->lchild->rchild = node->rchild;
    } else if( node->rchild->lchild == NULL ){               /* 5 */
        child = node->rchild;
        node->rchild->lchild = node->lchild;
    } else {                                                 /* 6 */
        child = node->rchild;
        if( stat == LCHILD )
            pred->lchild = node->rchild;
        else
            pred->rchild = node->rchild;
        bt_freenode( node );
        return( bt_insert2(node->lchild) );
    }
```

continued on p. 161

continued from p. 160

```
    /*

    *    Adjust predecessor's pointers
    */
    if( stat == LCHILD )
        pred->lchild = child;
    else
        pred->rchild = child;
    bt_freenode( node );

    return( OK );
}
```

Listing 6.6
Binary tree deletion.

its parent, and a status flag indicating whether the deleted node is the left or right child of its parent.

Note than the function **bt_insert2()**, used to reinsert a subtree, is different from its predecessor **bt_insert()**. This version takes as an argument a pointer to a node rather than a data value. We leave its implementation as an exercise for the reader.

Utility Functions

As with linked lists, there are several useful utility functions for processing binary trees. The function **bt_copy()**, presented in Listing 6.7, generates a copy of a binary tree. Note that the function is really just a modification of a preorder traversal.

The function **bt_equal()** (Listing 6.8) determines the equivalence of its two tree arguments. Defined recursively, the function descends both trees until it either encounters a difference or determines that the two trees are equivalent.

6.3 BALANCED TREES

Let's continue our discussion of ordered binary trees (OBTs). OBTs are fairly easy to implement. However, they can have one drawback: a worst-case running time of $O(n)$. As depicted in Figure 6.14, even an

```
struct     bt_node   *
bt_copy( struct bt_node *treeptr )
{
    struct     bt_node    *new;

    if( treeptr == NULL )               /* The 'out' */
        return( NULL );

    new = get_new_bt();
    new->data = treeptr->data;
    new->lchild = bt_copy( treeptr->lchild );
    new->rchild = bt_copy( treeptr->rchild );

    return( new );
}
```

Listing 6.7

Copying a binary tree.

ordered binary tree can degrade into a linear list if the insertion routine receives elements in ascending (or nearly ascending) order.

Several methods have been developed to prevent trees from becoming skewed. Some of the most powerful are so-called *AVL trees*. (Their name is derived from the scientists who first studied them: Adel'son-Vel'skii and Landis.)

Before we can understand AVL trees, we must define what we mean by *balanced*. Let's begin by defining *height* for some node n as

$$left\_height(n) = \begin{cases} 0, & \text{if } n \text{ has no left child} \\ 1 + height(left\_child(n)) & \text{for all other nodes} \end{cases}$$

$$right\_height(n) = \begin{cases} 0, & \text{if } n \text{ has no right child} \\ 1 + height(right\_child(n)) & \text{for all other nodes} \end{cases}$$

As you may recall, the height of any node in a tree is the length of the longest path from that node to a leaf node. Based on the preceding definitions, a leaf node has *right_height* and *left_height* both equal to 0.

Now let's define the *balance* of some node n as

$$balance(n) = right\_height(n) - left\_height(n)$$

```
#define      TRUE    1
#define      FALSE   0

int
bt_equal( struct bt_node *tree1, struct bt_node *tree2 )
{
    int  res;

    if( tree1 == NULL && tree2 == NULL )
        return( TRUE );

    res = FALSE;
    if( tree1->data == tree2->data ){
        res = bt_equal( tree1->lchild, tree2->lchild );
        if( res == TRUE )
            res = bt_equal( tree1->rchild, tree2->rchild );
    }

    return( res );
}
```

Listing 6.8
Binary tree equivalence.

Thus, a node's balance indicates the relative height of its right subtree as compared to its left. If the balance is positive, the right subtree has greater depth than the left; if the balance is negative, the reverse is true.

A binary tree is an AVL tree if, and only if, every node in the tree has a balance of -1, 0, or $+1$. Figure 6.15 provides some examples of both AVL and non-AVL trees.

AVL trees have a number of attributes that make them well suited for searching applications. First, an AVL tree with n nodes has height $O(\log_2 n)$. Second, we can insert and delete nodes in AVL trees with an efficiency of $O(\log_2 n)$, while still preserving the AVL properties of the tree. The sections that follow discuss the implementation of AVL trees.

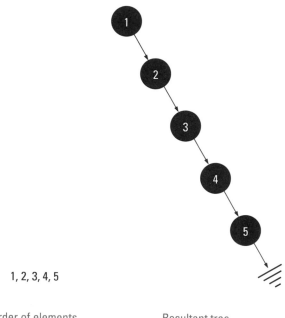

1, 2, 3, 4, 5

Figure 6.14
Ordered binary tree.

Order of elements
(*b*)

Resultant tree
(*b*)

AVL Tree Insertion

Because an AVL tree is essentially a binary tree, we can reuse our node structure. We will, however, need to add a field to store balances. Because there are only three balance values, we only need two bits of storage for this data element. However, for pedagogical clarity, we will implement this field as a full **int**. Listing 6.9 contains the new AVL node structure.

Conceptually, we insert new nodes into an AVL tree as follows:

1. Employ the same algorithm we used to insert a node into an ordered binary tree. That is, we trace a path from the root node to a leaf node (where we will perform the insertion).
2. Insert the new node.
3. Retrace the path back up to the root node, adjusting balances along the way.
4. If a node's balance should become ±2, readjust the node's subtrees so that its balance is in line with AVL requirements (i.e., ±1).

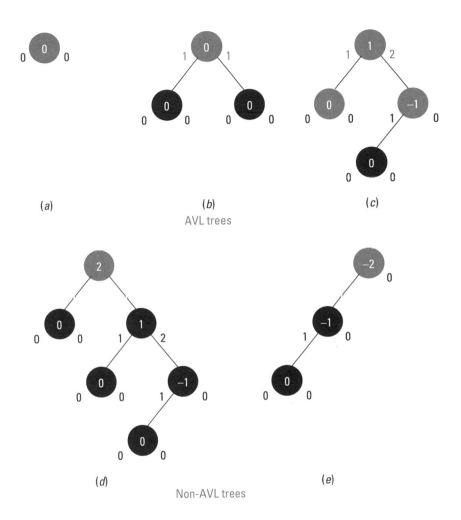

Figure 6.15
Examples of AVL and
non-AVL trees.

```
struct   avl_node    {
    int      bal;
    int      data;
    struct   avl_node  *lchild;
    struct   avl_node  *rchild;
};
```

Listing 6.9
AVL node structure.

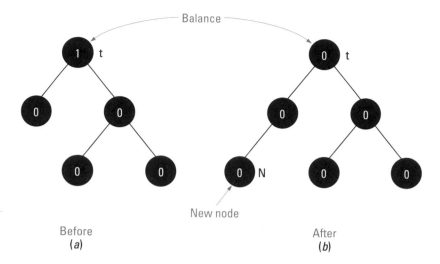

Figure 6.16
AVL insertion—
case 1.

Obviously, step 4 is the most difficult. Specifically, we need to decide how we can readjust a node's descendents such that all balances are in accord with AVL requirements. The problem decomposes into four distinct cases (and their mirror images).

Case 1   A node becomes balanced as a result of an insertion. As depicted in Figure 6.16, the balance of node t decreases from 1 to 0 as a result of the insertion of node n into the tree.

There is no reason to readjust node t's descendents because the overall height of the tree remains unchanged.

Case 2   A node becomes unbalanced by only ± 1. As depicted in Figure 6.17, the balance of node t changes from 0 to $+1$ as a result of the insertion.

Note that the height of the tree increases. As a result, we must adjust the balance of node r as well.

Case 3   In this case, a node becomes unbalanced by ± 2 because the right subtree of its right child increases in height. For example, when we insert a new element into the tree depicted in Figure 6.18a, we generate the tree contained in Figure 6.18b. Notice how the balance for node a increases from $+1$ to $+2$.

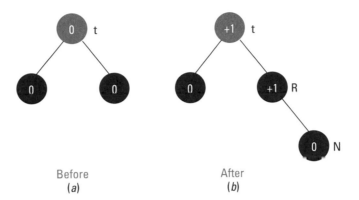

Figure 6.17
AVL insertion—
case 2.

Before
(a)

After
(b)

Unfortunately, we cannot readjust the balance by simply interchanging nodes *b* and *e*. This solution would undermine the ordered property of the tree.

However, as illustrated in Figure 6.18c, we can make *a* the left child of *c* and reposition the left child of *c* (node *d*) as the right child of the newly positioned node *a*. We call this type of transformation a *single left rotation*.

There are several important points that we should address regarding the transformation process:

- It preserves the ordered property of the tree.
- It restores all nodes to appropriate AVL balances.
- It preserves the inorder traversal of the tree. That is, an inorder traversal will access nodes in the same order after the transformation (as it would have prior to the reordering).
- We only need to modify three pointers to accomplish the rebalancing.

One final note: There is a mirror-image case in which a node becomes unbalanced by -2 because the left subtree of its left child increases in height. We rebalance the tree in this case with an equivalent *single right rotation*.

Case 4 A node becomes unbalanced by ± 2 because the right subtree of its left child increases in height. As illustrated in Figures 6.19a and 6.19b, when we insert the new node *n* as the right child

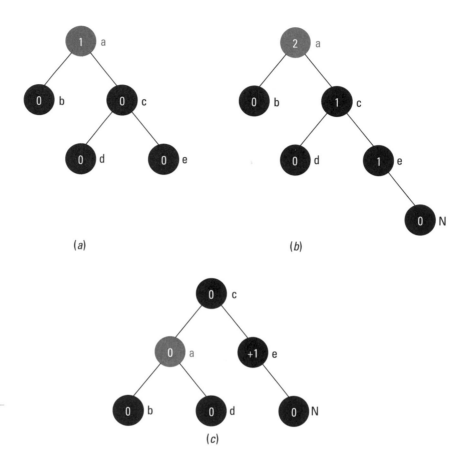

(a)   (b)

(c)

Figure 6.18
AVL insertion—
case 3.

of node *d*, the balance of node *a* increases to +2.

This case really has two subcases. In the first, the new node becomes the right child of *d*. This is the case we will describe. In the other, the new node becomes the left child of *d*. For both subcases, we undertake identical steps to rebalance the tree. The only difference is that the resulting node balances will differ slightly.

To rebalance the tree, we perform with a single right rotation at node *c* (Fig. 6.19c), followed by a single left rotation at node *d* (Fig. 6.19d). Because we need two rotations, we refer to this transformation as a *double rotation* or an *RL rotation* (due to the rotation order).

As with case 3, there is a mirror-image case. This would require an *LR rotation* to rebalance the tree.

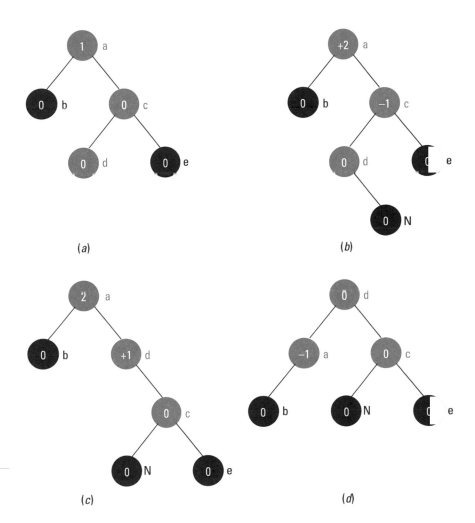

Figure 6.19
AVL insertion—
case 4.

Once the insertion process is understood, it is a straightforward
task to develop the actual algorithm. Listing 6.10 contains the code for a
C implementation of an AVL insertion algorithm. Contained in the
listing are routines to right balance and left rotate. The listing lacks the
complementary routines that left balance and right rotate; we leave
the implementation of these functions as exercise for the reader.

```
struct  avl_node    {
    int     bal;
    int     data;
    struct  avl_node  *lchild;
    struct  avl_node  *rchild;
};

struct avl_node *root = NULL;

#define NO      0
#define YES     1


#define BAL     0
#define LHIGH   -1
#define RHIGH   1


struct avl_node *
avl_insert( struct avl_node *root, struct avl_node *new,
            int *chg_hgt )
{
    if( root == NULL ){
        root = new;
        root->bal = BAL;
        root->lchild = NULL;
        root->rchild = NULL;
        *chg_hgt = YES;
    } else if( new->data < root->data ){       /* Insert Left */
        root->lchild = avl_insert( root->lchild, new, chg_hgt );
        if( *chg_hgt ){                         /* LCHILD grew *1
            if( root->bal == LHIGH )        /* Node's now 2 High */
                root = left_bal( root, chg_hgt );
            else if( root->bal == BAL )     /* Node is now LHIGH */
                root->bal = LHIGH;
            else {                          /* Was RHIGH now BAL */
                root->bal = BAL;
                *chg_hgt = NO;
            }
        }
```

continued on p. 171

continued from p. 170

```
    } else {                                  /* Insert Right */
        root->rchild = avl_insert( root->rchild, new, chg_hgt );
            if( *chg_hgt ){                   /* RCHILD grew *
            if( root->bal == LHIGH ){         /* Was LHIGH now BAL  */
                root->bal = BAL;
                *chg_hgt = NO;
            } else if( root->bal == BAL )     /* Node's now RHIGH   */
                root->bal = LHIGH;
            else                              /* Node's now 2 High */
                root = right_bal( root, chg_hgt );
        }
    }

    return( root );
}

struct avl_node *right_bal( struct avl_node *node, int *chg_hgt )
{
    struct  avl_node  *rsub,      /* Right subtree of node */
                      *lsub;      /* Left subtree of rsub  */

    rsub = node->rchild;
    switch( rsub->bal ){
    case RHIGH:                   /* Single rotation */
        node->bal = BAL;
        rsub->bal = BAL;
        node = rotate_left( node );
        *chg_hgt = NO;
        break;

    case LHIGH:                   /* Double rotation */
        lsub = rsub->lchild;
        switch( lsub->bal ){
        case RHIGH:
            node->bal = LHIGH;
            rsub->bal = BAL;
            break;

        case BAL:
            node->bal = BAL;
            rsub->bal = BAL;
            break;
```

continued on p. 172

```
        case LHIGH:                          continued from p. 171
            node->bal = BAL;
            rsub->bal = RHIGH;
            break;
        }
        lsub->bal = BAL;
        node->rchild = rotate_right( node );
        node = rotate_left( node );
        *chg_hgt = NO;
        break;
    }
    return( node );
}

struct avl_node *rotate_left( struct avl_node *node )
{
    struct avl_node *tmp;

    tmp = node->rchild;
    node->rchild = tmp->lchild;
    tmp->lchild = node;
    return( tmp );
}

struct avl_node *left_bal( struct avl_node *node, int *chg_hgt )
{
    /* Left as an exercise */
}

struct avl_node *rotate_right( struct avl_node *node )
{
    /* Left as an exercise */
}
```

Listing 6.10
AVL insertion algorithm.

The driving routine is called **avl_insert()**. It requires three arguments: a pointer to the root node of the AVL tree; a pointer to the new node that it will insert; and a pointer to an integer variable. This latter argument serves as a flag that will indicate when the height of the tree changes. (We must pass and return this value as a pointer due to C's call-by-value convention.)

Similar to an OBT function, this routine begins execution by recursively invoking itself until it locates the point of insertion. However, unlike an OBT insertion, **avl_insert()** must readjust the balance fields after it adds the new node. The function indicates a change in height by setting the **chg_hgt** flag to **YES**. If the balance becomes ±2, **avl_insert()** calls routines to rotate nodes and rebalance the tree.

AVL Tree Deletion

Deleting nodes in AVL trees requires that we employ the same basic principles we discussed for insertion. Specifically, we will need to perform single and double rotations.

We begin an AVL deletion by following the deletion algorithm for an ordered binary tree. Then, after we've located the node we wish to delete, we perform the following processing:

1. If the node is a leaf node, just delete it.
2. If the node has only one child, replace it with its child (i.e., have the node's parent point to the node's child).
3. If the deleted node has two children, replace it with (a copy of) its inorder successor; then delete the (original copy of the) inorder successor. This example is illustrated beginning with Figure 6.20e. Note that this processing preserves the ordered property of the tree.

Now that we have deleted the node, we must rebalance the tree:

4. If the balance of the deleted node's parent changes from 0 to ±1 (Fig. 6.20b), the algorithm terminates. That is, the tree does not require any additional rebalancing.
5. If the deleted node's parent changes from ±1 to 0 (Fig. 6.20c), the height of the tree has changed and the balance of the deleted node's grandparent is affected.
6. If the balance of a deleted node's parent changes from ±1 to ±2

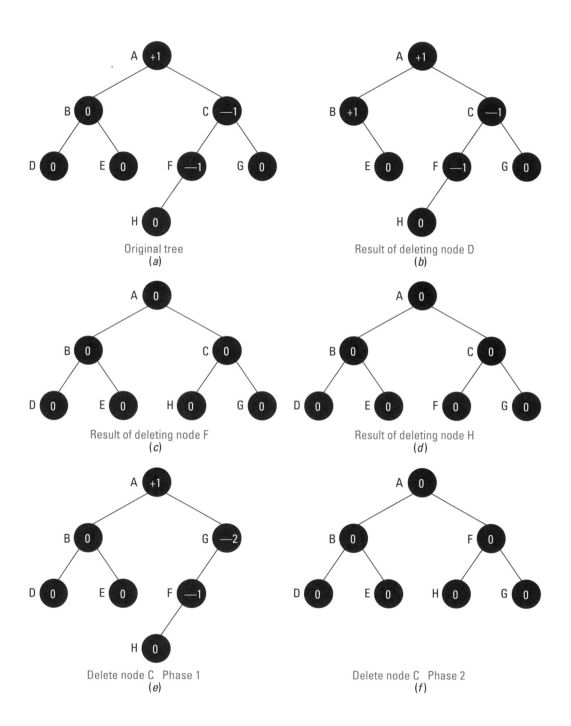

Original tree
(*a*)

Result of deleting node D
(*b*)

Result of deleting node F
(*c*)

Result of deleting node H
(*d*)

Delete node C   Phase 1
(*e*)

Delete node C   Phase 2
(*f*)

Figure 6.20
AVL tree deletion.

(Figs. 6.20e and 6.20f), it forces a rotation. After the rotation completes, the parent's balance may change. This, in turn, might force additional changes (and possible rotations) all the way up the tree as we retrace our path back to the root. In fact, we need to retrace our path until we encounter a node that changes from 0 to 1; then we can terminate the algorithm (as described in step 4).

Even in the worst case, when a deletion forces $O(\log_2 n)$ rotations, the algorithm's complexity remains $O(\log_2 n)$. This is because we can perform rotations in a constant amount of time. Completing the implementation is left as an exercise for the reader.

6.4 THREADED BINARY TREES

If you examine the structure of a binary tree, you will discover that the number of unused links (in leaf nodes) is greater than the number of pointers actually used. In fact, in a tree with n nodes, of the $2n$ available pointers, only $n - 1$ are used. This represents less than half of the total number of available pointers.

We can make use of these otherwise unused links by having them point to other nodes in the tree—in a predefined manner—to create a *threaded binary tree* (TBT). In a threaded binary tree, we assign addresses to leaf node pointers based on the following rules:

- If the pointer is the right child of a given node N, assign to it the address of the node that would follow N during an inorder traversal.
- If the pointer is the left child of a given node N, assign to it the address of the node that would precede N during an inorder traversal.

Figure 6.21a provides an example. With two exceptions, all the previously null links are now pointing to other nodes in the tree. The exceptions are the left child of node 4 and the right child of node 3. The nodes have, respectively, no predecessor or successor element in an inorder traversal. If we left the tree in this state we would require special-case processing for these two pointers. A better solution is to use a *head node* and have both of these links point to it. Figure 6.21b shows the tree with a head node and all of its pointers assigned.

There is one more point we must address: Now that every pointer

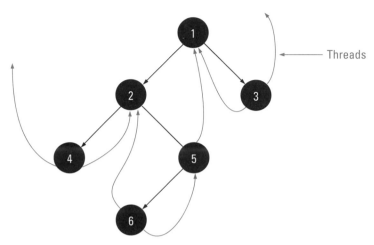

Figure 6.21a
Threaded binary tree.

In order traversal
4, 2, 6, 5, 1, 3

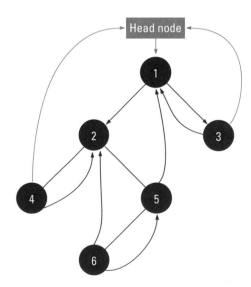

Figure 6.21b
Threaded binary tree
with head node.

has been put to use, it has become impossible to distinguish a leaf node from a non-terminal node. As a result, we must include a type field in the **bt_node** structure.

TBT Traversal

Inorder traversal is now greatly simplified. If, for a given node N, **rtype = BT_THREAD**, its inorder successor is **rchild**. Alternatively, if **rtype = BT_NORM**, we determine its inorder successor by traversing the left links of the **rchild** of N until we locate a node with **ltype = BT_THREAD**. A pseudo-code description of the algorithm follows.

```
tbt_inorder( root )        /* Inorder Traversal of TBT */
{
    /*
     * Find leftmost node
     */
    tmp = root;
    if( tmp != NULL )
        while( tmp->lchild != NULL )
            tmp = tmp->lchild;

    while( tmp != root )       /* Begin Traversal */
        visit( tmp );
        tmp = tbt_next( tmp );
}

tbt_next( node )     /* Locate Inorder Successor */
{
    /*
     * For a thread, successor is rchild
     */
    tmp = node->rchild;

    /*
     * For normal nodes, follow left hand path
     */
    if( node->rtype == BT_NORM )
        while( tmp->ltype != BT_THREAD )
            tmp = tmp->lchild;

    return( tmp );
}
```

Confirm your understanding of the algorithm by tracing its execution when locating the inorder successor of node 2 in Figure 6.21b. In much the same manner, we can use threaded binary trees to simplify preorder and postorder traversals. One minor drawback of threaded binary trees is that they commit you to a particular traversal methodology (e.g., inorder).

TBT Insertions

We now need to develop an insertion algorithm for threaded binary trees. To begin our discussion, let's consider how we would insert a node as the right child of a leaf node. In Figure 6.22a, the right subtree of node *C* is a thread. Therefore, to insert a new node *N*, we need to perform the following processing:

```
n->rchild = c->rchild;
n->rtype = c->rtype;
n->lchild = c;
n->ltype = BT_THREAD;
c->rchild = n;
c->rtype = BT_NORM;
```

Figure 6.22b demonstrates how we insert a new node when the **rchild** of *C* is not a thread. The **lchild** of *E*—which currently points to *C*—must end up pointing to *N*. The code, therefore, becomes

```
n->rchild = c->rchild;
n->rtype = c->rtype;
n->lchild = c;
n->ltype = BT_THREAD;
c->rchild = n;
c->rtype = BT_NORM;
if( t->rtype == T_NORM )
    tmp = inorder_succ( c );
tmp->lchild = n;
```

We will leave the case of left-child insertions as an exercise for the reader.

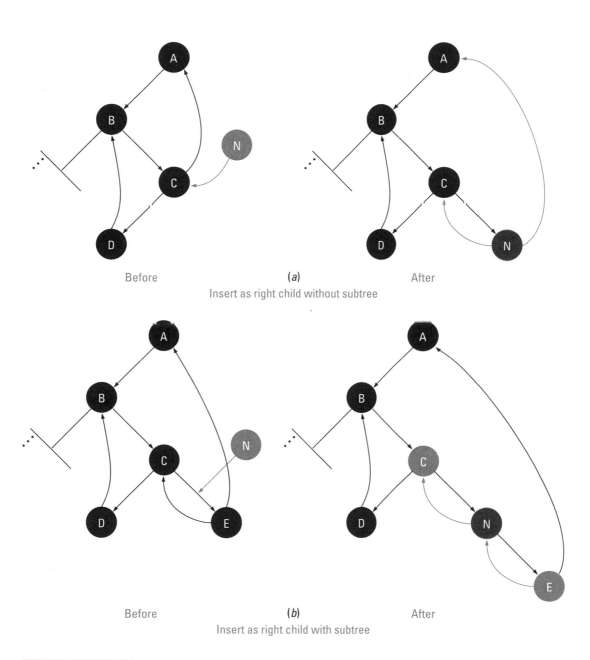

Before   (a)   After

Insert as right child without subtree

Before   (b)   After

Insert as right child with subtree

Figure 6.22
Threaded binary tree
insertion.

TBT Deletions

As with unthreaded trees, the deletion of nodes in a threaded binary tree is application dependent. However, with threaded trees we have the added concern of adjusting threads when elements are deleted. Exercise 7, p. 193 explores this topic further.

6.5 APPLICATIONS OF TREES

There are many uses for tree structures in program design. As we have seen, they can be used in the sorting and searching of data. Trees are also well suited for representing relationships among data. Let's look at some examples.

Decision Trees

Another of the classic problems studied by computer scientists is the Eight Coins Problem:

> There are eight apparently identical coins. However, one coin—a counterfeit—is of a different weight than the others. We must determine, with only three weighings on a balance scale, which coin is counterfeit, and whether it is heavier or lighter than the others.

There are 16 unique results: Coin 1 is heavier/lighter, Coin 2 is heavier/lighter, etc. You may find it beneficial to attempt to solve the puzzle before reading on.

The solution to the puzzle can be described as follows:

> Compare the weights of coins (1,2,3) with coins (4,5,6). There are three possible results:

> 1. Set (1,2,3) = Set (4,5,6)
>   Because both sets weigh the same, we can deduce that either coin 7 or coin 8 is counterfeit. We now compare one of them with a known standard (for example, coin 1). In the remaining two weighings, we can determine conclusively which coin is counterfeit and whether it is heavier or lighter.
> 2. Set (1,2,3) < Set (4,5,6)
>   We now know, based on this first weighing, that coins 7 and

8 must be genuine. To determine which of the first six coins are bad, we must switch two of them and isolate two others. That is, we compare coins (1,4) with (2,5). There are, again, three possible outcomes:

a. Set (1,4) < Set (2,5)

Because the relationship remained the same (i.e., the coins on the left weigh less than the coins on the right), we can surmise that coins 3 and 6 are genuine; we also know that coins 2 and 4 are good because switching them had no effect on the balance. Therefore, either coin 1 is light or coin 5 is heavy. We need only compare one of the coins to a standard to determine which one is counterfeit.

b. Set (1,4) = Set (2,5)

Either coin 3 or coin 6 is counterfeit. We also can surmise— from the original weighing— that if coin 3 is bad, it is heavy; if coin 6 is bad, it is light. Compare one against a standard to determine the result.

c. Set (1,4) > Set (2,5)

The switching of coins 2 and 4 caused the balance to change. Therefore, either coin 2 is light or coin 4 is heavy. Compare one against a standard to determine the result.

3. Set (1,2,3) > Set (4,5,6)

The solution is analogous to section 2, above.

Before we begin our discussion of an algorithmic solution, consider the problem-solving method we just described. After each weighing, we observed an outcome and decided on a new course of action. That is, each step served as a crossroads where we selected a new path until we finally reached a solution.

We can simulate this process in a computer program using a *decision tree*. Each node in a decision tree corresponds to a critical point in the solution of a problem. Typically, this is some action or test that must be performed. The children of a node represent the implications of a decision made at the parent's level (that is, a choice of actions based on the outcome of the test). Leaf nodes represent solutions to the problem (if attained via proper use of the tree).

Figure 6.23 depicts the decision tree for the Eight Coins Problem. Each non-terminal node represents a weighing. Each of a node's children represents additional comparisons that are required based on the out-

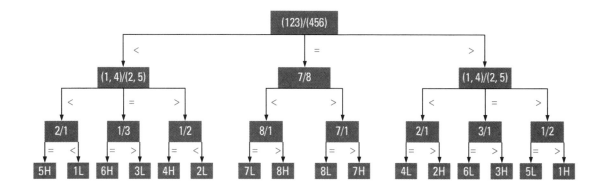

Figure 6.23
Eight Coins decision
tree.

come of a weighing. Each leaf node represents one of the 16 unique solutions.

There are essentially two ways to implement this problem-solving technique. First, after constructing a decision tree for a given problem, we can employ a traversal function to determine a solution. As it moves along the tree, the function uses the results of each test to select the next path to follow. A solution is attained when the function reaches a leaf node.

The other way is to code the decision tree implicitly. That is, embed the decision logic right into the code. As an example of this technique, Listing 6.11 presents the code for the function **eightcoins()**.

Game Trees

Another use for trees is in computer game simulations. To illustrate this technique, we will design a program that plays tic-tac-toe. To begin our discussion, assume that we have written a function called **board _eval()**. The purpose of this routine is to evaluate board positions. That is, the function computes a numerical value representing the relative strength of the position for one of the players. A winning position would yield the maximum value, a losing position the minimum.

For our tic-tac-toe program, **board_eval()** could determine for

```
#define    HEAVY      1
#define    LIGHT     -1

void eightcoins( int *coin, int *bad, int *stat )
{
    int  s1, s2;
    int  s3, s4;

    s1 = coin[0] + coin[1] + coin[2];
    s2 = coin[3] + coin[4] + coin[5];
    if( s1 == s2 ){              /* 6 or 7 bad */
        if( coin[6] > coin[7] )
            if( coin[6] != coin[0] ){
                *bad = 6;
                *stat = HEAVY;
            } else {
                *bad = 7;
                *stat = LIGHT;
            }
        else                          /* 6 < 7 */
            if( coin[7] != coin[0] ){
                *bad = 7;
                *stat = HEAVY;
            } else {
                *bad = 6;
                *stat = LIGHT;
            }
    } else if( s1 > s2 ){
        s3 = coin[0] + coin[3];
        s4 = coin[1] + coin[4];
        if( s3 == s4 )
            if( coin[2] != coin[0] ){
                *bad = 2;
                *stat = HEAVY;
            } else {
                *bad = 5;
                *stat = LIGHT;
            }
        else if( s3 > s4 )
            if( coin[0] != coin[2] ){
                *bad = 0;
                *stat = HEAVY;
```

continued on p. 184

```
                            } else {              continued from p. 183
                                *bad = 4;
                                *stat = LIGHT;
                            }
                    else                          /* s3 < s4 */
                        if( coin[1] != coin[2] ){
                            *bad = 1;
                            *stat = HEAVY;
                        } else {
                            *bad = 3;
                            *stat = LIGHT;
                        }
            } else {                              /* s1 < s2 */
                s3 = coin[0] + coin[3];
                s4 = coin[1] + coin[4];
                if( s3 == s4 )
                        if( coin[2] != coin[0] ){
                            *bad = 2;
                            *stat = LIGHT;
                        } else {
                            *bad = 5;
                            *stat = HEAVY;
                        }
                else if( s3 > s4 )
                        if( coin[1] != coin[2] ){
                            *bad = 1;
                            *stat = LIGHT;
                        } else {
                            *bad = 3;
                            *stat = HEAVY;
                        }
                else                              /* s3 < s4 */
                        if( coin[0] != coin[2] ){
                            *bad = 0;
                            *stat = LIGHT;
                        } else {
                            *bad = 4;
                            *stat = HEAVY;
                        }
            }
        }
```

Listing 6.11
Eight Coins function.

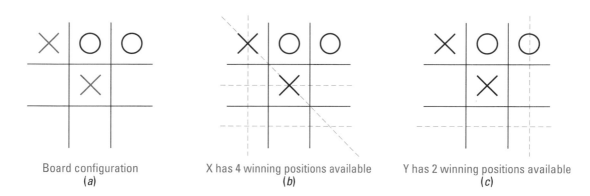

Board configuration
(a)

X has 4 winning positions available
(b)

Y has 2 winning positions available
(c)

Figure 6.24
Strength index
calculation.

each player the total number of rows, columns, and diagonals still open (i.e., locations where a win is still possible) and return the difference of the two values. For example, consider the board position depicted in Figure 6.24a. If evaluating this position on behalf of player X, **board_eval()** would compute four winning positions for X (Fig. 6.24b) and two for O (Fig. 6.24c) and return a strength index of 2 (i.e., $4 - 2$). Conversely, if evaluating the same position for player O, the function would return a strength index of -2 ($2 - 4$).

To determine the next move for a player, a program could evaluate every possible move from the current position and select the one that yields the highest strength index. However, this type of analysis does not always yield the best result. As depicted in Figure 6.25, if the selection were based solely on the strength index, the program would choose either b or c as the next move for player X. Nevertheless, despite their lower index, choices d or e—both of which yield directly to winning positions—are the best moves for X.

There are two ways to correct this problem. One is to build a better evaluation function. For simple games, such as tic-tac-toe, this is certainly possible. In fact, because the number of possible board positions is relatively small, we could examine every possible combination before selecting our next move. However, for more complex games—such as chess—this option is impractical.

The other way to solve the problem is to change our approach.

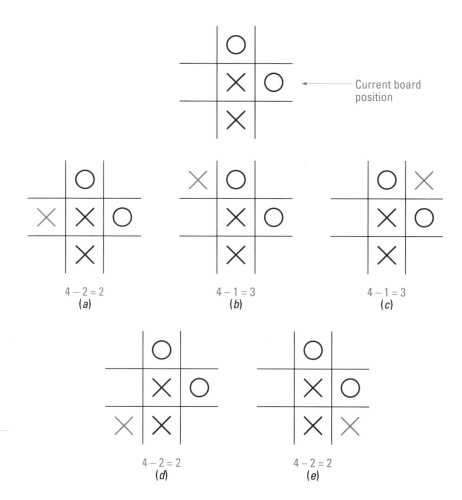

$4 - 2 = 2$
(a)

$4 - 1 = 3$
(b)

$4 - 1 = 3$
(c)

$4 - 2 = 2$
(d)

$4 - 2 = 2$
(e)

Figure 6.25
Move evaluation for
player *X*.

The shortcoming of a static evaluation function is that it cannot predict the outcome of the game. That is, it cannot determine the future effect of a given move. However, if it were possible for the function to look ahead several positions, it could improve its choice of moves.

We can effectively implement this approach using *game trees*. A game tree consists of all possible moves derived from a given position. Each node represents a move; each level represents, alternately, moves for each player. We define the *look-ahead* level as the maximum depth of the game tree (i.e., how many moves ahead we will look).

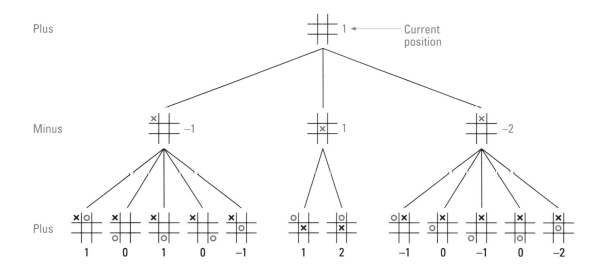

Figure 6.26

Game tree to select opening move for player *X*.

Figure 6.26 contains an example. (Note that because of symmetry, we need not consider all possible board configurations.) The root node of the game tree is the current position, and each subsequent level represents a choice of moves for one of the players. The player to move, in this case *X*, is designated as *plus*, the opponent as *minus*.

Before we describe how to use game trees, let's observe for a moment how humans play the game. When we select moves for ourselves, we obviously choose what we believe to be our best move. Our opponent will obviously try to do the same. Thus, when we attempt to predict opponents' moves, we must put ourselves in their position and pick the best move for them—that is, the *worst* move for us.

Now let's apply that same logic to our game tree. However, we must keep in mind that the evaluation function determines the value of each board position from the standpoint of the player whose turn it is to move. For example, let's assume it's *X*'s turn to move. For all levels in the game tree that represent moves for *X*, we choose a path that yields the highest value (that is, the best move for *X*).

Conversely, on levels representing moves for O, we select moves with the lowest index (i.e., the best moves for O). Therefore, at each *plus* level in the game tree, our algorithm must select the move with the maximum index; at each *minus* level it must select the move with the minimum index.

In summary, to select a move for a given player, our game program must

- Construct a game tree based on the current board position.
- Evaluate (using a static evaluation function) the position index for all leaf nodes.
- Bubble up—from leaf to root—the strength indexes by assigning each plus node the maximum value of its children, each minus node the minimum value of its children.

When this processing has completed, the function selects as its move the level two node (the child of the root) with the highest strength index. This process is then repeated, using the new board position, to choose the best response for the opposing player.

Implementation

Implementation of our game tree algorithm will require several data elements. Because the number of moves varies with each position, we will need the following node structure:

```
struct    gnode      {
    int     val;              /* Position value  */
    int     turn;             /* Whose turn?     */
    char    pos[3][3];        /* Board position  */
    struct  gnode   *cptr;    /* Child pointer   */
    struct  gnode   *sptr;    /* Sibling pointer */
};
```

To simplify processing, we will not use direct pointers to reference subtrees; rather, child nodes will be stored using linked lists. As depicted in Figure 6.27, **cptr** points to a list of children and **sptr** points a list of siblings. In addition, each node must provide storage for a board position, a position value (strength index), and a flag to indicate whether it is on a plus or minus level.

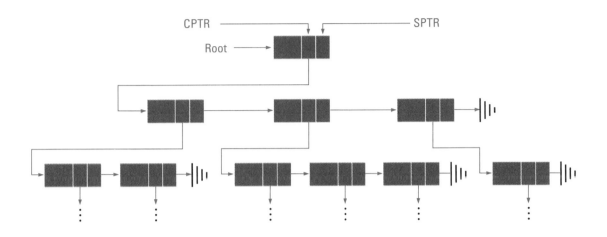

Figure 6.27
Game tree
implementation.

The driving loop of the program will be

```
who = 'X';
blank_board( board );
while( move(board, who, MAXLEVEL) != WIN ){
    print_board( board, who );
    if( who == 'X' )            /* Alternate Turns */
        who = 'O';
    else
        who = 'X';
}
print_board( board, who );
```

The program moves alternately for each player until it determines a winner; it then displays the results. The call to **print_board()** within the body of the loop is optional, but is useful to trace all the intermediate moves made by both players. The symbolic constant **MAX-LEVEL** determines the maximum look-ahead level for each move.

The function **move()** selects and records moves (i.e., updates the master board) for each player. It requires three arguments: the player ID, the current board position, and the maximum look-ahead level. It is defined as

```
int move( char *board[], char who, int level )
{
    int val;
    struct gnode *root;
    struct gnode *best;


    root = make_tree( board, level );   /* Build tree */
    best = best_move( who, root );
    move_board( board, best ->pos );    /* Store move */
    val = best ->val;
    free_all( root );                   /* Free nodes */


    return( val );
}
```

The function **make_tree()** constructs a game tree, of depth **level**, for the current board position; it returns a pointer to the root of the tree. The function **best_move()** takes two arguments: the player ID and a pointer to the game tree. It determines the best move for player **who** by computing the position index for each leaf node (using the function **board_eval()**) and then bubbling the values up the tree. It returns the child node of **root** with the highest value.

The functions **make_tree()**, **game_tree()**, and **best_move()** appear in Listing 6.12. We leave the completion of the program as an exercise for the reader.

```
struct gnode *
make_tree( char *board[], int lev )
{
    struct    gnode    *root;

    /*
     *    Setup root node of tree
     */
    root = get_gnode();
    root->cptr = NULL;
    root->sptr = NULL;
    root->turn = POSITIVE;
    move_board( root->pos, board );    /* Copy board pos */

    /*
     *    Build rest of game tree
     */
    game_tree( root, lev, 0 );
    return( root );
}

void
game_tree( struct gnode *root, int max_level, int cur_level )
{
    struct    gnode    *tmp;

    if( cur_level == max_level )  /* the 'out' */
        return;

    /*
     *    Generate all unique board positions
     *    (child nodes) for this level
     */
    gen_pos( root );

    /*
     *    Build the next level for each child
     */
    for(tmp = root->cptr;tmp != NULL;tmp = tmp->sptr){
        tmp->turn = -root->turn;
        game_tree( tmp, max_level, cur_level+1 );
    }
}
```

continued on p. 192

continued from p. 191

```
struct      gnode *
best_move( char who, struct gnode *root )
{
     int  bval, tval;
     struct     gnode      *tmp, *best, *tbest;

     if( root->cptr == NULL ){
          /*
           *    Leaf node
           */
          root->val = board_eval( root->pos, who );
          return( root );
     }


     /*
      *    Not a leaf node — process all child nodes
      *    select & return best
      */
     tmp = root->cptr;
     best = best_move( who, tmp );   /* Get first one */
     bval = best->val * tmp->turn; /* NEG node ? */
     for( tmp = tmp->sptr; tmp != NULL; tmp = tmp->sptr ){
          tbest = best_move( who, tmp );
          tval = tbest->val * tbest->turn;
          if( tval > bval ){
               bval = tval;
               best = tbest;
          }
     }

     return( best );
}
```

Listing 6.12

Tic-tac-toe game.

SUMMARY

Trees are very common structures found in everyday life. They can also serve as powerful models for problem-solving techniques in computer science.

Once constructed, trees can be traversed in many ways. We can also add threads to leaf nodes to further simplify tree traversal.

Applications typically restrict the number of branches each node in a tree may have. The most common example of this approach is a binary tree.

Trees are simple to implement and use. As a result, they can serve as the basis for many applications, including searching, sorting, parsing, expression analysis, decision making, and game theory. We will explore other uses for trees in subsequent chapters.

EXERCISES

1. Write the iterative forms of the functions `inorder()`, `preorder()`, `postorder()`.

2. Draw the tree produced by the function `bt_insert()` when presented with the following input:

   `1, 2, 3, 4, 5, 6, 7, 8, 9, 10`

3. Prove that a binary tree can be uniquely defined by its preorder and postorder traversals.

4. Design and code traversal routines for trees implemented as arrays.

5. Implement the tic-tac-toe program. Design it so that the computer can play against a human opponent.

6. Using a breadth-first traversal, write a program that will display graphically the structure of a binary tree.

7. Develop a complete set of functions (insert, delete, traversal, etc.) to implement a threaded binary tree.

8. Write a function that will thread an unthreaded binary tree. Can it be done in place?

9. For the binary tree depicted in Figure 6.28, determine the following:
   a. The number of terminal nodes

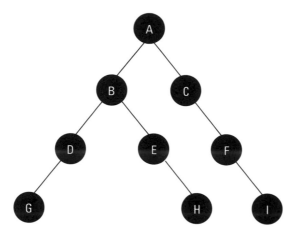

Figure 6.28
A binary tree.

b. The number of non-terminal nodes
c. The degree of each node
d. The level of each node

10. Write a function that will compute the information required in exercise 9 for any tree. Test your program using the tree shown in Figure 6.28.

11. How many different ways can we store the values 1 to 5 in an ordered binary tree?

12. Write a function that determines the maximum height of a binary tree.

13. Complete the omitted routines of the AVL insertion algorithm of Listing 6.10.

14. Implement an AVL deletion function.

15. For the binary tree depicted in Figure 6.28, depict the internal representation using list, array, linked, and threaded implementations.

Graphs and Digraphs

CHAPTER

One of the most widely used data structures in mathematics and computer science is the *graph*. Informally, we can define a graph as a finite set of points, some of which are connected by lines (called *edges*). A *digraph*—short for directed graph—is a finite set of points, some of which are connected by *arrows;* the arrows determine the *orientation* (direction) of the edges.

Graphs are useful abstractions for modeling many types of problems. Examples include airline route maps, electronic circuits, data flow diagrams, etc. An example graph depicting an airline route map appears in Figure 7.1. Although the carrier does not service it, note that Portland is part of the graph.

7.1 INTRODUCTION

Definitions and Terminology

Formally, a graph consists of two sets, V and E, where V is a finite, possibly empty, set of vertices and E is a set of subsets of V (of order 2) that represent edges. For example, the graph depicted in Figure 7.1

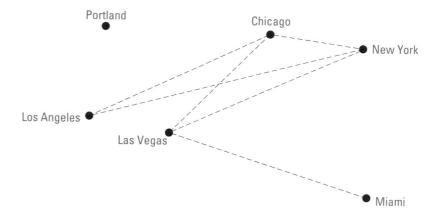

Figure 7.1
Graph representation
of an airline route
map.

has V defined as {PT, LA, LV, NY, FL, CHI} and E defined as {(CHI, LA), (LA, NY), (CHI, LV), (NY, LV), (LV, FL)}. The graph is written as $G = (V, E)$; additionally, we refer to the set of vertices of graph G as $V(G)$ and to the set of edges in G as $E(G)$.

Edges connecting two vertices in a graph are unordered. This means that the pairs (v_1, v_2) and (v_2, v_1) represent the same edge. However, edges in a digraph (which have orientation) are ordered so that $\langle v_1, v_2 \rangle$ and $\langle v_2, v_1 \rangle$ represent two distinct edges. (We will use angle brackets to denote edges in digraphs.) For any directed edge $e = \langle v_1, v_2 \rangle$ in a digraph we say that e *departs* from v_1 and *enters* v_2; in addition, we refer to v_1 as the *tail*, and v_2 as the *head* of the edge. A tree is an example of a digraph; refer to Figure 7.2 for additional examples.

An edge cannot connect a vertex to itself (these are sometimes referred to as *self-loops*). In addition, no more than one edge may connect a given pair of vertices in a graph, nor can there be more than one edge with the same orientation connecting two vertices in a digraph. However, these restrictions may be relaxed for practical applications. For example, Figure 7.2c depicts a *multigraph* wherein vertices may be connected by more than one edge. We can use this type of structure to model applications such as communication networks that contain more than one link (e.g., fiber and microwave) between locations.

The maximum number of edges in a graph with n vertices is $n(n - 1)/2$; digraphs have at most $n(n - 1)$ edges. A graph (or digraph) is considered *complete* if it contains the maximum number of edges. Figure 7.3 contains two examples.

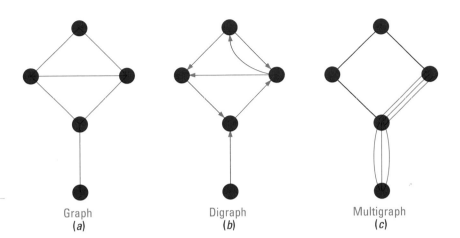

Figure 7.2

Three graphs.

Graph
(*a*)

Digraph
(*b*)

Multigraph
(*c*)

Given an edge (v_1, v_2) in a graph G, the vertices v_1 and v_2 are considered *adjacent* to each other; the connecting edge is *incident* to the vertices. For a digraph with edge $\langle v_1, v_2 \rangle$, v_1 is *adjacent to* v_2; v_2 is *adjacent from* v_1. We define the *degree* of a vertex v_i as the number of edges incident to it. For a digraph, the notion of degree is partitioned into *indegree* and *outdegree*: Indegree is the number of edges for which v_i is the head, and outdegree is the number of edges for which v_i is the tail.

A *subgraph* S_1 of graph G is defined as

$$V(S_1) \subset V(G)$$

$$E(S_1) \subset E(G)$$

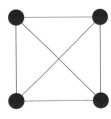

Figure 7.3

Two complete graphs.

Complete graph
(*a*)

Complete digraph
(*b*)

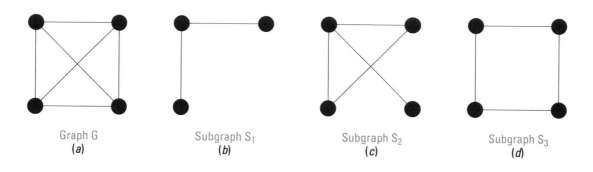

Graph G
(a)

Subgraph S₁
(b)

Subgraph S₂
(c)

Subgraph S₃
(d)

Figure 7.4
Subgraphs.

That is, S_1 is a subset of G *iff* (if and only if) $V(S_1)$ is a subset of $V(G)$ and $E(S_1)$ is a subset of $E(G)$. Figure 7.4 provides some examples.

A *path* from vertex v_1 to vertex v_n is a sequence of edges v_1, v_2, v_3, ..., v_n such that all pairs (v_1, v_2), (v_2, v_3), ..., (v_{n-1}, v_n) are edges in G. We define its length to be n, the number of edges comprising the path. A *simple path* is one in which all the vertices are distinct (refer to Fig. 7.5a). A *cycle* is a simple path wherein the first and last vertices are identical (see Fig. 7.5c). A graph that does not contain any

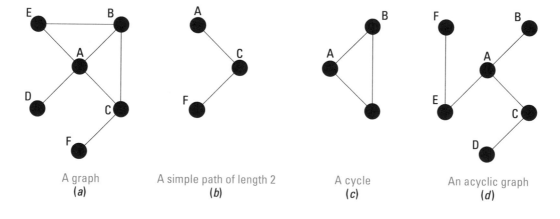

A graph
(a)

A simple path of length 2
(b)

A cycle
(c)

An acyclic graph
(d)

Figure 7.5
Paths and cycles in graphs.

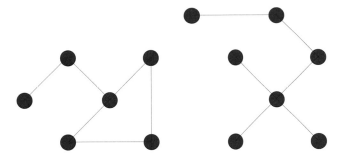

Figure 7.6
A graph with two connected components.

cycles is termed *acyclic*. A tree is an example of an acyclic graph; refer to Figure 7.5d for another example of an acyclic graph.

If a path should exist from v_1 to v_2, the vertices are *connected*. Furthermore, an entire graph is considered connected if, for each pair of vertices (v_i, v_j), there exists a path from v_i to v_j. A *connected component* of a graph G is a maximal connected subgraph of G. Figure 7.6 contains a graph with two connected components.

A directed graph is considered *weakly connected* if, for each pair of vertices (v_i, v_j), there exists a path from v_i to v_j such that $v_1 = v_i$ and $v_n = v_j$ and for each component of the path $\langle v_x, v_y \rangle$ either $\langle v_x, v_y \rangle$ or $\langle v_y, v_x \rangle$ is in $E(G)$. In other words, a path exists between the two vertices but you might not be able to traverse it because of the orientation of some of the edges.

Alternatively, we consider a digraph *strongly connected* if, for each pair of vertices $\langle v_i, v_j \rangle$, there is a directed path (i.e., one you could traverse) from v_i to v_j. A *strongly connected component* of a digraph D is a subgraph of D that is strongly connected.

Applications of Graphs

Graphs are among the most powerful modeling tools in computer science. Although simple in concept, graphs can model many complex physical and logical problems. Some examples include:

- We can use graphs to model and implement map-based applications. For example, we could model an airline company's route map. The graph would serve as the basis for fare and routing systems.

- As another example of using graphs to model maps, consider a company that specializes in home delivery of food. The firm might maintain many food preparation centers located throughout a geographical area. However, to minimize costs, only one location would serve as the central point for orders. Thus, when customers telephone the central site to request a delivery, graph-based algorithms could determine which preparation center should produce the order and estimate for the customer the expected delivery time.
- One of the classic map studies is the traveling salesperson problem. Given a list of cities and distances, determine the most economical route for the salesperson to travel.
- We can model process flow using graphs. For example, a manufacturing firm could model an assembly-line process using a graph. Each vertex in the graph could represent one stage of the production cycle.
- Graphs can represent electrical circuits. Each vertex in the graph could represent an electrical component, and edges could represent the type of connection between pairs of components.

7.2 INTERNAL REPRESENTATION

Now that we've dispensed with the definitions and terminology, let's start to see how we can use graphs to model problems. Before we can work with them, however, we must develop a set of data structures suitable for representation in a computer. For the following discussions, assume a graph $G = (V, E)$ with $n = |V|$ and $m = |E|$.

Adjacency Matrix

The first data structure we will discuss is an *adjacency matrix*. An adjacency matrix is a two-dimensional matrix a, such that for each edge (v_i, v_j) in $E(G)$, $a[i, j] = 1$. All other index pairs are set to 0. Note that for a non-directed graph, we must also set $a[j, i] = 1$ as well. The size of the array will be n^2 elements (optimally bits), but for non-directed graphs we can save half the storage (i.e., $a[i, j] = a[j, i]$). Figure 7.7 contains an example graph and its associated adjacency matrix.

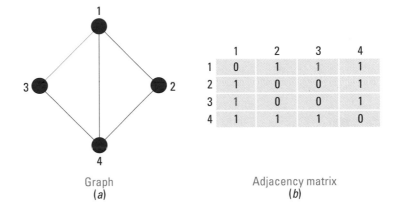

Figure 7.7
Example graph and
adjacency matrix.

In a non-directed graph G, we compute the degree of a given
vertex i as its row sum:

$$\sum_{j=1}^{n} a[1,j]$$

For each vertex in a digraph, the row sum is its outdegree and
the column sum is its indegree.

Adjacency Lists

We can also represent graphs as *adjacency lists*. An adjacency list is an
array of n pointers to linked lists. Specifically, each array element,
$a[i]$, represents one vertex and points to a linked list; each node in
the linked list represents a vertex adjacent to v_i. Refer to Figure 7.8 for
an example. A graph containing n vertices and m edges requires $a[n]$
array elements and $2m$ list nodes; a directed graph will require
only m list nodes.

For non-directed graphs, the degree of any node, i, can be computed by just counting the number of elements in list $a[i]$. The
outdegree of any vertex in a digraph can be computed in a similar
manner. However, calculating the indegree of a digraph is somewhat more problematic. A program must scan the entire array of lists
(from $a[0]$ to $a[n]$) counting references to i. We can simplify this process
by maintaining a separate list to track indegree (the equivalent of a

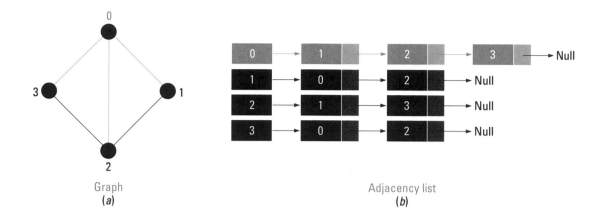

Figure 7.8
Example graph and
adjacency list.

column in the adjacency matrix). However, this will add to the size and
processing time of our data structure.

7.3 TRAVERSALS

Like trees, there are several methods we can employ to traverse graphs.
The most common are the *depth first* and the *breadth first* searches.
However, unlike trees, graphs do not contain root nodes. As a result,
the traversal methods we are about to discuss require that we define (or
arbitrarily select) a vertex to serve as the starting point for the
algorithms.

Depth First Search

Given the root node of a graph, a Depth First Search (DFS) proceeds
as follows:

- Begin processing at the root node v_0.
- Select a previously *unvisited* node v_i, adjacent to v_0, and process it.
- Select an unvisited node adjacent to v_i and visit it.

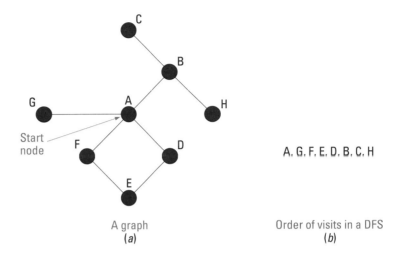

Figure 7.9
Example DFS
traversal.

A graph
(*a*)

A, G, F, E, D, B, C, H

Order of visits in a DFS
(*b*)

- Continue in this manner until we encounter a node that does not have any unvisited adjacent vertices.
- Back up to a node that has an unvisited adjacent vertex and continue the processing from that point.

A DFS can be likened to a tree traversal in that we visit all of a node's descendents before visiting any of its siblings. Figure 7.9a contains an example graph, and Figure 7.9b displays the output generated by a DFS beginning at node *A*. The order in which we select adjacent nodes is essentially arbitrary. However, note that we vist node *D* as a descendent of node *E*, not node *A*.

Listing 7.1 contains an implementation of a DFS. The function, **dfs()**, performs depth first traversals on graphs implemented using adjacency lists. Each node in the graph corresponds to an index in a structure array called **alist[]**. Each element of **alist[]** contains two members: a flag field (**tag**) to indicate whether the node has been visited, and a pointer (**ptr**) to the node's adjacency list.

To implement the adjacency list, we used a linked list of type **struct adj_node**. This structure also contains two fields: **vertex** is the name (ID) of the adjacent vertex and **next** is a pointer to the next element in the list. Each adjacency list terminates with a **NULL** pointer.

We invoke **dfs()** with one argument, namely the index of the

```
#define VISITED    1
#define MAX_NODES 100

struct  adj_node {
        int     vertex;
        struct  adj_node *next;
};

struct  adj_list {
        int     tag;
        struct  adj_node *adj;
} alist[ MAX_NODES ];


struct  adj_node *getnode();

void dfs( int vertex )
{
        struct  adj_node *ptr;

        print_vertex( vertex );
        alist[ vertex ].tag = VISITED;

        ptr = alist[vertex].adj;
        while( ptr != NULL ) {
                if( alist[ptr->vertex].tag != VISITED )
                        dfs( ptr->vertex );
                ptr = ptr->next;
        }
}
```

Listing 7.1
Depth First Search.

first node. The function begins its processing by visiting—and setting the **tag** field of—the initial vertex. Next, it searches the initial node's adjacency list for any unvisited vertices. When it locates one, **dfs()** invokes itself recursively to process the unvisited vertex. When the recursive call eventually returns, the original instantiation continues with its scan of the adjacency list.

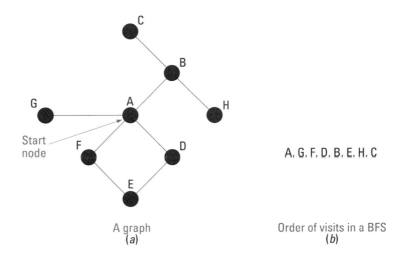

Figure 7.10
Example BFS
traversal.

Start node

A graph
(a)

A, G, F, D, B, E, H, C

Order of visits in a BFS
(b)

The complexity of this algorithm depends on the data structure employed. In this case, having used adjacency lists, the function can locate adjacent vertices by simply traversing a linear list. Thus, because the algorithm will examine each list node only once, and because there are at most $2|E|$ list nodes, the performance of the algorithm is $O(|E|)$. Alternatively, let's assume we used an adjacency matrix to implement the graph. The work required to identify all vertices adjacent to a given vertex is $O(n)$. Therefore, because the function will process at most n vertices, the performance of the algorithm becomes $O(n^2)$.

Breadth First Search

Another important traversal method for graphs is the Breadth First Search (BFS). A BFS differs from a DFS in that the BFS visits nodes in order of increasing distance from the start node. That is, it processes all nodes adjacent to the start node first, then all nodes adjacent to those, and so on. It can be likened to traversing a tree by levels.

Figure 7.10 depicts a sample BFS traversal. It uses the same graph contained in Figure 7.9a. However, note the different order in which a BFS visits nodes.

Obviously, as developers of a BFS algorithm, we must ensure that the function processes nodes in the correct order. The example function,

bfs(), presented in Listing 7.2, demonstrates how we can accomplish this. The routine begins by placing the start node of the graph on a work queue. (In this example, we arbitrarily selected **alist[0]** as the beginning point of our search. We could easily adapt the function to receive this value as an argument instead.) It then iteratively removes the next element from the queue, processes it, and enqueues all nodes adjacent to that element. It continues in this manner until the queue becomes empty. The function assumes all the declarations from Listing 7.1 and two queue routines from Chapter 3.

As with a DFS traversal, this algorithm's complexity is determined by its underlying data structure. For this implementation, the outer **while** loop will iterate exactly once for each vertex: $O(n)$. If, as with this implementation, we use adjacency lists, the inner loop will be iterated $O(m)$ times (the number of edges in the graph). If an adjacency matrix is used, the inner loop will be executed $O(n)$ times, yielding a complexity of $O(n^2)$.

Connected Graphs

As you may recall, a graph is considered connected if, for each pair of vertices (v_i, v_j), there exists a path from v_i to v_j. If you were to consider the problem for a moment, you would discover that there is an easy way to determine algorithmically whether a graph is connected. Simply perform either a BFS or a DFS and then determine whether any unvisited vertices remain. The code for such a function, **conn_graph()**, appears in Listing 7.3.

Weighted Graphs

Graphs can become even more functional if we assign values to edges. These values, referred to as *weights*, represent a relative cost (or benefit) associated with each edge. For example, the graph in Figure 7.11 represents the route map of an air carrier. The weights represent the air miles between each node (city).

Formally, a weighted graph is a triple $G = (V, E, W)$, where (V, E) is a graph (or digraph) and W is a function that maps edges to weights. That is, if $e \in E$, then $W(e)$ yields its weight. The weight of a path

```
#define VISITED 1

void bfs( void )
{
    int     node;
    struct  adj_node    *tmp;

    /*
     *   Put first element on queue
     */
    addqueue( 0 );
    alist[0].tag = VISITED;

    /*
     *   Begin the BFS
     */
    while( (node = delqueue()) != QUEUE_EMPTY )
    {
        prt_node( node );    /* The Visit */

        /*
         *   Add adjacent nodes to queue
         */
        tmp = alist[node].adj;
        while( tmp != NULL )
        {
            if( alist[tmp->vertex].tag != VISITED )
            {
                addqueue( tmp->vertex );
                alist[tmp->vertex].tag = VISITED;
            }
            tmp = tmp->next;
        }
    }
}
```

Listing 7.2
Breadth First Search.

```
#define MAXNODES 100
#define TODO      0
#define VISITED   1

#define TRUE      1
#define FALSE     0

int conn_graph( void )
{
    int   i;

    /*
     *    Initialize tag fields
     */
    for( i = 0; i < MAX_NODES; i++ )
        alist[i].tag = TODO;

    dfs( 0 );

    for( i = 0; i < MAX_NODES; i++ )
        if( alist[i].tag != VISITED )
            return( FALSE );

    return( TRUE );
}
```

Listing 7.3
Connect graph
function.

in a weighted graph is the sum of the weight of its component
edges.

7.4 SPANNING TREES

As we have seen, both DFS and BFS traversals visit all vertices in a
graph. However, they do not necessarily traverse all the edges. Let's
examine this point more closely. At any given moment during a traversal, we can envision the edges of the graph as belonging to one
of two distinct sets:

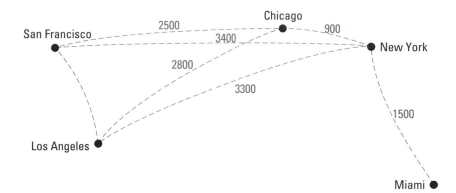

- *S*—set of edges already traversed (used) during the search
- *B*—the remaining (*back*) edges.

Throughout the traversal, the algorithm moves edges from set *B* to set *S*. When the traversal completes, the function has visited all vertices; however, not all edges are in set *S*. That is, *S* contains only the edges minimally required to visit all vertices.

A closer examination reveals that the edges in *S* form a tree (i.e., no cycles exist). This tree is of special interest and is called a *spanning tree*. A spanning tree is composed of all the vertices in *G* and only the edges in *S*. Graphs may have more than one spanning tree. Figure 7.12 contains a sample graph and several of its spanning trees. Note that in each example, the *back edges* (i.e., the edges not included in *S*) would form cycles in the spanning tree.

Formally, a spanning tree for a connected graph $G = (V, E)$ is a subgraph of *G* that forms a tree connecting all vertices in *G*. The number of edges in a spanning tree is $n - 1$, where *n* represents the number of vertices in *G*. As mentioned earlier, a graph may have more than one spanning tree.

We can easily modify and adapt the traversal routines to generate a spanning tree for a given graph. Simply add a statement to either `dfs()` or `bfs()` that stores all traversed edges so that they may be printed or processed later. The two types of trees derived from the modified algorithms are referred to as a *depth first spanning tree* and a *breadth first spanning tree*, respectively.

There are many uses for spanning trees. For example, consider

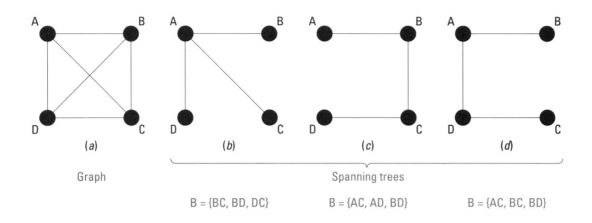

Figure 7.12
Graph and spanning
trees.

implementing a broadcast facility for a communications network.
A spanning tree could represent the set of paths required to ensure
that a message will be transmitted to every node in the network.

Minimal Spanning Trees

Extending the preceding example, we could add weights to the graph
representing our communication network. The weights could be used to
represent the cost of sending a message between any two nodes. If
we anticipated using the broadcast facility extensively, it would
be to our advantage to analyze the structure of the network to determine a broadcast path of minimal cost. If we define the weight of a
spanning tree as the sum of the weights of its component edges, then
what we need to determine is a spanning tree of minimal weight. We call
this a *minimal spanning tree* (MST). Note that a weighted graph may
have more than one MST.

MST Construction

The construction of an MST begins with the selection of an initial
vertex. We then repeatedly add to the tree edges of minimal weight until
all vertices in the graph are represented. At any given moment during

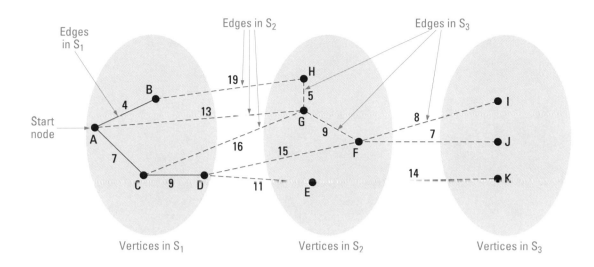

Figure 7.13
Minimal spanning tree
construction.

the construction, the edges and vertices are partitioned into three disjoint sets:

Set S_1 The set of vertices and edges already part of the MST

Set S_2 The set of vertices (and incidental edges) adjacent to the vertices in S_1. Specifically, each vertex in S_2 connects to a vertex in S_1 via an edge of *minimal* weight. In other words, a given edge in S_2 might be adjacent to more than one vertex in S_1; the S_2 set contains the incidental edge of minimal weight. We will select the next member of S_1 from this set.

Set S_3 All the remaining edges and vertices.

The function constructs the MST one edge at a time; it terminates as soon as all vertices are in S_1. Edges are considered for inclusion into S_1 (from S_2) in order of increasing weight, and only if they do not create a cycle in the MST. Figure 7.13 depicts an intermediate point in the processing of an MST; Listing 7.4 presents a pseudocode description of the algorithm. (Note that for programming convenience, we have divided each S set into companion v and e sets.)

The algorithm functions as follows (see Fig. 7.14):

```
mst( G )
{
1:    S1 = {i};               /* Starting point */
      S3 = V(G) − v1;         /* Remove i from S3 */
      S2 = {};                /* Null set */

2:    while( v1 != V(G) ){
            forall( j in v2 adjacent to i ){
3:                /*
                  *   W(x, j) == weight of edge x
                  *   incident to j in S2. Vertices
                  *   in S2 may be adjacent to more
                  *   than one S1 vertex. We must find
                  *   the edge of minimal weight.
                  */
                   if( W(i, j) < W(x, j) ){ /* Adjust S2 set */
                        e2 = e2 − (x, y);
                        e2 = e2 + (i, i);
                   }
            }

4:          forall( k in S3 adjacent to i ){ /* Adjust S3 set */
                  v2 = v2 + {k}; v3 = v3 − {k};
                  e2 = e2 + (i, j);
            }

5:          if( e2 == {} )
                  return( NO_SPANNING_TREE );

6:          e = MIN( e2 );    /* Select edge w/ min weight */
7:          i = vertex( e );  /* Set i = the v2 vertex of e */

8:          /* Adjust sets */
            e1 = e1 + e;
            e2 = e2 − e;
            v1 = v1 + i;
            v2 = v2 − i;
      }
}
```

Listing 7.4

MST algorithm—pseudo-code description.

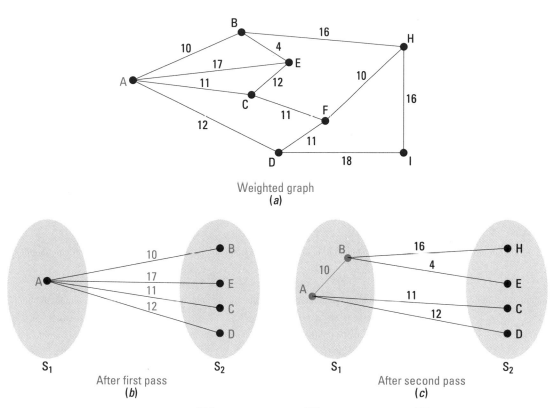

Note: Shortest edge $\overline{AB}$ added to S_1. Edge $\overline{AE}$ is replaced by edge $\overline{BE}$ in S_2

Figure 7.14
Operation of MST
algorithm.

1. Variables are initialized. **i** represents an arbitrary vertex where
   we will begin construction of the MST. (We could obviously modify
   the function to receive this value as an argument.)
2. The **while** loop iterates until the **v1** set is equal to *G*. (That is,
   until all vertices are included in the spanning tree).
3. The algorithm adjusts the **v2** set with respect to **i**. At this point,
   i represents a vertex that has just been moved into the **v1**
   set. The function must therefore adjust the **v2** set to ensure that
   it contains all vertices in *G* adjacent to vertices in **v1**.

4. After adjusting the **v2** set, the function must also update the **v3** set.

5. If, at this point, **e2** is empty, G has no spanning tree and the function returns to its caller.

6. In this step, the function selects the **e2** edge with minimal weight for inclusion into the MST.

7. This step determines the **v2** vertex of the selected edge.

8. Adjust the S_1 and S_2 sets.

Figures 7.14b and 7.14c illustrate the first two passes of the algorithm when processing the graph of Figure 7.14a. Note that after the second pass the shortest edge $\overline{AB}$ was moved to the S_1 set and that $\overline{BE}$ replaced $\overline{AB}$ in S_2.

Analysis

An analysis of the algorithm shows that the critical steps are 3, 4, and 6. Assuming $n = |V|$ and $m = |E|$, the total time required for steps 3 and 4 is $O(m)$. However, in the worst case, step 6 might require $n - 1$ comparisons, and because it will execute n times (step 2), the overall complexity becomes $O(n^2)$.

Implementation

There are several operations in the MST that are critical to its performance. The function must

- Determine to which set a given vertex belongs
- Access all members of the **v2** set
- Determine the **v1** component of a vertex in **v2**
- Reference the weight of each edge
- Reference the adjacency list for a given vertex.

Keeping the foregoing criteria in mind, we see that Listing 7.5 contains data structures suitable for implementing the MST algorithm. We represent each vertex as an entry in a structure array of type **mst_graph**. The field, **set**, identifies the set to which the vertex belongs (initially S_3). For values of 1 or 2 (indicating inclusion in either S_1 or S_2), **v1node** contains the node's adjacent vertex and **weight** contains the weight of the incidental edge. When the algorithm termi-

```
int   s2list = −1;              /* Head ptr for V2 list */

struct    nadj_list {
     int     node;             /* ID of adjacent node      */
     int     weight;           /* Weight of incident edge */
     struct  nadj_list *next;/* Pointer to next element */
};

struct    mst graph {
     int     set;              /* S1, S2, or S3                */
     int     s2link;           /* Points to next S2 node       */
     int     v1node;           /* V1 node of an (E1, E2) edge */
     int     weight;           /* Weight of E1 or E2 edge      */
     struct  nadj_list *adj; /* Pointer to adjacency list    */
} graph[ MAX_NODES ];
```

Listing 7.5
MST data structure.

nates, we can determine the edges that are part of the MST by indexing through the structure array and printing: (**i, graph[i].v1node**).

The adjacency list for each vertex is headed by the member **adj**, which points to elements of type **struct nadj_list**. The remaining field, **s2link**, provides quick access to vertices in the S_2 set. It forms a linked list headed by **s2list**. Figure 7.15 depicts the state of the data structure when processing the graph in Figure 7.14c. (Note that, for the sake for brevity, the adjacency lists are not included.) The final implementation of the algorithm is discussed in the exercises at the end of this chapter.

7.5 SHORTEST PATH ALGORITHM

Another common problem associated with graphs is determining the shortest path between two vertices. As you may recall, the weight of a path is the sum of the weights of its edges. We will define the shortest path as the path of minimal weight connecting two vertices.

The direct approach to this problem is to write an algorithm that

SAVE

Vertex	Set	S_2 Link	V_i Node	Weight	ADJ list
A	1	–	*	*	——→ ...
B	1	–	A	10	——→ ...
C	2	D	A	11	——→ ...
D	2	–1**	A	12	——→ ...
E	2	C	B	4	——→ ...
F	3	–	–	–	——→ ...
G	3	–	–	–	——→ ...
H	2	E	B	16	——→ ...

Figure 7.15

State of data structure for Figure 7.14c.

S_2 List = H
*   Root node
** End of list

enumerates all possible paths between two vertices, and then selects the one of minimal weight. This approach, however, is inefficient. (Consider the number of paths connecting any two nodes in a complete graph.) Alternatively, we will design a solution that functions in much the same manner as the MST algorithm. In short, it will begin at some point v_α and create minimal paths of increasing magnitude until it reaches the destination vertex v_β.

As with the MST algorithm, edges and vertices be partitioned into three disjoint sets:

S_1 The set of vertices (and connecting edges) for which a shortest path from v_α to some intermediate vertex has been found

S_2 The set of vertices (and incidental edges) that are not yet part of the path but which are adjacent to vertices in S_1. As with our MST function, each vertex in S_2 is connected to a vertex in S_1 via an edge of minimal weight.

S_3 The remaining edges and vertices of the graph.

As the function executes, it must repeatedly select an S_2 vertex for inclusion into the S_1 set. At first glance, it might appear tempting just to choose the S_2 vertex of minimal weight. However, keep in mind that we are trying to build the shortest path, not the shortest edge. Thus, the selected edge is the one that minimizes the following:

$$weight(v_\alpha, v_i) \ + \ weight(v_i, v_\beta) \qquad \text{for all edges } (v_i, v_\beta) \text{ in } S_2$$

where *weight*(v_α, v_i) represents the weight of an edge in S_1, and *weight*(v_i, v_β) represents the weight of the edge of an adjacent vertex in S_2.

Figure 7.16 shows an example of how the algorithm functions. Given the state depicted in Figure 7.16b, the next edge selected will be $\overline{MC}$ (even though $\overline{BD}$ is shorter). This is because $\overline{AMC}$ (weight value of 12) is shorter than $\overline{ABD}$ (weight value of 14).

After moving $\overline{MC}$ into S_1, we must reorganize the sets as depicted in Figure 7.16c. Note that $\overline{AF}$ was considered for inclusion into S_2 but was supplanted by $\overline{CE}$.

Listing 7.6 presents a pseudo-code description of the Shortest Path algorithm. A careful review of the code should prompt the question, How does it work? The function actually constructs and maintains multiple paths until it determines the one that ultimately passes through the destination vertex. During any given iteration of the **while** loop, the algorithm selects, and will add an edge to, the shortest path currently contained in S_1.

But, you may ask, what if that path does not pass through destination vertex? If you consider this problem carefully, you will observe that, as we continue to add edges to that path, it will eventually become larger than other paths contained in S_1. Thus, during a subsequent iteration of the loop, the function will select some new, smaller path for processing. Eventually one of the paths will include an edge incident to the destination vertex and the algorithm will terminate. The exercises at the end of this chapter discuss the implementation in more detail.

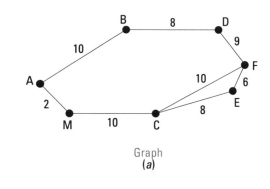

Graph
(*a*)

Intermediate step.
Note that $\overline{MC}$ will be the next edge selected.
(*b*)

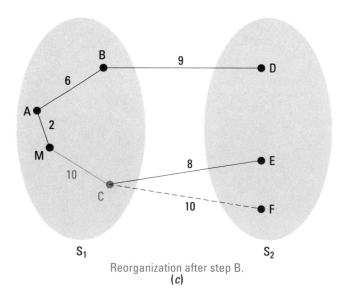

Figure 7.16
Example of Shortest
Path algorithm.

Reorganization after step B.
(*c*)

```
sp( G, b, e )           /* Shortest path from b to e */
{
    v1 = {b};
    i = b;
    W(i) = 0;
    v3 = V(G) - v1;
    v2 = {};
    e1 = {};
    e2 = {};

    while( i != 3e ){      /* Until destination */
        forall( j adjacent to i ){
            if( j in v2 AND W(i) + W(j) < W(b, j) ){
                /* Replace edge */
                e2 = e2 - {x, j};
                e2 = e2 + {i, j };
            }

            if( j in v3 ){   /* Move into v2 */
                v3 = v3 - j;
                v2 = v2 + j;
                e2 = e2 + {i, j};
            }
        }
        if( v2 == {} )          /* No spanning tree */
            return( NO_PATH );

        x = MIN_PATH( e2 );
        v₂ = v₂ - x;            /* Adjust sets */
        v₁ = v₁ + x;            /* Remove x from v₂ */
        i = x;                  /* Add x to v₁ */
    }
}
```

Listing 7.6
Shortest Path algorithm—a psuedo-code description.

SUMMARY

Graphs are powerful data models that we can use to solve a wide variety of problems in mathematics and computer science. They have been in existence for many years and have developed a unique and extensive nomenclature.

In computer programs, graphs are usually implemented using either adjacency lists or adjacency matrices. A basic requirement of all graph algorithms is a traversal method. The two most common are called depth first and breadth first traversals.

We can add weights to edges in a graph. This imbues graphs with even more functionality. Two common problems associated with weighted graphs include generating a minimal spanning tree and finding the shortest path between two vertices.

EXERCISES

1. Write routines that insert and delete edges in a graph implemented using an adjacency matrix. Do the same for a digraph. Compare/contrast implementation differences.

2. Repeat exercise 1 using adjacency lists.

3. Draw a complete graph with seven vertices.

4. Apply both DFS and BFS traversals to the graph of exercise 3. Using the same beginning vertex for each traversal, list the order in which the vertices are visited.

5. Write algorithms to calculate the indegree and outdegree for any given node in a graph. Assume an adjacency list implementation.

6. Rewrite both the DFS and BFS traversal functions using an adjacency matrix.

7. Show that when we perform a DFS or a BFS traversal on a connected graph, the resulting edges form a tree.

8. Write an algorithm that determines whether a given graph is a tree. (Do not assume a connected graph.)

9. What is the maximum number of paths between two vertices in a complete graph?

10. Design and implement a function that computes all spanning trees for a given graph. What is its complexity?

11. Implement the minimal spanning tree algorithm. Test with several graphs/paths.

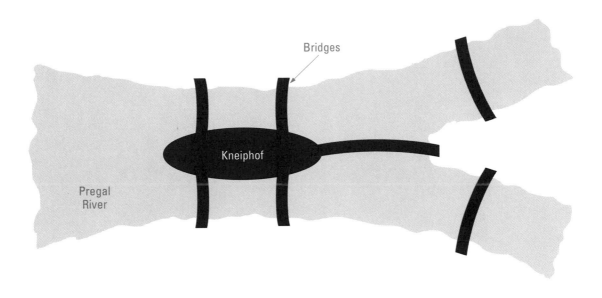

Figure 7.17
The Koenigsberg
bridges.

12. Implement the Shortest Path algorithm using the data structures from the previous exercise. Test your program using several graphs/ paths.

13. What is the complexity of the function **conn_graph()** (see Listing 7.3)?

14. Write a function that computes *all* the connected components of a given graph. (*Hint:* Extend the function **conn_graph()**.)

15. Consider the diagram in Figure 7.17. It depicts a section of a town in East Prussia called Koenigsberg. The river Pregal flows around the island Kneiphof and then splits in two. This forms the four land areas that are connected by the seven bridges.

    Your problem is to determine whether it is possible to begin and end a walk at the same spot while crossing each bridge exactly once. (Swimming is not a viable option.)

    This problem was originally solved—using a graph—in 1736 by the mathematician Euler and became known as Euler's Walk. Euler used vertices to represent the land areas and edges to represent the bridges.

Searching

8.1 INTRODUCTION

In this chapter we examine efficient methods to search for information. Searching is a common task in our everyday lives: We look up telephone numbers in a directory; locate words in a dictionary; determine if we are free for an appointment on a given day; the list is endless. Searching is also a common task in computer applications; it can also be one of the most time-consuming. As a result, it is to our advantage to do it as efficiently as possible.

Before we begin, we should introduce some terminology. In a computer program, searching is the task of locating a particular *record* within a collection of records. Records are composed of one or more *fields* or elements. For example, an employee record might include fields for *name, address, and social security number,* among others. A collection of records is commonly referred to as a *table*.

Records are usually identified by one of their fields called the *key*. Keys are usually exclusive; this implies that each key uniquely identifies one record. Records may also have more than one key. For example, an employee table may be keyed on both social security number and last name. In such cases, we may initiate searches using either

```
int seq_srch( int data[], int size, int key )
{
        int     i;

        i = size - 1;           /* C arrays have a 0 offset */
        while( i >= 0 && data[i] != key )
                i--;

        return( i );
}
```

Listing 8.1
Sequential search.

key. We need not store records in any particular order, but, as we will see, if we sort tables by key, we can increase the efficiency of some searching algorithms.

To simplify our examples, simple integer arrays will serve as our data records. Each element in the array will represent one key. Please keep in mind, however, that we can apply all the principles we will discuss to larger, more complex record formats.

8.2 SEQUENTIAL SEARCHING

The simplest and most direct approach to this problem is the exhaustive or *sequential search*. Given an unsorted table of records, we can write a function that scans an entire table, one record at a time, searching for a given key. Listing 8.1 contains an example.

The function, **seq_srch()**, requires three arguments: **key** is the search key, **data[]** is the table, and **size** indicates the number of entries in the table. The algorithm begins its search at the end of the list and iteratively compares each record with **key** until it either finds a match or exhausts all possibilities. In the former case, it returns the index of the record; in the latter case it returns the value −1.

Complexity We will partition the discussion of this algorithm's complexity into two parts. For a successful search, the number of comparisons depends on the position of the key within the table. Assuming an equal probability for all keys, the average number of comparisons in a successful search will be

$$\frac{1 + 2 + 3 + \cdots + n}{n} = \frac{n + 1}{2}$$

or roughly $O(n/2)$. If the desired key is not in the table, the function performs n comparisons. The following sections discuss improvements to this basic algorithm.

8.3   SEARCHING ORDERED TABLES

Before we introduce our first refinement, let's observe how humans search for information. For example, consider how we might look up the word *processor* in the dictionary. We would not begin at the A's and scan every entry (as suggested by the preceding algorithm). Rather, using the thumb tabs, we would begin our search at (or near) the P's. Nonetheless, we know intuitively that we will not overlook our word when we skip past the earlier entries. Why? Because words in the dictionary are *ordered* (sorted). We can apply this same principle to improve the performance of our basic searching algorithm. (Chapter 9 will discuss sorting methods in detail; throughout the discussions in this chapter, we will assume that our tables have been sorted.)

Ordered Linear Search

Assuming an ordered table, the first improvement we can make to **seq_srch()** is to terminate the search whenever **data[i]** < **key**. That is, we do not have to search the entire table to determine that a key is not present. We can terminate the search as soon as we reach a point where the remaining data values are less than the search key. An example algorithm, **seq_srch2()**, is presented in Listing 8.2.

Complexity The discussion of complexity again assumes that all keys are equally likely. For a successful search, the performance of

```
#define NOT_FOUND  -1

int seq_srch2( int data[], int size, int key )
{
        int     i;

        i = size - 1;
        while( i >= 0 && data[i] != key )
                if( data[i] < key )           /* Terminate Early */
                        return( NOT_FOUND );
                else
                        i--;

        return( i );
}
```

Listing 8.2
Modified sequential search algorithm.

`seq_srch2()` remains the same (i.e., $O(n/2)$). We have, however, improved—by half—the time required to determine that a given key is not part of the table.

Indexed Sequential Search

Our next improvement increases efficiency at the expense of additional space. This method, referred to as an *indexed sequential search*, uses a second table, called an *index*, to point to entries in the main data table. See Figure 8.1 for an example.

The index array effectively partitions the main data table into subarrays. If there are *n* entries in the index, and *size* elements in the main data table, then each index entry represents a subarray of *size/n* elements in the main table. Note that the entries in both tables must be ordered by key.

The idea behind this algorithm is very simple. The function begins with a scan through the index array searching for the case where

`index[i] <= key < index[i+1]`

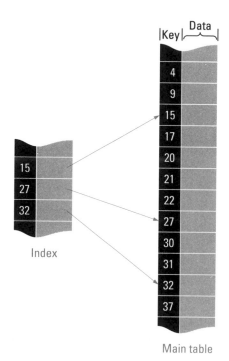

Figure 8.1
Indexed sequential
tables.

That is, the function scans the index to determine which subarray in the main table would contain **key** (if it exists). It then uses the value stored in **index[i]** as the point at which to begin a sequential search of the main table. Note that, as the function scans the index, it is skipping over large chunks of the main data table. An example algorithm, **indx_seq()**, appears in Listing 8.3.

The function **indx_seq()** begins with an initial test to determine whether its key argument is smaller than the smallest key in the data table; if it is, the function immediately returns the value **NOT_FOUND** to indicate an unsuccessful search.

The first **while** loop scans the index to determine in which subarray of the main data table **key** would reside. The index, **idx[]**, is an array of type **struct index**. This structure contains two members: **val** is the key value each index element represents; **slot** is an index that points into the main data table.

After scanning the index, **indx_seq()** invokes **seq_srch2()** to search the main table. The function calculates the boundary limits of

```
#define NOT_FOUND  -1

struct     index     {
    int  val;
    int  slot;
};

int indx_seq( int key, struct index idx[], int idx_size,
              int data[], int data_size )
{
    int     i, size, ret;

    if( key < idx[0].val )          /* Initial test for bad key */
        return( NOT_FOUND );

    /*
     *   Scan index for key
     */
    i = 0;
    while( i < idx_size && key >= idx[i+1].val )
        i++;

    /*
     *   Determine segment size
     */
    if( i == idx_size-1 )           /* i points to last slot */
        size = data_size - idx[i].slot;
    else
        size = idx[i+1].slot - idx[i].slot;

    /*
     *   Scan data table
     */
    ret = seq_srch2( &data[ idx[i].slot ], size, key );
    if( ret >= 0 )
        ret = ret + idx[i].slot;

    return( ret );
}
```

Listing 8.3
Indexed sequential search algorithm.

the subarray based on the values contained in the index. Note that the arguments we pass to **seq_srch2()** only delineate the subarray that we want it to search. As a result, if the search is successful, the function must add the slot offset contained in the index to the value returned by **seq_srch2()**.

Complexity The efficiency of this algorithm is a function of the size of the index. As we decrease the size of the index array, we increase the size of the sublists each index entry represents; this, in turn, increases the size of the sublist that we must search in the main table. Increasing the size of the index results in an increase in the number of comparisons required to search the index itself. In general, if k represents the size of the index and n represents the size of the table, the complexity of this method is

$$O\left(\frac{k}{2} + \frac{n/k}{2}\right)$$

If the index begins to grow so large that it becomes inefficient, we can use a *secondary index*. A secondary index functions in much the same manner as a primary index except that it points into the primary index, not the main table. Searching begins with a scan through the secondary index; this points us to a subarray in the primary index, and then processing continues as described earlier. An example of such a data structure appears in Figure 8.2.

Binary Search

As highlighted in the previous section, searching algorithms perform fewer comparisons if they can skip over some elements. We can extend this idea to the point where we can eliminate half of the remaining list with each unsuccessful comparison. We call this technique a *binary search*.

We begin a binary search by comparing the search key with the middle entry of an ordered table. If they match, the function returns the index of this element. Otherwise, processing continues using either the lower or upper half of the table (depending on the value of the key). In essence, we eliminate half the table with only one

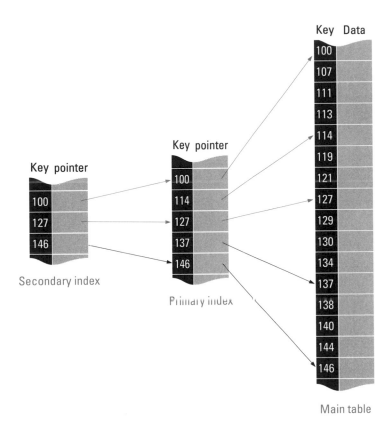

Figure 8.2
Secondary index.

comparison. This is the most efficient method of searching an ordered list without the use of additional tables or indices.

An example binary search function, **binsrch()**, appears in Listing 8.4. The variables **upper** and **lower** delineate the portion of the array that the function has not yet searched. Initially, their values are set to the upper and lower bounds of the array. The value stored in the variable **middle** is the index of the middle entry of the current sublist. With each iteration of the **while** loop, the function compares **key** with **data[middle]**. Based on the result, **binsrch()** either returns the location of **key** in the table or adjusts its index variables accordingly. If the function fails to locate **key**, it returns the value **NOT_FOUND**.

Complexity The complexity of **binsrch()** is not as obvious as some of the other algorithms we have been discussing. To begin our analysis,

```
#define NOT_FOUND  -1

int binsrch( int data[], int size, int key )
{
        int      lower, middle, upper;

        lower = 0;
        upper = size - 1;
        while( lower <= upper ){
                middle = (lower + upper) / 2;
                if( key == data[middle] )
                        return( middle );
                else if( key > data[middle] )
                        lower = middle + 1;
                else
                        upper = middle - 1;
        }

        return( NOT_FOUND );
}
```

Listing 8.4
Binary search
algorithm.

notice that if the function fails to locate a key during the first iteration
of its loop, it divides the list in half and repeats the process. At this
point, we can compute the performance of the algorithm as 1 (the cost
of the first comparison) plus the cost of processing the remaining half.
This is best expressed by the formula $O(1 + O(n/2))$ (where n represents the number of elements in the table).

We can compute the cost of a failed second pass in much the same
way: 1 plus the cost of processing half the remaining entries. Note that
at this point, half the remaining entries is equivalent to one fourth of
the array or $n/4$. The total complexity at this point is $O(1 + 1 + O(n)/4)$.

We can continue in this manner building each seccessive term. In
other words, with each failed iteration, we add 1 to our formula and
divide n again by the next power of 2. However, this formula does not
provide a definitive complexity. That is, it defines the value of $O(n)$ in
terms of n. This is an example of a *recurrence relation*.

We can define a recurrence relation as

an equation or inequality that relates the value of a function on successively smaller values of the function.

A recurrence relation does not adequately describe the complexity of an algorithm. That is, to be useful, we must define complexity in a way that does not express $f(n)$ in terms of n. Thus, we must transform the recurrence relation into its equivalent *closed form*. In closed form, we evaluate a function $f(n)$ without referring to other values of n.

We begin the transformation of a recurrence relation by examining its *boundary* conditions. A boundary condition yields a definitive value for a particular function argument. In our example, if $n = 1$, then $f(1) = 1$. Thus, we now have two formulas that describe the relation:

$$f(1) = 1$$

$$f(n) = 1 + f\left(\frac{n}{2}\right)$$

Now let's expand the second formula:

$$f(n) = 1 + f\left(\frac{n}{2}\right)$$

$$= 1 + 1 + f\left(\frac{n}{2^2}\right)$$

$$= 1 + 1 + 1 + f\left(\frac{n}{2^3}\right)$$

$$\vdots$$

Note that as we add each new term, we divide n by the next power of 2. Relating this back to the binary search algorithm, each term in the formula corresponds to a failed comparison. Therefore, for an array of size n, there will be (in the worst case) approximately $\log_2(n)$ terms, each of which has a complexity of 1. This yields a final closed form of

$$f(n) = \log_2(n) + 1$$

The additional 1 term is to compensate for the fact that, in general, $\log_2(n)$ might not compute to an even integer. As a result, a binary search function might perform one additional comparison. Thus, this yields a complexity of $O(\log_2 n)$.

Modified Binary Search

There is an interesting variation of the **binsrch()** algorithm. Instead of using—and computing the value of—three variables, we only require the use of two: one to track the current position in the array (**middle**), and a second to track a rate of change (**delta**). The idea is that after each unsuccessful comparison, the algorithm will apply the value in **delta** to **middle** to compute the next slot; it then divides **delta** by 2. The direction of the change is reflected as a positive or negative value for **delta**. The algorithm **binsrch2()** is presented in Listing 8.5.

Interpolation Search

There is another interesting variation on the binary search algorithm. In this version, we try to guess more precisely where the search key resides in the array. Before we describe the method in detail, let's again consider how we look up words in a dictionary. If the word we are searching for begins with a *w*, we begin our search near the end of the book; if the word begins with a *c*, we search near the front. In short, we begin our search near the location where we expect to find our word. We call this technique an *interpolation search*.

We can simulate an interpolation search in a computer program with a small modification to our binary search algorithm. Instead of simply calculating **middle** as

    (lower + upper) / 2

we instead estimate the location of the record based on the search key and the current **lower** and **upper** bounds of our array. The formula we use is

$$middle = lower + \frac{(key - data[lower]) \times (upper - lower)}{(data[upper] - data[lower])}$$

```
#define HALF(x)    ( ((x)+1)/2 )
#define NOT_FOUND  -1

int binsrch2( int data[], int size, int key )
{
        int     delta, middle;

        delta = size / 2;
        middle = delta;
        while( key != data[middle] ){
                if( delta == 0 )
                        return( NOT_FOUND );
                else if( key > data[middle] )
                        middle += HALF( delta );
                else
                        middle -= HALF( delta );
                delta = delta / 2;
        }

        return( middle );
}
```

Listing 8.5
Modified binary
search.

In essence, we are *weighting* our formula so that the new value of **middle** will be closer to the expected location of our key.

For example, suppose that a data array contains the values 1, 2, 3, . . . , 10, and that the search key is the value 8. The basic binary search algorithm would compute *middle* as

$$middle = \frac{lower + upper}{2} = \frac{1 + 10}{2} = \frac{11}{2} = 5.5$$

An interpolation search computes *middle* as

$$middle = lower + \frac{(key - data[lower]) \times (upper - lower)}{(data[upper] - data[lower])}$$

$$= 1 + \frac{(8 - 1) \times (10 - 1)}{(10 - 1)} = 8$$

Even though the calculation is somewhat more complex, an interpolation search can provide a significant improvement over a binary search for large datasets with evenly distributed keys.

Fibonacci Search

As we have observed, a binary search algorithm divides the data array in half with each loop iteration. Now let's consider another way to partition the dataset using the Fibonacci sequence.

To begin our discussion, assume that the size of our data array is some Fibonacci number $F(n)$. Our search algorithm will make its first comparison using element $data[F(n-1)]$. There are three possible results:

$key = data[F(n-1)]$ The search is successful and the function returns the index of the record.

$key < data[F(n-1)]$ The key, if it exists, resides in the subarray indexed from $lower$ to $data[F(n-1)] - 1$. The next comparison will use element $data[F(n-2)]$.

$key > data[F(n-1)]$ The key, if it exists, resides in the subarray indexed from $data[F(n-1)] + 1$ to $data[F(n)]$. Note that the size of this subarray, $F(n) - F(n-1)$, is also a Fibonacci number. The next comparison will use element $data[F(n-1) + F(n-3)]$.

The advantage of this technique is that the algorithm uses only addition and subtraction rather than the division called for in a binary search. Thus, a Fibonacci search might outperform a binary search on machines where division is significantly slower than addition.

The only practical item we have not addressed is the (likely) event that the size of the array is not an exact Fibonacci number. We can overcome this problem by adjusting our index variable before the first iteration of the loop. The complete algorithm appears in Listing 8.6.

Note that the function **fibsrch()** requires the help of a routine to compute Fibonacci numbers. The code for this function, called **fibnum()**, is presented in Listing 8.7.

```
#define NOT_FOUND -1

int fibsrch( int data[], int size, int key )
{
      int      tmp, index, adj, fmin2, fmin3;

      tmp   = fibnum(size);
      adj   = size - fib(tmp);
      index = fib(tmp-1);
      fmin2 = fib(tmp-2);
      fmin3 = fib(tmp-3);

      if( key > data[index] )          /* adj for size != fib numb */
            index = index + adj;

      while( index >= 0 && index < size ){
            if( key == data[index] )
                  return( index );
            else if( key < data[index] ){
                  index = index - fmin3;
                  tmp   = fmin2;
                  fmin2 = fmin3;
                  fmin3 = tmp - fmin3;
            } else {
                  index = index + fmin3;
                  fmin2 = fmin2 - fmin3;
                  fmin3 = fmin3 - fmin2;
            }
      }

      return( NOT_FOUND );
}
```

Listing 8.6
Fibonacci search.

```
int fibnum( int num )
{
        int       i, p, q, tmp;

        if( num == 0 )
                return( 0 );
        if( num == 1 )
                return( 1 );

        p = 0;
        q = 1;
        for( i = 1; p+q <= num; i++ ){
                tmp = q;
                q += p;
                p = tmp;
        }

        return( i );
}
```

Listing 8.7
Compute a Fibonacci
number.

Binary Tree Searching

As you may recall, in Chapter 6 we discussed the construction of an ordered binary tree (OBT). An OBT has the property that for a given node n, the data values contained in its left subtree are less than $data(n)$ and the data values contained in its right subtree are greater than $data(n)$.

Once the tree is constructed, we can search for keys in an OBT in a straightforward manner. Compare the search key with the data value stored in the root node; if they are equal return. If $key < data(root)$, traverse the left subtree; otherwise, traverse the right subtree. Recursively reapply this logic until you either locate the desired key or encounter a terminal node. In the latter case, the function returns a value indicating that it could not locate the key.

Listing 8.8 contains the code for the algorithm **treesrch()**. A brief inspection will show that it is very similar to the traversal

```
struct      bt_node    {
    int   data;
    struct      bt_node *lchild;
    struct      bt_node *rchild;
};

struct bt_node *
treesrch( struct bt_node *node, int key )
{
    if( node == NULL )
        return( NULL );
    else if( key == node−>data )
        return( node );
    else if( key < node−>data )
        return( treesrch(node−>lchild, key) );
    else
        return( treesrch(node−>rchild, key) );
}
```

Listing 8.8
Ordered binary tree
search.

algorithms discussed in Chapter 6. The function assumes that its search
tree was constructed using an insertion algorithm similar to the
one presented in Listing 6.5. Upon success, it returns a pointer to the
matching node; otherwise it returns the value **NULL**.

Complexity The complexity of this algorithm depends on the shape of
the search tree. For a full or complete binary tree, we can expect an
$O(\log_2 n)$ complexity (where n represents the number of nodes in the
tree). However, as noted in Chapter 6, insertion algorithms can produce
skewed trees. (This typically occurs when the insertion routine receives
keys in relatively sorted order.) Thus, in the worst case, complexity can
degrade to $O(n)$ (linear). In practice, however, keys are usually random
enough that we may expect a fairly balanced tree. This fact, combined
with its relatively easy implementation, makes **treesrch()** the
algorithm of choice for many applications.

8.4 HASHING

The searching techniques we have discussed thus far share one common attribute: Their efficiency is inversely proportional to the number of comparisons they perform. As highlighted in the preceding sections, as we eliminate comparisons, we improve the performance of the algorithms.

There is, however, another way in which we can improve the performance of searching algorithms. Consider a scenario in which the keys themselves point directly to records. That is, information encoded directly within a key can point us to its associated record. Thus, we would no longer require multiple searches to access a record; rather, we could simply examine the key and *know* where to look.

We can effectively achieve this capability using a technique called *hashing* or *scatter storage*. With hashing, we determine the location (or address) of a record by performing an arithmetic computation on its key. The result of this computation (called a *hashing function*) yields the location of the record in a table (called a *hash table*). Specifically, a hash function maps all possible key values into specific slots in the hash table. Once we store a record in the table, we can retrieve it using the same process. That is, the hashing function we use initially to insert keys into the hash table is the same one we use to search for records later.

Hash tables are sequential and contiguous. Each slot in the table is called a *bucket*. The contents of buckets can either be the record itself or a pointer to where the record actually resides (out on disk, for example). The latter is a common approach used by many professional database management systems. Buckets may hold (or reference) more than one key.

Although, as we will see, there are some difficulties that we must address, the justification for studying hashing techniques should be obvious. Hashing allows us to search and retrieve records quickly and efficiently.

Simple Hashing Example

As alluded to earlier, there are several concerns we must address. The best way to highlight them is by way of example.

Let's assume we have to build an application that supports a

```
#define DIGIT1 5
#define DIGIT2 6

int hash_tel( char tel_number[] )
{
        int   digit1, digit2;

        digit1 = tel_number[DIGIT1] - '0';   /* Convert to int */
        digit2 = tel_number[DIGIT2] - '0';   /* Convert to int */

        return( digit1*10 + digit2 );
}
```

Listing 8.9
Hashing function.

customer service department for some company. To simplify the operation, for both representatives and customers, we will key account records by telephone number. Thus, when answering a call, the service representative will retrieve account information by entering the customer's telephone number into the system.

Because access time is important to us—we do not want customers to endure a long wait while the system retrieves their account information—we will use a hashing-based solution. Specifically, we will hash on the right-most two digits of the customer telephone number. Because our hash function can only return values in the range of 0 through 99, we build a hash table with 100 buckets. Thus, our first hashing function might be similar to the one presented in Listing 8.9.

The day finally comes and our application cuts live: We enter our first customer, 5551024, into slot 24 of our table. We then enter our second customer, 5552048, into slot 48. The application continues along quite smoothly until the day customer 5554048 calls to open an account. We then realize that our hashing function is not perfect. That is, the function maps keys 5552048 and 5554048 into the same bucket. This is called a *collision*. A collision occurs whenever a hash function maps two distinct keys to the same bucket.

As simple as this example might seem, it highlights some of the more important issues surrounding hashing:

- Hashing functions must generate bucket addresses quickly. If the hashing algorithm is too inefficient it will overshadow the advantages this technique provides, and we would likely use one of the other searching techniques discussed in this chapter.
- Along with being efficient, our hashing function should minimize the number of collisions that might occur. That is, we would like the algorithm to distribute keys evenly throughout the entire hash table.
- Regardless of the type of hashing function, we will likely experience collisions because the domain of keys is usually larger than the number of buckets we can (or wish to) allocate in our hash table.

The following sections address these concerns in more detail. We will begin by discussing collision resolution and then continue with a discussion of efficient hashing functions.

Collision Resolution Strategies

As mentioned earlier, a collision occurs whenever a hashing function maps two (or more) distinct keys into the same bucket. Regardless of its relative sophistication, a hashing function will likely generate its share of collisions. The main reason is that the size of the key domain is typically larger than we can (or want to) make the hash table. For example, we probably could not allocate enough buckets for all potential accounts if we did index customer records by their complete telephone numbers.

Theoretically, we could develop a hashing function that guarantees a one-to-one mapping of keys to buckets. However, it will likely negate one of the major advantages of hashing: speed.

Thus, because it is effectively a foregone conclusion that collisions will occur, our only recourse is to develop methods to resolve them. In the sections that follow, we will discuss two important collision resolution strategies: chaining and open addressing.

Chaining

Separate Chaining

Stated simply, the problem with collisions is that the hash function maps more than one key to the same bucket. A direct solution to the

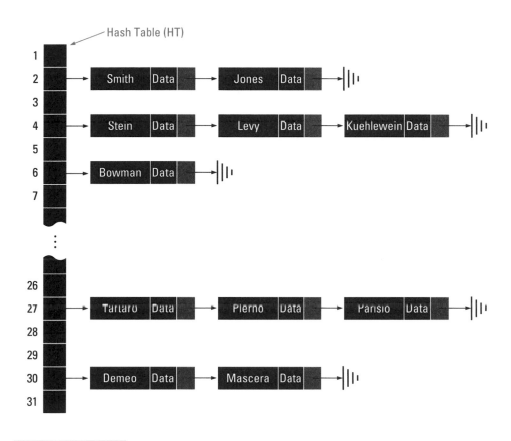

Figure 8.3
Hash chains.

problem is to allow buckets to hold more than one key. We can effectively accomplish this by employing a technique called *chaining.*

With chaining, hash table slots do not hold data; rather each element in the table is a pointer to a linked list. Thus, if our hashing function maps two (or more) keys to the same bucket, we just insert them into a linked list.

An example of this technique is depicted in Figure 8.3, wherein we use chaining to resolve collisions in an employee database. The hashing algorithm is based on the hire date of each employee. Specifically, the hash function returns the day of the month each employee was hired.

```
struct hash_node {
     int data;                   /* The data we need to store */
     char key[ MAX_KEY ];        /* The 'key' for this record */
     struct hash_node *next;     /* Ptr to next node in chain */
};

struct hash_node *hash_table[ HASH_SIZE ];

struct hash_node *get_hash( char *key )
{
     int    slot;
     struct hash_node *first_elem;

     slot = hash_function( key );
     first_elem = hash_table[ slot ];
     return( mod_seq_srch(first_elem, key) );
}

void ins_hash( struct hash_node *new_elem )
{
     int slot;

     slot = hash_function( new_elem->key );
     new_elem->next = hash_table[slot];
     hash_table[slot] = new_elem;
}
```

Listing 8.10
Example chaining functions.

Thus, if we hired another employee on the second day of some month, we would insert the new individual's record in the chain currently headed by the element *Smith*.

Listing 8.10 contains examples of some routines that manage chained hash lists similar to the one presented in Figure 8.3. Central to this algorithm is the structure **hash_node**. Its members include key and data fields, as well as a link field that points to the next element in the chain. Note that a definition for macro, **MAX_KEY**, is application dependent.

The hash table, **hash_table[]**, is an array of pointers to **hash_node** structures. In effect, each element in the array is a head pointer for a linked list. We defer the discussion of appropriate values for the macro **HASH_SIZE** until we discuss hashing functions later; for now, just assume some reasonable size.

The function **ins_hash()** inserts new elements into a hash chain; the slot is determined by a call to the routine **hash_function()**. (We will discuss hashing functions in detail later in this section.) We have omitted a complementary deletion function; its implementation is similarly straightforward and is left as an exercise for the reader.

The function **get_hash()** returns a pointer to an existing hash element determined by its one argument. Note that it uses a modified version of a sequential search routine—called **mod_seq_srch()**—to scan the chain. This version performs an exhaustive search on a linked list, rather than an array; it returns either a pointer to the matched element or the value **NULL**, signifying a failed search. Its implementation is also left as an exercise.

Complexity To simplify our discussion of the complexity of chaining, let's define the term *probe* to denote every reference we make to our hash structure. For example, we require three probes to access the record *Jones* (Fig. 8.3): one to select the list pointer (slot 2), and two additional probes for list elements (one each for *Smith* and *Jones*). In a similar manner, referencing the record *Tartaro* requires two probes, and *Parisio* requires four probes. For a given hash structure, the time we need to process a query will be proportional to the number of probes it requires. As a result, we will use probe count as the metric for measuring hashing complexity.

Assume that the only records currently in our employee database are the 11 that are represented in Figure 8.3. We can begin to compute the average number of probes by noting that there are

- Five chains that require at least two probes (all non-empty chains)
- Four chains that require at least three probes (chains 2, 4, 27, and 30)
- Two chains that require at least four probes (chains 4 and 27).

Thus, we can compute the average number of probes as follows:

$$\frac{(5 \times 2) + (4 \times 3) + (2 \times 4)}{11} = 2.73$$

Note that the preceding value is specific to this one table and its current contents. As an alternative, we can provide a more general description of hashing complexity. To begin, let n denote the number of records we need to store and let m denote the size of the hash table. We can now define the *load factor* λ of a hash table as follows:

$$\lambda = \frac{n}{m}$$

The load factor represents the average length of a chain. For our example, the load factor for the table of Figure 8.3 is

$$\frac{11}{31} = .035$$

Note that when using chaining, load factors may be greater or less than 1.

If we assume that our hash function generates a relatively even distribution of keys throughout the entire hash table, and that every key is equally likely, then we can define the following:

$S(\lambda)$: The expected number of probes required for a successful search
$U(\lambda)$: The expected number of probes required for an unsuccessful search.

As stated earlier, chaining requires one probe for the list header and one probe for each referenced list element. If λ represents the average chain length and we must inspect every element in a chain during an unsuccessful search, then $U(\lambda)$ becomes

$$U(\lambda) = 1 + \lambda$$

Computing $S(\lambda)$ is only slightly more problematic. First, recall from our complexity analysis of a sequential search that a successful search will access, on average, half the elements in the chain. Thus, if k represents the length of a given chain, a successful search requires $\frac{1}{2}(k + 1)$ probes. However, we know that the expected length of a chain, on average, is no longer than λ. Thus, $S(\lambda)$ becomes

$$S(\lambda) = \frac{1}{2}(k + 1) = \frac{1}{2}(1 + \lambda + 1) = 1 + \frac{1}{2}\lambda$$

Note that the worst case occurs when all keys (most likely due to a poor choice of hashing function) hash to the same bucket. If n represents the number of keys in the table, worst-case complexity can be computed as follows:

$$U(\lambda) = 1 + n$$

$$S(\lambda) = 1 + \frac{1}{2}n$$

Advantages/Disadvantages Some of the advantages of chaining include easy insertion and deletion of nodes. The costs include the extra space required for the pointers and the additional coding required for the dynamic links. If records are large as compared to the size of pointers, the advantages of chaining usually outweigh the disadvantages.

Improvements and Extensions

Ordered Chains

We can improve on the basic chaining strategy. First, we can order the chains. As in the case of **seq_srch2()** (Listing 8.2), we can improve—by half—the time required to determine that a given key is not part of the chain.

Modified Hash Table

For our next improvement, note that even if the element we are searching for is first in its chain, we still require two probes: one for the hash table slot and one to access the first element. We can eliminate the need for that initial probe if we store the first element in the hash table itself. That is, the hash table is no longer just an array of pointers; rather, it is an array of list structures. Figure 8.4 provides an example. It depicts the hash table of Figure 8.3 as it would appear if we had employed this technique.

This technique not only saves us the cost of a probe, it also reclaims the additional space required by the pointers in the original hash table. However, we should use this strategy only when the keys are relatively small and when we expect our hash table to be relatively

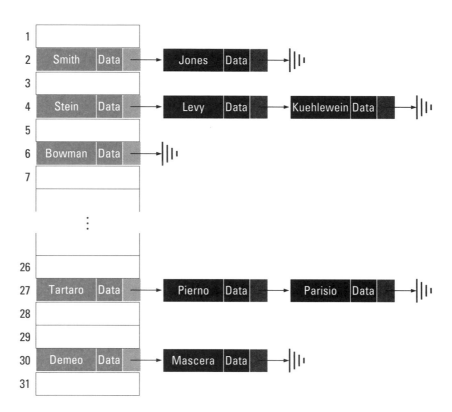

Figure 8.4
Modified hash table.

full; otherwise, we will waste too much space on empty slots. (Records are usually larger than pointers.)

Coalesced Chaining

The final improvement we will discuss is an extension of the previous idea. If the modified hash table is composed of node structures, why use separate chains to handle collisions? We could use empty slots in the hash table itself. We illustrate an example of this technique, referred to as *coalesced chaining*, in Figure 8.5, which depicts the hash table of Figure 8.3 as it might appear if we employed coalesced chaining.

With coalesced chaining, we no longer allocate new nodes with each collision; rather, we just appropriate the next available slot in the hash table. However, there is a price to pay for this feature in that a later arriving element might be displaced as a result of a prior

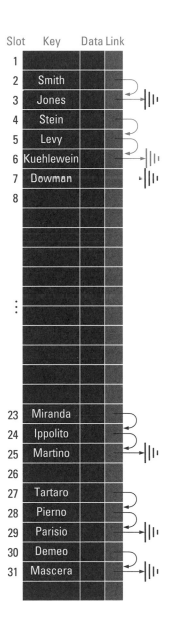

Figure 8.5
Coalesced chaining.

appropriation. For example, note that in Figure 8.5 the key *Bowman* is no longer in slot number 6. This is because the *Kuehlewein* record arrived first and appropriated the bucket that would have otherwise been used by *Bowman*.

The way we handle such an event is to add the new record to the list that contains the element that appropriated its slot. This is how the technique derives its name: Keys with different hash values merge into the same chain; thus, the chains coalesce.

Insertion operations remain similar to that of separate chaining. The only difference is that we allocate new nodes in the table rather than from a separate buffer pool (or dynamic memory).

We implement retrieval operations exactly as in the case of separate chaining. Chains will likely contain elements with different hash values. However, all keys with the same hash value will reside in the same chain. Thus, we need to search only one chain to locate a given key.

At first glance, deleting coalesced elements might seem as easy as deleting elements from a linked list: Locate the deleted node's predecessor and have it point to the deleted node's successor. However, a closer inspection reveals that it is not that easy. For example, let's assume we wanted to delete *Kuehlewein* from the hash table of Figure 8.5. After we performed the aforementioned processing, the hash table would appear as depicted in Figure 8.6. Obviously, the problem that arises is that after the deletion, we can no longer access the key *Bowman*. That is, because its hash value is 6—and that slot appears empty—we have no chain to follow.

To overcome this problem, we can use a special key value that denotes *deleted*. Thus, a deleted node's pointer remains in place and maintains the continuity of the chain. This is illustrated in Figure 8.7.

Open Addressing

The second method that we use for collision resolution is called *open addressing*. As in the modified hash table, this technique calls for us to store keys directly in the hash table. However, rather than using linked lists, we will store (and search for) colliding keys directly within the hash table itself. That is, we will use some alternate means by which we will determine a secondary bucket address for a colliding

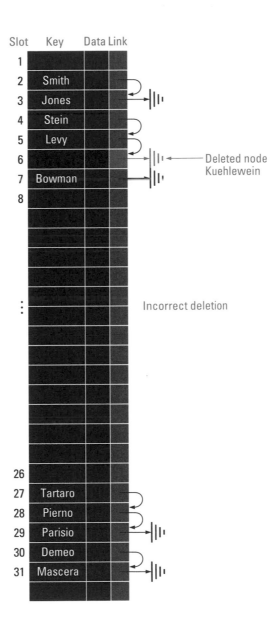

Deleted node
Kuehlewein

Incorrect deletion

Figure 8.6
Coalesced chain—
incorrect deletion.

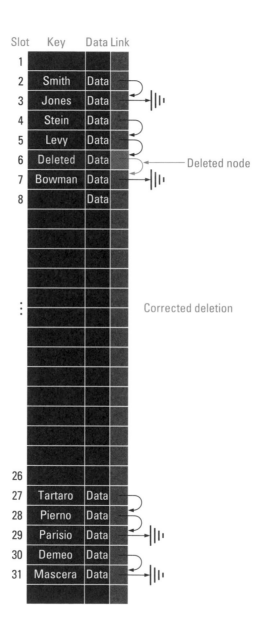

Figure 8.7
Coalesced chain—
correct deletion.

key. For example, we might use a secondary hashing function to generate a new index.

With open addressing, the order in which we search through buckets is called the *probe sequence*. A probe sequence begins with the initial bucket address generated by the primary hashing algorithm. If this address results in a collision, we repeatedly generate secondary bucket addresses until we either locate the key we are searching for or locate an empty slot for an insertion. The two methods we will discuss for generating secondary probe sequences are called linear probing and rehashing.

Linear Probing

The first open addressing technique we will discuss is called *linear probing*. It derives its name from the fact that, when a collision occurs, we simply search successive slots in the hash table. If we are inserting a key, we search for the next free bucket; if we are searching for a key, we continue until we encounter an empty slot. When we reach the end of the table, we simply wrap around back to the beginning. Thus, we search buckets in the following order:

$$\text{SLOT}_{initial} = primary\_hash(key)$$
$$\text{SLOT}_{next} = (\text{SLOT}_{current} + 1) \bmod m$$

where m represents the size of the hash table.

For an example of this technique, refer to Figure 8.8. Figure 8.8a depicts the initial state of our data structure. We are about to insert *Jones* and *Baker* into the table; assume both keys have a primary hash value of 2. However, the key *Smith* already occupies that position. As a result, we begin searching the table for the next available position to perform the insertion. In the case of *Jones*, the next free bucket is slot 3 (Fig. 8.8b); for *Baker*, the next available bucket is slot 7 (Fig. 8.8c).

Clustering Linear probing is a very simple technique and performs well if the hash table remains relatively empty. However, it has one major drawback: As the hash table becomes about half full, it suffers from a phenomenon that we refer to as *clustering*. That is, once a block of contiguous slots develops in the table, it becomes a likely candidate for additional collisions. Moreover, as clusters grow, they tend to merge and form even larger clusters.

Figure 8.8
Linear probing.

As an example of this phenomenon, consider an empty hash table and an associated hashing function. The probability of selecting any given bucket, say slot 10, is $1/m$, where m is the size of the hash table. However, if we enter a record into slot 9, we increase the probability of filling slot 10 on the next insertion: A key can hash to either bucket 9 or 10, and we would fill slot 10. If both buckets 8 and 9 were filled, the probability would increase again.

Linear Probing Complexity Obviously, the problem with clustering is that it increases search times. This is true for both successful and unsuccessful searches. In general, for a successful search, $S(\lambda)$ is the average of the number of probes required to locate each individual key. The analysis for $U(\lambda)$ (an unsuccessful search) can be divided into two components. If a slot is empty, we only require one probe. Otherwise, we must examine every slot in the cluster. The following are the final formulas, based on the load factor, for $S(\lambda)$ and $U(\lambda)$ when using linear probing. (The derivations are beyond the scope of this text; consult the bibliography for a list of references that provide a comprehensive discussion of the derivations.)

$$S(\lambda) = \frac{1}{2}\left(1 + \frac{1}{1 - \lambda}\right)$$

$$U(\lambda) = \frac{1}{2}\left(1 + \frac{1}{(1-\lambda)^2}\right)$$

Rehashing

One might think that we could minimize clustering by changing the probe offset to a value other than 1 (for example, i). However, we just end up with clusters of the form

$$s, \quad s + i \bmod m, \quad s + 2i \bmod m, \quad \ldots$$

where s is the original hash slot and m is the size of the table.

The only way we can minimize clustering is to generate the probe sequences in a manner that is independent of a key's primary position in the table. We can accomplish this by using a technique called *rehashing* (sometimes referred to as *double hashing* or *secondary hashing*). With this technique, we use an alternate hashing function to generate an increment. We then repeatedly apply the increment to the previous slot address until we locate the element or encounter an empty bucket.

As an example of this technique, recall that for our employee database the primary hash function was based on the employee's date of hire. We could develop a secondary hashing function based on the employee's date of birth. That is, we could use the day as an increment to scan through the hash table. However, because we only rehash once, we must ensure that the secondary hashing algorithm generates an increment that will eventually probe *every* slot in the hash table. As a trivial example, consider what would happen if our secondary hashing function was

$$newpos = oldpos + 2 \bmod m$$

and that our table size m was an even number. The increment generated by the secondary function would only probe the even-numbered slots in the table.

In general, to ensure that our probe sequence will reach every slot in the table, the secondary hashing function ($hash_2(key)$) should return a value that is greater than zero and relatively prime with respect to m. Specifically, if m and $hash_2(key)$ share a common divisor d, then

$$\left(\frac{m}{d} \times hash_2(key)\right) \bmod m = \left(m \times \frac{hash_2(key)}{d}\right) \bmod m = 0$$

if that were the case, then the probe m/d would be the same as the first, and we will not visit all the buckets in the hash table. The way to ensure that this will not happen is to choose a table size that is a prime number (as we have done, using the value 31, in our example). Thus, we can improve the performance of open addressing–based hash functions and minimize the effects of clustering.

Hashing Functions

The hashing strategies we discussed earlier are only as good as their associated hashing algorithms. We look for two important features in a hashing function: It should be easy to compute and it should distribute keys evenly over the entire range of the hash table.

In some cases, applications themselves will suggest a particular hashing algorithm—other times we must experiment. If we know, a priori, what keys we will process, we can develop a very efficient hashing algorithm specific to our needs. This is not typically the case, however, and we are thus forced to build generalized functions. In the following sections, we will describe several methods.

Truncation

The first method we will discuss is called *truncation*. Using this technique, we selectively ignore parts of the key. This is similar to our first example wherein we used the last two digits of customer telephone numbers as our hash key. Although fast, truncation typically fails to distribute keys evenly.

Division

If we have an integer-based key, we can divide the key by the size of the hash table and use the remainder as our bucket address. Simply put, we can compute the hash slot as

```
#define HASH_TABLE_SIZE 'some_value'
        .
        .
        .
int hash_function( int key )
{
     return( key % HASH_TABLE_SIZE );
}
```

As mentioned earlier, the distribution of keys depends heavily on the value selected for the modulus operation. The best choice is a prime number. Thus, do not use a hash table size of 1000; use 997 or 1009 instead.

Another concern that we must address is that keys are often alphabetic. However, we can easily convert alphabetic keys into integer values using the following formula:

$$K_{\text{integer}} = \sum_{i=1}^{i=L} c_i \cdot R^i$$

where L represents the length of the key, c represents characters in the original key, and R represents the base (radix) of the character set (typical values include 128 and 256). Listing 8.11 contains the example function, **str_to_int()**, which converts string keys into integer values. In addition, it shows an example of how we might incorporate the function into a hashing algorithm.

Hashing by this method is simple and fast. However, there is one minor consideration. Because it uses division, this technique might be too slow on small processors or on machines lacking hardware support for arithmetic computations.

Folding

One disadvantage of the division method discussed earlier is that some string keys may convert to integer values larger than the processor's word size. One way to address this problem is to apply a technique called *folding*.

With folding, we partition the key into several parts and then recombine the pieces in some convenient way to reconstruct a key that will fit within a given size restriction. (Note that we can also incorporate

```
#define RADIX   128
#define HASH_TABLE_SIZE 1009

long str_to_int( char key[] )
{
        long    i, nkey = 0;

        for( i = 0; key[i] != NULL; i++ )
                nkey = nkey * RADIX + key[i];

        return( nkey );
}

int new_hash_function( char key[] )
{
        return( str_to_int(key) % HASH_TABLE_SIZE );
}
```

Listing 8.11
Function to convert string keys to numeric.

truncation to eliminate unwanted—or unneeded—components of the key.)

To demonstrate this technique, let's return to our telephone number example. We could partition a number into its area code, exchange, and extension. We could then add the pieces together before we hashed. For example, we can partition the telephone number 800-555-1000 into the segments 800, 555, 1000; adding them yields a key value of 2355.

Because all segments have an effect on the resultant key, folding typically achieves a greater distribution of key values as compared to using truncation alone. As a result, this folding is often chosen in lieu of truncation (even in cases where it is not explictly needed).

SUMMARY   Searching is a common task in computer programs. In many cases, the perceived usefulness of an application will be predicated on the speed at which it can locate and retrieve information.

We can improve the performance of searching algorithms by ordering the datasets. This allows us to search for elements in a much more intelligent manner. Examples include binary search, interpolation search, and indexed sequential search.

The complexity of some algorithms is expressed in terms of a recurrence relation. To be of practical value, we must transform such complexities into their equivalent closed form.

Another method by which we can store and retrieve data quickly is called hashing. The basic principle behind hashing is that the key, after undergoing a transformation, points directly to the location of a given record. Despite its efficiency, hashing introduces several unique problems. First, we must address the problem of collisions. The two major techniques for resolving collisions are chaining and open addressing.

Second, we must develop an efficient hashing function. Specifically, the hashing routine must not only be fast, it must distribute keys evenly across the entire hash table.

EXERCISES

1. Implement all the searching routines discussed in this chapter. Compare execution times and the number of actual comparisons they each require. Be sure to vary the size and distribution of your test datasets.

2. Implement a secondary index routine based on the function `indx_seq()` (Listing 8.3).

3. Design and implement a function that build indexes for sorted tables.

4. Rewrite the binary search algorithm using recursion. Which method is faster?

5. Determine the number of different ways the data 1, 2, 3, . . . , 10 can be arranged in an ordered binary tree.

6. Write a recursive function that determines the maximum number of comparisons required to locate a record in a given OBT. (*Hint:* Consider the tree's height.)

7. Design and implement a function that performs an interpolation search on ordered arrays.

8. Compare the execution efficiency of your function from the previous exercise with that of **binsrch()**. Be sure to vary the size and distribution of your sample datasets.

9. While searching for the keys (A, C, M, P, W, Z) on a dataset consisting of the alphabet, trace the execution of both the interpolation and binary searching techniques.

10. Design and implement an iterative version of **treesrch()**.

11. Discuss the relative advantages and disadvantages of the two major collision resolution strategies used in hashing.

12. Assume a hashing function that returns the last digit of a telephone number. Practically speaking, what should be the maximum size of our hash table?

13. Draw the state of a hash table after inserting the following telephone number keys (in the order presented): 5551212, 5551001, 5552001, 5552223, 5556001. Assume that we are using a strategy of linear probing and that we have, as a hashing algorithm, a function that returns (as an integer) the last digit of the key. Count the number of probes each key requires.

14. Repeat the preceding exercise, but this time assume we are using chaining.

15. Implement the modified sequential search algorithm introduced in Listing 8.10.

16. Design and implement a deletion function for coalesced chaining.

17. Assume a hashing implementation that uses coalesced chaining, and design and implement a function that reorganizes all the keys after a deletion.

18. Design and implement a deletion function for linear probing.

Sorting Techniques

C H A P T E R

9.1 INTRODUCTION

In this chapter, we will focus our attention on the design and implementation of efficient sorting techniques. Sorting is the process whereby we arrange data (records) based on some sorting criteria (rules). Sorting criteria range from the obvious (alphabetical, numerical, etc.) to the not so obvious (some disk controllers prioritize I/O requests based on the proximity of the data blocks with respect to the current position of the drive's read/write head).

Records are usually ordered based on their key values. Note that keys may be complex (spanning several fields) and the sorting criteria may specify more than just one key (e.g., sort by last name, then by first name). We refer to the additional sort keys as *subkeys*.

There are several important attributes that we must consider when discussing sorting algorithms:

Execution time Determine an algorithm's complexity and compare it to the complexity of other sorting algorithms. Moreover, determine if the algorithm's performance is affected by the composition (the relative order) of its dataset. For example, some

Initial state:	5	4	1	3	2
After 1st pass:	4	1	3	2	5
After 2nd pass:	1	3	2	4	5
After 3rd pass:	1	2	3	4	5

Figure 9.1
Bubble sort example.

sorting routines perform efficiently when the data are sorted (or nearly so); others perform poorly.

Space requirements   Can the algorithm sort in place or does it require additional storage? Optimally, we would like an efficient algorithm that does not require additional space.

Stability   Does the algorithm preserve the original order of records with equal keys? For example, two distinct records could have the same key (e.g., *Smith, John*). In such cases, a sorting routine could position them in any order relative to each other. If the algorithm preserves their original order—that is, the order in which they appeared in the input stream—it is considered *stable*.

The sections that follow discuss a number of sorting techniques.

9.2   BUBBLE SORT

One of the most direct methods of sorting is a *bubble sort*. We can describe the technique as follows:

- Step through an array of unsorted elements, comparing adjacent cells.
- If they are out of order, switch them.
- When you complete an entire scan without switching any elements, the data are sorted and processing may terminate.

Figure 9.1 illustrates a bubble sort making several passes over a dataset. The function begins by comparing key_1 with key_2, then key_2 with key_3, and so on. After the first pass completes, the largest element is in its final position; after the second pass, the second largest element is in its final position. This is how the technique derives it name: During the first pass the largest element bubbles to the top; during

```
void bbl_sort( int data[], int no_elems )
{
     int   top, flag, tmp, i;

     top = no_elems;
     do {
          flag = 0;
          top--;
          for( i = 0; i < top; i++ ){
               if( data[i] > data[i+1] ){
                    tmp = data[i];
                    data[i] = data[i+1];
                    data[i+1] = tmp;
                    flag++;
               }
          }
     } while( flag > 0 );
}
```

Listing 9.1

Bubble sort algorithm.

the second pass the second largest element bubbles into position; and so on. Processing continues in this manner until all elements have been moved into their final position. It might require a moment's reflection to convince oneself that the technique indeed works.

An example of this sorting technique appears in Listing 9.1. The function **bbl_sort()** requires two arguments: the array to sort and its size. The outer **do** loop controls execution. That is, the function will iterate until the inner loop makes a pass without swapping any elements. This is indicated by the value stored in the variable **flag**. The inner loop does most of the work; it steps through each cell of the array, swapping adjacent elements as required.

Analysis

The inner loop executes n times, once for each element of the array. In the worst case, the outer loop will also iterate once for each element. This yields a complexity of $O(n^2)$. Average-case behavior of

Initial state:	4	2	5	3	1
1st pass:	1	2	5	3	4
2nd pass:	1	2	5	3	4
3rd pass:	1	2	3	5	4
4th pass:	1	2	3	4	5

Figure 9.2
Selection sort
example.

`bbl_sort()` is predicated on its input. For example, if the data are sorted, then only one pass is required. However, it turns out that the average-case behavior of this algorithm is only slightly better than the worst-case behavior and still yields a complexity of $O(n^2)$. (The actual analysis is beyond the scope of this text.) Also note that, because it never exchanges the positions of equal keys, `bbl_sort()` is a stable sorting algorithm.

9.3 SELECTION SORT

Another simple sorting method is called *selection sort*. The idea behind this technique is as follows:

- Search the data array for the smallest element.
- Exchange that element's position with the element in slot 1.
- Now locate the second smallest element and exchange its position with the element in slot 2.
- Continue in this manner, searching for each successive element, until the entire array is sorted.

Obviously, the algorithm derives its name from the fact that it *selects* the element it will position during each pass through the array.

Figure 9.2 depicts several passes of the algorithm on a sample dataset. During the first pass, the function identified the element 1 as the smallest and switched its position with that of element 4. No exchange occurred during the second pass because element 2 was already in its final position.

Note that, by virtue of its design, selection sort may move the same element several times. This is highlighted in passes 1 and

```
void sel_sort( int data[], int no_elems )
{
    int  i, j, min, tmp;

    for( i = 0; i < no_elems; i++ ){
        min = i;
        for( j = i+1; j < no_elems; j++ )
            if( data[j] < data[min] )
                min = j;
        tmp = data[i];
        data[i] = data[min];
        data[min] = tmp;
    }
}
```

Listing 9.2
Selection sort
algorithm.

4, where the function repositions element 4 during both passes. However, the algorithm will only perform, at most, one exchange during each pass.

Listing 9.2 contains the code for the function **sel_sort()**. Its two arguments indicate the data array and its size. During each iteration of the outer loop, the inner loop locates the smallest remaining element and saves its index in the variable **min**. The actual exchange occurs when the inner loop terminates. Note that as the outer loop moves through the list, the low-order elements (i.e., index values less than **i**) are in sorted order.

Analysis

The outer loop iterates n times; with each iteration of the outer loop, the inner loop performs a comparison for each unsorted element. This yields a complexity of $O(n^2)$. Due to its design, the function's behavior remains constant regardless of the composition of its dataset. Thus, the average-case complexity is also $O(n^2)$. **sel_sort()** is not a stable algorithm. That is, during the exchange, the relative position of equal keys can be reversed.

Figure 9.3
Insertion sort
example.

Initial state:	4	2	3	1	5
1st pass:	2	4	3	1	5
2nd pass:	2	3	4	1	5
3rd pass:	1	2	3	4	5

One other point. As noted earlier, only one exchange takes place with each iteration of the outer loop. Thus, despite its simplicity and somewhat poor performance, `sel_sort()` is useful for datasets with large records and small keys.

9.4 INSERTION SORT

Another straightforward method of sorting is called *insertion sort*. This sorting method can be likened to the way some people arrange a hand of playing cards. To begin, the first card is placed into the hand. Then, as each successive card is received, it is inserted into the hand in order. The player makes room for each new card by shifting cards of higher value to the right.

We can mimic this sorting technique in a computer program (see Fig. 9.3). The element in slot 1 of the array will serve as the first card. New elements are dealt by scanning the array from slots 2 to *n*. We then determine where the new element belongs and insert it into the hand (i.e., the low-order portion of the array).

Listing 9.3 contains the code for the function `ins_sort()`. Its outer loop, which selects elements for insertion, indexes from `1` to `no_elems − 1`. Note that we initialize `i` to the value `1`; thus, the element in slot `0` serves as the initial card. The actual insertion takes place in the inner loop. This section of code scans the already sorted portion of the array (i.e., the low-order indices) in reverse order, shifting elements to the right as required. This both determines the correct location of, and makes room for, the new element. When the inner loop terminates, the function stores the new element into the vacated slot. Note that like `sel_sort()`, the low-order elements are sorted; however, unlike `sel_sort()`, this algorithm may move (shift) elements several times.

```
void ins_sort( int data[], int no_elems )
{
    int i, j, tmp;

    for( i = 1; i < no_elems; i++ ){
        tmp = data[i];
        j = i - 1;
        while( (data[j] > tmp) && (j >= 0) ){
            data[j+1] = data[j];
            j--;
        }
        data[j+1] = tmp;
    }
}
```

Listing 9.3
Insertion sort
algorithm.

Analysis

It should be obvious that **ins_sort()** is stable. Specifically, the **while** loop does not move equal keys across each other.

As with the preceding algorithms, **ins_sort()** has both worst-case and average-case complexities of $O(n^2)$. However, observe that when the dataset is ordered (or nearly so), it performs comparatively few shifts. As a result, it can be the algorithm of choice for applications that must add new elements to pre-existing, sorted lists.

At this point you might be wondering whether $O(n^2)$ is the fastest we can sort. The sections that follow address that issue and discuss more efficient sorting techniques.

9.5 QUICKSORT

We will begin our discussion of advanced sorting techniques with one of the most popular sorting algorithms: *quicksort* (also called *partition sort*). Quicksort was originally developed in 1960 by C. A. R. Hoare and has been studied, analyzed, and 'tweaked' ever since. We begin our discussion with a description of the basic algorithm; we will then address several improvements and extensions.

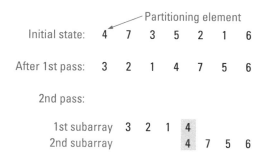

Figure 9.4
Quicksort example.

Unfortunately, quicksort has no real-life analogue from which we can derive a pedagogical metaphor. We are compelled, therefore, to jump right in. So let's begin with a brief overview of the algorithm (assume n is the size of our data array):

- Select one element, x, from the array. We will refer to this element as the *partitioning element* for reasons that will become clear shortly. (Initially, the choice of partitioning element will be arbitrary; we will discuss and refine the selection criteria later.)
- Determine the final position of x in the sorted array. For now assume it is some location *data*[i].
- Rearrange all the other elements of the array such that all elements in slots *data*[0] through *data*[$i - 1$] are $\leq x$, and all elements in slots *data*[$i + 1$] through *data*[n] are $\geq x$.
- Recursively apply the algorithm on the two subarrays *data*[0], . . . , *data*[$i - 1$] and *data*[$i + 1$], . . . , *data*[n] until all elements are sorted.

Figure 9.4 provides an example. During the initial pass, the function arbitrarily selects the element in array slot 0 (value 4) as the partitioning element. When the first pass completes, this element is in its final position and the function can proceed with recursive calls on the two subarrays.

If you consider the problem at all, it quickly becomes obvious that the most difficult task is determining the final position of the partitioning element. Specifically, how can we determine the final position of some element x unless we sort the entire array? After a moment of reflection you might observe that we do not need to sort the array to determine x's final position. All we need to know is the *number* of other

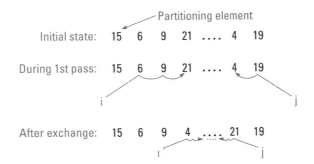

Figure 9.5
Quicksort: Partitioning the elements.

elements that will be positioned either above or below *x* in the array. It then becomes a simple calculation to determine *x*'s final location.

At this point, you are probably ready to start coding. Select a partitioning element *x*, count the number of elements less than *x*, move *x* into its final position, and recursively process the two subarrays on either side of *x*. We have, however, one more problem. When it processes each subarray, the function assumes that the values they contain are logically positioned. That is, all values in the left subarray are ≤ *x*; all values contained in the right subarray are ≥ *x*. Once the partitioning element is in position, there is no provision for moving elements between the newly created subarrays. Therefore, we cannot position *x* without also rearranging the other array elements.

The solution to this problem is the very heart of the quicksort algorithm. Consider the following scenario: Select two index variables *i* and *j*. Simultaneously, move *i* through the array from *left to right* (i.e., from 0 to *n*), and move *j* through the array from *right to left* (i.e., from *n* to 0). When *i* encounters a condition where $data[i] > x$ and *j* encounters a condition where $data[j] < x$, exchange elements (i.e., $data[i] \Leftrightarrow data[j]$.) The function continues in this manner until the indices cross (i.e., when $j \leq i$). This ensures that all elements are partitioned correctly. Thus, when *x* is finally positioned, all elements $< x$ will be positioned below *x* in the array, and all elements $> x$ will be positioned above *x* in the array. See Figure 9.5 for an example.

Note that the elements, as they are rearranged, are not sorted. Rather, the algorithm decides whether to reposition elements based solely on their value relative to the final position of the partitioning element. Sorting only occurs as a result of recursively reapplying the algorithm on all subarrays.

```
void qck_sort( int data[], int lo, int hi )
{
    int  i, j, tmp, part_elem;

    if( hi > lo ){
        part_elem = data[hi];
        i = lo-1;
        j = hi;
        while( 1 ){
            while( data[++i] < part_elem )
                ;
            while( data[--j] > part_elem )
                ;
            if( i >= j )
                break;

            tmp = data[i];
            data[i] = data[j];
            data[j] = tmp;
        }

        tmp = data[i];
        data[i] = data[hi];
        data[hi] = tmp;

        qck_sort( data, lo, i-1 );
        qck_sort( data, i+1, hi );
    }
}
```

Listing 9.4
Quicksort algorithm.

We are now ready to implement the basic algorithm. As presented in Listing 9.4, the function **qck_sort()** requires three arguments. The first points to the data array and the latter two are, respectively, its lower and upper bounds. (The need for an index to track the lower bound will be made clear shortly.) The initial call sets these values to 0 and *n* respectively (the size of the array). Note that, when using languages that support zero-based arrays (e.g., C), we must set **hi** to $n - 1$ (i.e., the index of the high-order slot).

The initial **if** statement is a sanity check to ensure that **qck_sort()** was invoked with reasonable arguments. The function then selects the partitioning element (**data[hi]**) and initializes its index variables. The outer **while(1)** statement is an infinite loop that drives the main body of the function. Contained in that loop are two nested **while** loops. Their purpose is to step their respective index variables through the data array searching for elements that need repositioning. When the inner loops terminate, the function tests whether **i** and **j** have crossed. If they have, the outer loop terminates; **qck_sort()** then repositions the partitioning element and recursively invokes itself on the two newly created subarrays. If **i** and **j** have not crossed, the function swaps elements in positions **data[i]** and **data[j]** and continues with the next iteration of the outer **while** loop.

Analysis

Let's begin with the average-case analysis of quicksort. Assume a random dataset of size n. The time required to partition elements is $O(n)$ (linear). Each time we partition a subarray, we create two additional subarrays. If we assume that each partition will generate subarrays of about the same size (e.g., $n/2$), the overall complexity of quicksort can be expressed by the following recurrence relation:

$$f(1) = 1$$

$$f(n) = n + 2f\left(\frac{n}{2}\right), \qquad \text{for } n > 1$$

Based on our discussions in Chapter 8, the closed form of this recurrence relation is

$$f(n) = n \log_2 n$$

Thus, quicksort has an average-case complexity of $O(n \log_2 n)$.

For quicksort, the worst case occurs when the data are sorted (or nearly so). Each recursive call would only sort one element. The function would thus require n recursive calls, each requiring $O(n)$ time to partition the elements. This yields an overall worst-case complexity of

$O(n^2)$. In the sections that follow we discuss simple ways to ensure that quicksort will not encounter the pathological case. One final point: It should be obvious that quicksort is not a stable sorting method.

Improvements to Quicksort

Remove Recursion

As you may recall from Chapter 4, all recursive algorithms have an equivalent iterative solution. Thus, the first improvement we can make to quicksort is to tranform the basic algorithm from recursive to iterative.

The driving loop of this new function will use a stack to track unprocessed subarrays. The values pushed and popped will be the upper and lower bounds of each subarray; initially, the stack contains values denoting the entire array.

With each iteration of the loop, the function

- Pops a subarray off the stack
- Processes it (as discussed earlier)
- Pushes the two resulting subarrays onto the stack.

The function terminates when the stack becomes empty.

Secondary Sorting Routine

For our next improvement, consider that regardless of the size of the original array, quicksort will ultimately begin processing small subarrays. (We will define *small* shortly.) In a recursive solution, the overhead required to process these small subarrays is obvious. However, iterative versions of the algorithm will also be affected by this overhead.

This begs the obvious question: How can we minimize the impact of small subarrays? Approaching the problem directly, you might try optimizing quicksort for small arrays. However, let's be more clever. Instead of trying to *fix* quicksort, let's just choose another algorithm. The idea is that when subarrays become smaller than some given size *m*, we will employ a secondary sorting algorithm.

Two questions now arise: Which algorithm should we use? And what are suitable values for *m*? Let's begin with the first question. Observe that as a result of the partitioning that has taken place, ele-

ments in subarrays are close in value. Thus, we would want to use
an algorithm that works efficiently on datasets that are nearly sorted.
As noted earlier, **ins_sort()** works well in such cases and is an appropriate choice here. As for the second question, an exact value for *m*
is implementation dependent. However, it need not be perfect. Versions
of quicksort modified in this manner will perform approximately the
same for values of *m* in the range of 10 to 25.

We can carry this idea one step further. Quicksort does not need
to invoke the secondary sorting routine for each subarray of size < *m*.
Consider that if each subarray is nearly sorted, then the entire set of
subarrays of size < *m* is also nearly sorted. We can modify quicksort to
ignore all small subarrays during its partitioning phase. That is, it will
not invoke any sorting routine whatsoever. When it completes the
partitioning phase, quicksort can then invoke the secondary sorting
routine just once and have it complete the sort for the entire array.

Median-of-Three Partitioning

The final improvement we will discuss focuses on the selection of the
partitioning element. In our complexity analysis, we noted that quicksort's
performance degrades when its dataset is already (or nearly) sorted.
This problem is a direct result of repeatedly using the same relative
element for array partitioning.

For example, consider a case in which quicksort is processing a
dataset that is already sorted. With each recursive call, the function
selects **data[hi]** as its partitioning element. Based on this selection,
the function will partition the array into two subarrays: one of size **lo** to
hi − 1 and one of size **0**. In effect, the function creates only *one*
subarray for each element because there are no elements greater than
data[hi]. This causes the performance to degrade toward $O(n^2)$.

We could be assured of better overall performance if we could
improve the selection of the partitioning element. Specifically, the
closer the partitioning element is to the middle of the array, the better
the function will perform. A first suggestion might be to use a random
number to select a partitioning element. However, the cost associated
with a pseudo–random number generator might be prohibitive.

A better solution is a technique referred to as *median-of-three* parti-

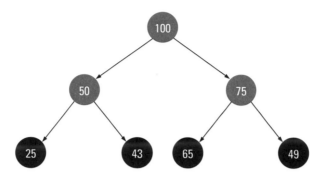

Figure 9.6
Example heap.

tioning. This method calls for the function to select the partitioning element from a set of three: `data[lo]`, `data[middle]`, `data[hi]`. Specifically, the algorithm selects the median of those three elements based on key value. This technique is an inexpensive way to ensure that the partitioning element is not located at either extreme of the array.

Final Remarks

The three modifications we have discussed can result in a 20% to 30% overall improvement in the performance of quicksort. There have been a number of other improvements suggested (e.g., median-of-five), but they result in only a marginal gain in performance. That is, the improvement in performance is not commensurate with the added complexity.

9.6   HEAPSORT

The next sorting method we will discuss is called *heapsort*. This algorithm derives its name from the data structure it employs. Before we discuss the sorting technique itself, let's take a look at its data structure.

A *heap* is a complete binary tree with the property that the key associated with any given node *n* is greater than the keys of its children. Figure 9.6 provides an example.

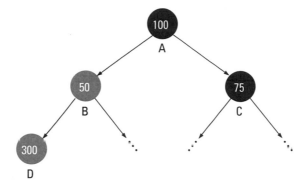

Figure 9.7
Binary tree prior to heap.

A heap has many uses; one of the most common is to implement priority queues. Referring back to Figure 9.6, we see that the element positioned at the root always has the highest priority. This can be a convenient way for applications—such as a print spooler—to schedule prioritized tasks.

When we remove an element from a heap, we must *re-heap* the tree. That is, one of the deleted node's children (the greater) will become the new parent; one of that node's children will replace it; and so on. Thus, implementing a heap is a two-stage process. Initially, we must transform a complete binary tree into a heap. Then, as elements are inserted and removed, we must maintain the integrity of the heap.

Let's take a closer look at the process of transforming a complete binary tree into a heap. Consider the tree depicted in Figure 9.7. To transform it into heap, we would have to switch node *D* with node *B*; once moved, we would again need to switch node *B* with node *A*. Although simple in theory, this technique has one shortcoming in that a child cannot easily access its parent. One solution is to add back pointers to each node. However, this treats a symptom, not the problem. A better solution is to use an array. Recall from Chapter 6 that when using an array implementation of a binary tree, the children of any node i are located at $2i$ and $2i + 1$; its parent is located at $\lfloor i/2 \rfloor$. Thus, via simple formulas, we can reference any node's parent and children.

In Chapter 6 we also noted one negative aspect of using arrays to implement trees. The problem concerned sparse trees and the programming difficulties associated with the empty array slots. However, by definition, a heap is based on a *complete* binary tree, which guarantees that there will be no empty slots within the array.

```
void buildheap( int data[], int size )
{
    int  i;

    for( i = size/2; i >= 0; i-- )
        form_heap( data, i, size );
}

void form_heap( int data[], int lo, int hi )
{
    int  tmp, desc;

    if( 2*(lo+1)-1 > hi )                    /* Nothing to do */
        return;

    if( (2*(lo+1)) <= hi && data[2*(lo+1)] > data[2*(lo+1)-1] )
        desc = 2 * (lo+1);              /* Right Child */
    else
        desc = 2 * (lo+1) - 1;        /* Left Child */

    if( data[lo] < data[desc] ){
        tmp = data[lo];
        data[lo] = data[desc];
        data[desc] = tmp;
        form_heap( data, desc, hi );
    }
}
```

Listing 9.5
Functions to create a heap.

To transform a binary tree into a heap, start at the end of the array and move up toward the root, switching elements as required. The code appearing in Listing 9.5 automates this task using two functions: **form_heap()** and **buildheap()**.

The function **form_heap()** takes three arguments: a pointer to the data array and two integer variables that delineate its lower and upper bounds. Its task is to form a heap beginning at element **lo**. The first

if statement determines whether **lo** has any children; the function returns immediately **lo** it has none. The function then decides which child to process—the greater of the two—and assigns its index to **desc**. Then, if the child is greater than its parent, it switches the two elements and invokes itself recursively to continue the process at the next level in the tree. Note that **form_heap()** assumes that if no switch is required, the rest of the tree below this point is already in heap form. Keep this in mind as we discuss **buildheap()**.

The function **buildheap()** is the driving routine for **form_heap()**. It requires two arguments: the array and its size. Its one loop begins by calculating the middle of the array. Then, while decrementing its control variable, the function iteratively invokes **form_heap()** with **i** as its middle parameter (i.e., **form_heap()**'s **lo** argument). This means that from node **i** through all of **i**'s descendants, the tree will be formed into a heap. Again keep in mind that **form_heap()** will terminate as soon as it identifies a case where the parent is greater than both of its children. The entire array is in heap form when **buildheap()** terminates.

These two functions can now serve as the foundation for a heapsort. Consider that after the initial heap of the array, the largest element is in the root position. If we were to remove that element and re-heap the tree, the second largest element would now be in the root position. We could proceed in this manner until we had processed all elements.

Note that the process we just described sorts elements in reverse order. We could make quick work of this problem by simply inverting the heap. However, this solution does not address one other problem: Where should we store the records as we remove them from the heap? We could create and maintain a separate array, but that is wasteful.

As an alternative, consider that when we remove the root node from the heap, the tree has one less element. After we re-heap, we can reuse this otherwise empty slot to store the removed element. We continue in this manner with each successive element; when the processing completes, the entire array will have been sorted in place.

We can now formalize our presentation of the heapsort algorithm:

1. Build the initial heap.
2. Exchange the root node with the (current) last node of the array.

```
void heap_sort( int data[], int size )
{
     int   tmp, i;

     buildheap( data, size );
     for( i = size; i > 0; i-- ){
          tmp = data[0];
          data[0] = data[i];
          data[i] = tmp;
          form_heap( data, 0, i-1 );
     }
}
```

Listing 9.6
Heapsort function.

3. Re-heap the tree.
4. Repeat steps 2 and 3 until all elements have been processed.

  Listing 9.6 contains the code for the function **heap_sort()**. This is the driving routine for the heapsort algorithm. It uses both **buildheap()** and **form_heap()** to create and maintain the heap; it tracks the current end of the array via its loop counter **i**.

Analysis

Initially (via **buildheap()**), **form_heap()** is called once for each node that has a child: $O(n)$. In **heap_sort()**, **form_heap()** is called $n - 1$ times with a maximum depth of $\lceil \log_2(n + 1) \rceil$. As a result, the overall complexity becomes $O(n \log_2 n)$. Note that, because of the way the heap is formed, **heap_sort()** is not naturally stable.

9.7 MERGESORT

  The final sorting technique we will study is called *mergesort*. As its name implies, merging plays a major role in this sorting algorithm. Merging is the process by which we combine two (or more) datasets into one. For example, consider two sorted arrays: A of size m, and B of size n. Merging these two datasets would create a third sorted array—C of

```
merge( C, A, B, m, n )
{
    i = 1;                         // Index into array A
    j = 1;                         // Index into array B
    k = 1;                         // Index into array C

    while( i <= m and j <= n ){
        if( A[i] <= B[j] )
            C[k++] = A[i++];
        else
            C[k++] = B[j++];
    }

    if( i <= m )                   // Process remaining elements
        while( i <= m )
            C[k++] = A[i++];
    else
        while( j <= m )
            C[k++] = B[j++];
}
```

Listing 9.7

Merging algorithm—pseudo-code.

size $m + n$—that contains all elements from both arrays. Listing 9.7 presents a pseudo-code description of such an algorithm.

The function **merge()** begins processing by initializing its control variables. With each iteration of the initial **while** loop, the function selects and stores into C the next largest element from A or B; it then advances control variables as appropriate. Note that the first loop terminates when *one* of the control variables reaches the end of its corresponding array. Therefore, **merge()** must determine which array has not been exhausted and then copy all of its remaining elements into C.

To understand how merging can help us sort, we need to alter our view of array storage temporarily. Just for a moment, imagine an array not as a set of elements, but rather as a set of adjacent subarrays. For

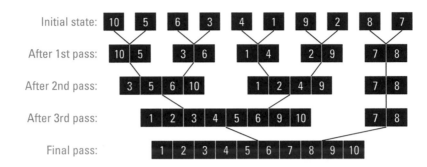

Figure 9.8
Mergesort example.

example, we could view an array of size *n* as *n* adjacent arrays of size 1.

Obviously, if the subarrays are of size 1, they are, in effect, sorted. Now consider what would happen if we were to merge adjacent pairs of subarrays. This would create adjacent subarrays of size 2 (also sorted). We could repeat this process to create adjacent subarrays of sizes 4, 8, and so on. Eventually, we would reach a case where only two subarrays remain; when we merge these, the entire array is sorted. Figure 9.8 illustrates this process.

Implementation

Our first task is to modify the function **merge()**. Previously, it required two separate source arrays. We will now modify it so that it will merge adjacent subarrays within the same array. Listing 9.8 contains the code for the modified algorithm. Note that in this version, **merge()** requires five arguments: The first two are the destination and source arrays; the latter three are index variables that denote which adjacent pair of subarrays to merge in the source array.

Listing 9.9 contains two other functions that complete the implementation of the mergesort algorithm. The first, **mrg_pass()**, is the function that drives **merge()**. It is invoked with four arguments: The first two are the arrays (destination and source); **size** is the size of the array and **len** is the length of the subarray for each pass. The function divides the array **from[]** into subarrays of size **len** and invokes **merge()** once for each adjacent pair. Take note of the special proc-

```
void
merge( int to[], int from[], int low,
       int mid, int high )
{
    int  ilow, ihigh, ito;

    ilow = ito = low;
    ihigh = mid + 1;
    while( ilow <= mid && ihigh <= high ){
        if( from[ilow] < from[ihigh] ){
            to[ito] = from[ilow];
            ilow++;
        } else {
            to[ito] = from[ihigh];
            ihigh++;
        }
        ito++;
    }

    while( ilow <= mid )
        to[ito++] = from[ilow++];

    while( ihigh <= high )
        to[ito++] = from[ihigh++];
}
```

Listing 9.8
Mergesort algorithm.

essing for cases where the **from[]** array cannot be partitioned into an even number of subarrays.

The second function, **mrg_sort()**, is the driving routine for the entire mergesort algorithm. It is invoked with two arguments: the array to sort and its size. Its driving loop calculates the length of the subarray and calls **mrg_pass()**.

Note that during each iteration of its **while** loop, **mrg_sort()** calls **mrg_pass()** twice, alternating the first two arguments. That is to say, during the first call **mrg_pass()** sorts from **data[]** into **tmp[]**; the second call reverses that order. This saves the time that we would

```
void
mrg_pass( int to[], int from[], int size, int len )
{
      int low = 0;

      while( low < size − 2*len ){
            merge( to, from, low, low+len−1, low+2*len−1 );
            low += 2 * len;
      }

      if( low+len−1 < size ){
              merge( to, from, low, low+len−1, size );
      } else {
            while( low <= size ){
                  to[low] + from[low];
                  low++;
            }
      }
}

void mrg_sort( int data[], int size )
{
      int        tmp[ 2048 ];              /* malloc */
      int len = 1;                         /* len of subfile */

      while( len < size ){
            mrg_pass( tmp, data, size, len );
            len *= 2;
            mrg_pass( data, tmp, size, len );
            len *= 2;
      }
}
```

Listing 9.9
Mergesort algorithm.

otherwise spend copying elements from **tmp[]** back to **data[]** after each pass.

One final note: In this version, **mrg_sort()** allocates auxiliary storage statically (i.e., **int tmp[2048]**). A more practical approach would be to allocate the additional storage dynamically using a function similar to **malloc()**. (Refer to Chapter 5 for a more detailed discussion of this topic.)

Analysis

As depicted in Figure 9.8, mergesort requires several passes:

Pass No.	Subarray Size
1	1
2	2
3	4
i^{th}	2^{i-1}

This yields a total of $\lceil \log_2 n \rceil$ passes. Each call to **merge()** requires one scan of the array $O(n)$. Thus, the overall complexity of mergesort is $O(n \log_2 n)$. Note that the function requires additional space proportional to n.

The algorithm is also stable. The function only moves records during merges. Thus, we can ensure that the relative position of the keys remains unchanged during processing.

SUMMARY

There is a wide variety of internal sorting techniques available to programmers. They range in complexity from $O(n \log_2 n)$ to $O(n^2)$. In addition, they vary with respect to storage requirements and stability.

Many sorting algorithms are affected by the organization of their data-sets. Some perform well when the data are (nearly) sorted; others do not. As a result, the behavior of sorting algorithms is expressed using two complexities: worst case and average case.

One of the most popular sorting algorithms is called quicksort. Although comparatively efficient, its complexity can be improved using simple modifications. It also has the virtue of sorting data in place. Two other popular techniques are called heapsort and mergesort.

1. We can improve the performance of the bubble sort algorithm by eliminating unnecessary comparisons. For example, consider an array of 50 elements. If during one scan of the array the last exchange occurred at location 35, we can assume that slots 36 through 50 are sorted. Therefore, the function can terminate the next pass at slot 34. Add the necessary code to the function **bbl_sort()** to implement this feature. Compare the new algorithm's performance to that of the original.

2. How does the function **qck_sort()** (Listing 9.4) put an end to its recursion?

3. At the end of its outer **while** loop, the function **qck_sort()** exchanges the partitioning element (**data[hi]**) with **data[i]**. Explain why we can place the partitioning element at the ith location.

4. Implement both the secondary sorting routine and the median-of-three improvements to the basic quicksort algorithm.

5. Modify your function of the previous exercise to use a pseudo–random number generator, rather than median-of-three partitioning, to select its partitioning element. Compare the performance of the two functions.

6. Which of the algorithms in this chapter are stable? Which are not? Provide example datasets to support your claims. Are your answers implementation dependent? If so, provide examples.

7. Analyze the behavior of all the sorting algorithms presented in this chapter when presented with sorted data. Perform the same analysis for datasets sorted in reverse order.

8. Implement a recursive version of the quicksort algorithm that uses a selection sort for small subfiles. Use an array size of 1000. Begin with $M = 15$ as your performance metric; then vary its value and note the results.

9. Carry out the same tasks as described in the previous exercise on an iterative implementation of quicksort. Compare your results.

10. Consider a complete binary tree wherein the data value for each node is equal to its index. Is this tree a heap?

11. Given an array containing the values 10, 9, . . . , 1, show the state of the heap after the initial call to **buildheap()**.

12. Design and implement a version of mergesort that sorts in place.

13. Write a general-purpose routine to insert and delete elements in a heap.

Acrostic Puzzle

In Chapter 4, we briefly described a backtracking algorithm that solved *acrostic* puzzles. In this appendix, we undertake a more thorough examination of the program.

Simply stated, an acrostic puzzle is a crossword puzzle without the clues: You are supplied the words and the diagram and, through trial and error, you must enter all the words into their appropriate slots (see Fig. A.1). We urge you—if you are not familiar with these types of puzzles—to try solving one manually before reading on.

Before we can describe an automated solution, we need to address some basic details. First, we must develop a way to input a puzzle description to our program. To simplify this example, we will place puzzle descriptions in files (the format of which will be described later). Thus, to invoke our program, we will type a command similar to the following:

```
kross puzzle_file
```

The puzzle description file is divided into two sections. Section I contains the layout of the puzzle. As depicted in Figure A.2, it begins with a line that contains the identifying string **@puzzle**. Following that, there is a series of lines—one for each row of the puzzle—that contain a combination of blanks and dashes. These characters represent the black boxes and the character locations of the puzzle, respectively. Note that you must ensure that all puzzle-description lines are of equal length (the program checks for this).

Section II of the puzzle description file begins with a line containing the identifying string **@words** (refer to Fig. A.2). Immediately following begins the list of words, one per line, that the program will

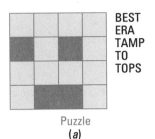

Puzzle
(*a*)

Solution
(*b*)

Figure A.1
A sample acrostic
puzzle and solution.

```
@puzzle          (Section I)
----
x-x-             ('x' = Blank)
----
-xx-
@words           (Section II)
best
tamp
tops
era
to
```

Figure A.2
Sample input file.

insert into the puzzle. You may enter words in any order. However, take the time to ensure that all words are spelled correctly. The program, as you might expect, is rather unforgiving in this regard.

The overall operation of the program is as follows:

• Read the puzzle and word list into internal data structures.
• Attempt to find a solution for the puzzle.
• If there is a solution, print it.

Figure A.3 contains sample program output for the puzzle presented in Figure A.2.

Let's begin our analysis of the program by examining its data structures. The program uses a two-dimensional character array, called **puzzle[][]**, to store the internal representation of the puzzle. The array is initialized by the function **readpuz()** as it scans Section I

Figure A.3
Sample program
output.

```
best
xrxo             ('x' = Blank)
tamp
oxxs
```

of the description file. By convention, a hyphen (-) represents a character location; a blank denotes a black box.

After loading the diagram, **readpuz()** reads and stores the word list into a structure array called list**[]**. Each element of this array represents words of the same length. The words themselves are stored in a subarray referred to by the simple appellation **w**, which is an array of type **struct words**. Each element of this structure contains two members:

word   This is a character array that holds the actual word.

flag   This is a status field that indicates the state of the word (i.e., used, free, etc.).

As an example of how the program uses these structures, consider how it might search for a five-letter word to fill a particular slot in the puzzle. It begins by indexing into the fifth slot of **list[]**. It then scans each element of the subarray **w** until it locates a free word that fits into the desired puzzle slot. Note that, as a programming convenience, we have offset the array index to eliminate unneeded entries (e.g., words of length 1 or 2).

Once **kross** has completed initializing its data structures, it invokes the function **solve()** to solve the puzzle. This is where we find all the backtracking logic (see Listing A.1). **solve()** is a recursive procedure that performs the following processing:

1. It begins each invocation by choosing, and determining the size of, the next puzzle slot it must fill (horizontal or vertical). This processing is performed by the function **next()** and is, by necessity, a rather messy bit of code.

2. It then selects, at random (i.e., sequentially), an appropriately sized word from the available list. It uses the function **itfits()** to determine whether the word fits into the slot (in typical crossword puzzle fashion).

3. If it fits, **solve()** enters the new word into the puzzle. Just prior to doing so, **solve()**, with the aid of the function **enter()**, takes a *snapshot* of the current puzzle state.

4. The function then invokes itself recursively, continuing toward a solution.

5. If, at any point, the function completes the puzzle (i.e., there are no more slots to fill), it returns the value **SOLVED**.

```
 1: solve( length, width )
 2: int      length, width;
 3: {
 4:          int      l, w, i, len, tmp, type;
 5:          char     old[ WORDLEN - MINWORD + 1 ];
 6:
 7:          w = width;
 8:          l = length;
 9:          len = next( &l, &w, &type );
10:          if( len == 0 )
11:                  return( SOLVED );
12:
13:          for(i = 0;i<MAXWORD&&WORD(len,i)[0]!=NULL;i++){
14:                  if( FLAG(len, i) == FREE
15:                      && itfits(l, w, WORD(len, i), type) ){
16:                          FLAG(len, i) = USED;
17:                          enter( old, l, w, WORD(len,i), type );
18:                          prev = type;
19:                          tmp = solve( l, w );
20:                          if( tmp == SOLVED )
21:                                  return( SOLVED );
22:                          restore( old, l, w, type );
23:                          FLAG(len, i) = FREE;
24:                  }
25:          }
26:
27:          return( FAIL );
28: }
```

Listing A.1
The function `solve()`.

6. If a given recursive call fails to find a solution, **solve()**

- Restores the puzzle to its previous state. This is accomplished via a call to the function **restore()**.
- Returns the word that it just tried back to the free list.
- Repeats the steps 2–5 with the next available word. If none remains, **solve()** returns the value **FAIL**.

Let's trace the execution of the function **solve()** as it begins to solve our sample puzzle from Figure A.2. All the line numbers referenced throughout the discussion correspond to Listing A.1. Also, to simplify our example, the random selection of words is the order in which they appear in Figure A.2.

First, we need a four-letter word to fill the *1 across* position. The function randomly selects *best* (line 14), marks it as **USED** (line 16), and inserts it into the puzzle (line 17). **Solve()** then calls itself recursively to continue processing (line 19).

The next invocation of the function needs a three-letter word for the *2 down* position; it selects *era* and inserts it into the puzzle. The next call to **solve()** must now fill the *3 down* position. Thus, it selects the next available four-letter word, *tamp* (line 13), checks to see that it fits (line 14), and inserts it into the puzzle (line 17).

The next slot the function needs to fill is *4 across*. As usual, it selects the next available four-letter word—in this case, *tops*. This time, however, the **itfits()** test (line 15) fails. Recognizing that the last four-letter word has been used (line 13), the function restores the puzzle to its previous state (line 22) and then initiates a backtrack (line 27).

After backtracking, the immediately preceding invocation of the function now resumes processing at the point where it, again, needs to fill the *3 down* position. It discards what was its first choice, *tamp* (lines 22 and 23) and selects the next available word, *tops* (line 14). Note that the function put the word *tops* back on the available list just prior to performing the backtrack. From this point on, the function solves the puzzle without any additional difficulties. The complete program appears in Listing A.2.

EXERCISES

1. Implement and test the operation of the **kross** program.

2. Create several puzzles of your own and test them with the **kross** program.

3. Rewrite the **kross** program to use dynamic data structures.

4. Modify the word search routines used by **kross** to utilize the hashing techniques discussed in Chapter 8.

```
#include        <"stdio.h">
#include        <"stdlib.h">
#include        <"string.h">

#define ALL     1
#define PUZ     2
#define DOWN    1
#define ACROSS  2

#define MINWORD 2
#define MAXPUZ  25
#define MAXWORD 50
#define WORDLEN 15

#define EMPTY   0
#define FREE    1
#define USED    2

#define FAIL    -1
#define SOLVED  3

#define BLANK   ' '
#define PADCHAR '-'
#define WORDS   "@words"
#define PUZZLE  "@puzzle"

#define FLAG(x, y)      list[ x - MINWORD ].w[ y ].flg
#define WORD(x, y)      list[ x - MINWORD ].w[ y ].word

int main( int ac, char *av[]);
int solve( int length, int width );
int next( int *len, int *wht, int *t );
int itfits( int l, int w, char *word, int t );

void readpuz( FILE *fp );
void puz_print( void );
void restore( char *old, int l, int w, int t );
void enter( char *old, int l, int w, char *word, int t );

int     length, width;
char    puzzle[ MAXPUZ ][ MAXPUZ ];

struct  words   {
        int     flg;
        char    word[ WORDLEN ];
};
```

continued on p. 290

continued from p. 289

```
struct   wordlist {
        struct   words   w[ MAXWORD ];
} list[ WORDLEN - MINWORD ];

int main( int ac, char *av[] )
{
     int i, j;
     FILE *fp;
        if( ac != 2 ){
                fprintf( stderr, "usage: kross puzzlefile\n" );
                exit( 1 );
        }
        if( (fp = fopen( av[1], "r" )) == NULL ){
                fprintf( stderr, "Cannot open '%s' to read!\n",
                av[1] );
                exit( 1 );
        }

        readpuz( fp );
        if( solve(0, -1) == SOLVED )
                puz_print();
        else
                printf( "No Solution!!\n" );

        return( 0 );
}

/*
 *
 *   ============================================================
 *        READPUZ(): read puzzle into memory from file
 *   ============================================================
 */
void readpuz(FILE *fp)
{
        int     i;
        char    buf[ 85 ];


        /*
         *      Puzzle Section
         */
        length = 0;
        if( fgets( buf, sizeof buf, fp ) == NULL ){
                fprintf( stderr, "%s: Premature EOF!\n", PUZZLE );
                exit( 1 );
        }
```

continued on p. 291

continued from p. 290

```
if( strncmp(buf, PUZZLE, strlen(PUZZLE)) ){
        fprintf( stderr, "%s: BAD FORMAT!\n", PUZZLE );
        exit( 1 );
}

if( fgets(buf,sizeof buf,fp) == NULL
    || !strncmp(buf,WORDS,strlen(WORDS)) ){
        fprintf( stderr, "%s: Premature EOF!\n", PUZZLE );
        exit( 1 );
}
width = strlen( buf ) - 1;

do {
        if( (strlen( buf ) - 1) != width ){
                fprintf( stderr, "Line %d: bad width!\n",
                        width );
                exit( 1 );
        }
        for( i = 0; i < width; i++ ){
                if( buf[ i ] == BLANK )
                        puzzle[ length ][ i ] = NULL;
                else if( buf[i] == PADCHAR )
                        puzzle[ length ][ i ] = buf[ i ];
                else {
                        fprintf( stderr,
                                "BAD CHAR %d L# %d\n",
                                buf[i], length );
                        exit( 1 );
                }
        }
        puzzle[ length ][ width ] = NULL;
        length += 1;
} while(fgets(buf,sizeof buf,fp)!=NULL &&
        strncmp( WORDS, buf, strlen(WORDS) ) != 0 );

/*
 *      Words Section
 */
```

continued on p. 292

continued from p. 291

```
        while(fgets(buf, sizeof buf, fp) != NULL ){
            for( i = 0; i < MAXWORD; i++ ){
                    if( FLAG(strlen(buf)-1, i) == EMPTY ){
                            strncpy( WORD(strlen(buf)-1, i),
                                    buf, strlen(buf)-1 );
                            FLAG(strlen(buf)-1, i) = FREE;
            break;
                    }
            }
            if( i >= MAXWORD ){
            fprintf( stderr, "Out of space %d %s\n",
                    strlen(buf)-1, buf );
            exit( 1 );
            }
        }
    }
}


/*
 *
 *    ================================================================
 *       PUZ_PRINT(): display solved puzzle
 *    ================================================================
 */
void puz_print()
{
    int     i, j;

    for( i = 0; i < length; i++ ){
        for( j = 0; j < width; j++ ){
            if( puzzle[i][j] )
                putchar( puzzle[i][j] );
            else
                putchar( BLANK );
        }
        putchar( '\n' );
    }
}
```

continued on p. 293

```
/*                                                          continued from p. 292
 *      ============================================================
 *           SOLVE(): function that searches for a solution
 *      ============================================================
 */
static  int     prev = −1;

int solve( int length, int width )
{
        int     l, w, i, len, tmp, type;
        char    old[WORDLEN − MINWORD + 1];

        w = width;
        l = length;
        len = next( &l, &w, &type );
        if( len == 0 )
                return( SOLVED );

        for( i=0; i<MAXWORD && WORD(len, i)[0] != NULL; i++ )
        {
                if( FLAG(len, i) == FREE
                    && itfits(l, w, WORD(len, i), type) ){
                        FLAG(len, i) = USED;
                        enter( old, l, w, WORD(len, i), type );
                        prev = type;
                        if( solve(l, w) == SOLVED )
                                return( SOLVED );
                        restore( old, l, w, type );
                        FLAG(len, i) = FREE;
                }
        }

        return( FAIL );
}
```
continued on p. 294

```
/*                                                     continued from p. 293
 *    =================================================================
 *          NEXT(): locate next slot to fill
 *    =================================================================
 */
int next( int *len, int *wht, int *t )
{
        /*
         *         Return the next slot in the puzzle to attempt
         *         to be solved. DOWN has precedence.
         *
         *         The new values for len & wht will be updated.
         *         The returned value for the 'w' coordinate for
         *         an across 'hit' will have to be the value + 1.
         */
        int     l, w, tmp;

        l = *len;
        w = *wht;

        /*
         *         Check current position for across: down would
         *         have been done already.
         */
        if( w != -1 &&  ((w - 1) < 0 || puzzle[l][w-1] == NULL )
            && puzzle[l][w] && (w + 1) < width && puzzle[l][w+1] ){
                /*
                 *        Across!
                 */
                *t = ACROSS;

                /*
                 *        Necessary evil!
                 */
                *wht = w + 1;

                tmp = 0;
                while( puzzle[l][w] != NULL && w < width ){
                        w += 1;
                        tmp += 1;
                }
                return( tmp );

        } else if( prev == DOWN || w == -1 )
                w += 1;
```

continued on p. 295

```
/*                                                       continued from p. 294
 *        Check for next possible position
 */
for(; l < length; l += 1 ){
        for(; w < width; w += 1 ){
                if( ( (l - 1) < 0 || puzzle[l-1][w] == NULL)
                    && puzzle[l][w] != NULL && (l+1) < length
                    && puzzle[l+1][w] != NULL ){
                        /*
                         *  Down!
                         */
                        *t = DOWN;
                        prev = DOWN;
                        *wht = w;
                        *len = l;
                        tmp = 0;
                        while(puzzle[l][w]!=NULL&&l<length){
                            l += 1;
                            tmp += 1;
                        }
                        return( tmp );
                }
                if( ((w - 1) < 0 || puzzle[l][w-1] == NULL)
                    && puzzle[l][w] && (w+1) < width
                    && puzzle[l][w+1] ){
                        /*
                         *        Across!
                         */
                        *t = ACROSS;
                        prev = ACROSS;
                        *len = l;
                        *wht = w + 1;

                        tmp = 0;
                        if( w == -1 ) w = 0;
                        while(puzzle[l][w]
                        !=NULL&&w<width){
                                w += 1;
                                tmp += 1;
                        }                           continued on p. 296
```

```
                                    return( tmp );        continued from p. 295
                               }
                       }
                       w = 0;
               }

               /*
                *       Puzzle completed!
                */
               return( 0 );
       }

       /*
        *   ================================================================
        *       ITFITS(): determine if a word fits into a given slot
        *   ================================================================
        */
       int itfits( int l, int w, char *word, int t )
       {
               char    *cp;

               if( t == ACROSS && w != -1 )
                       w -= 1;

               cp = word;
               while( *cp ){
                       if( *cp != puzzle[l][w]
                       && puzzle[l][w] != PADCHAR )
                               return( 0 );
                       if( t == ACROSS )
                               w += 1;
                       else
                               l += 1;
                       cp++;
               }
               return( 1 );
       }

       /*
        *   ================================================================
        *       ENTER(): enter a word into the puzzle
        *   ================================================================
        */
       void enter( char *old, int l, int w, char *word, int t )
```

continued on p. 297

continued from p. 296

```
{
        char    *cp;

        if( t == ACROSS )
                w -= 1;

        cp = word;
        while( *cp ){
                *old++ = puzzle[1][w];
                puzzle[1][w] = *cp;
                if( t == ACROSS )
                        w += 1;
                else
                        1 += 1;
                cp++;
        }
        *old = NULL;
}

/*
 *
 *      ================================================================
 *          RESTORE(): restore puzzle to its previous state
 *      ================================================================
 */
void restore( char *old, int 1, int w, int t )
{
        char    *cp;

        if( t == ACROSS )
                w -= 1;

        cp = old;
        while( *cp ){
                puzzle[1][w] = *cp;
                if( t == ACROSS )
                        w += 1;
                else
                        1 += 1;
                cp++;
        }
}
```

Listing A.2
The complete kross program.

C for Programmers

B

B.1 INTRODUCTION

This appendix provides a brief introduction to the C programming language. It is not intended to serve as an exhaustive tutorial. It will, however, acquaint readers with the basic features of the language. We assume the reader has had some prior programming experience in a high-level language. In addition, we also assume that the reader has reviewed the section in Chapter 1 titled "What You Need to Know." The grammar specified throughout this appendix adheres to the American National Standards Institute (ANSI) definition for C.

Quick Tour of C

To highlight many of the features we will discuss, Listing B.1 contains a simple, somewhat contrived, C program. All the program does is scan an array to locate and print the value of its largest element. An example of the program's output appears in Figure B.1.

Program Structure

A C program is composed of one or more functions, one of which must be named **main()**. Listing B.1 contains two function definitions, **main()** and **find_max()**. Program execution begins with the first executable instruction in **main()** and continues until either **main()** executes a **return** statement or the program invokes one of the standard exit routines (e.g., **exit()**).

A complete C program can—and usually does—span more than

```c
#include <stdio.h>                        /* Preprocessor Directive */

/*
 *        Preprocessor Macros & Symbolic Constants
 */
#define NO_OF_ELEMENTS 10
#define MAX(A, B)        ( (A) > (B) ? (A) : (B) )

int find_max( int beg, int end );        /* Function Declaration */

int data[ NO_OF_ELEMENTS ];              /* Variable Definition   */

int main()                               /* Function Definition   */
{
        int max;                         /* Automatic Class Vars */
        int i = 0;

        while( i < NO_OF_ELEMENTS )      /* While Loop */
        {
                data[ i ] = i;
                i = i + 1;
        }

        max = find_max( 0, NO_OF_ELEMENTS );

        printf( "The value of max is: %d\n", max );

        return( 0 );
}

int find_max(int beg, int end)           /* Definition of find_max() */
{
        int i, max;

        max = data[ beg ];                       /* External Variable   */
        for( i = 0; i < end; i++ )
                max = MAX( max, data[i] ); /* Macro Reference   */

        return( max );
}
```

Listing B.1
Sample C program.

Figure B.1
Sample program
output.

The value of max is: 9

one source module (file). That is, you can define functions in more than one source file and then compile and link the modules together to form one executable program. For example, we could have placed the function **find_max()** in its own, separate source file.

During compilation, source files can include additional C and preprocessor statements from other files, usually called *header files*. We refer to the resulting code, passed onto the C compiler, as a *compilation unit*. In Listing B.1, we included one header file **stdio.h**.

B.2 DATA TYPES

Basic Types

C supports several basic data types

char A variable large enough to hold any character of the native character set. It is usually one byte in size and may store other (small integer) values as well.

int An integer type that reflects the natural word size of the execution environment. For example, **int**s are typically two bytes on 16-bit processors, four bytes on 32-bit processors.

float Single-precision floating-point values. The size and precision of this data type is machine dependent.

double Double-precision floating-point values. The size and precision of this data type is machine dependent.

In the program of Listing B.1, we declared several variables of type **int**.

Qualifiers

The basic types may have qualifiers applied to them. Two that apply only to **int**s are **short** and **long**. The intent of these two qualifiers is to provide integers of different sizes where appropriate. For example, on most processors a **short** is typically 16 bits, a **long** is 32 bits. Compiler vendors may choose sizes that befit the execution environment with the proviso that **short**s are at least 16 bits and **long**s are at least 32 bits. You may omit the keyword **int** when you use these qualifiers. For example, both of the following type declarations are equivalent:

```
short i;
short int i;
```

Programmers may apply the qualifier **long** to **double**s as well. A declaration of type **long double** (both keywords are required in this case) implies extended-precision floating point. However, as with **double**s, the actual size is machine dependent.

The qualifiers **signed** and **unsigned** may be applied to any integer or **char** type. Values that are **unsigned** may only hold positive values or zero; **signed** values may hold negative quantities.

Constants

C recognizes several types of constants. An integer constant is a sequence of digits; its data type is **int**. If the digit sequence begins with a leading zero, the compiler interprets its value in octal; a leading **0x** (zero followed by an *x*—either case) signifies hexadecimal. The characters **a** through **f** (in either case) represent the hexadecimal digits 10 through 15, respectively. In Listing B.1, we use an integer literal in the declaration of the variable **i**.

If a digit sequence terminates with either an upper- or lowercase L, the value is treated as a **long**. A trailing U (either case) indicates **unsigned**. Programmers may combine both suffixes to signify **unsigned long**. Several examples follow.

```
15        /* Decimal int, value = 15                */
017       /* Octal int, value = 15                  */
0xF       /* Hexadecimal int, value = 15            */

15u       /* Decimal — unsigned int, value = 15     */
017L      /* Octal — long, value = 15               */
0xFul     /* Hex — unsigned long, value = 15        */
```

Character Constants

A character constant is a sequence of one or more characters enclosed within single quotes ('). To express the literal value *x* we write `'x'`. We may also use the following so-called *escape* sequences to express characters that are otherwise difficult to represent:

```
Newline             \n
Horizontal Tab      \t
Vertical Tab        \v
Carriage Return     \r
Formfeed            \f
Audible Bell        \a
Backspace           \b
Backslash           \\
Question Mark       \?
Single Quote        \'
Double Quote        \"
Octal Value         \ddd
Hexadecimal Value   \0xdd
```

We can use the octal and hexadecimal escape sequences to represent any character using its value in the native mode character set. For example, we could specify an ASCII bell character using any of the following forms: `\a`, or `\007`, or `\0x7`. We may use escape sequences anywhere a character would otherwise be expected. For example, we used an `\n` sequence in the call to **printf()** in Listing B.1.

String Constants

A string constant is a sequence of characters enclosed within double quotes ("). For an example, refer to the first argument in the call to **printf()** in Listing B.1. Please note that there is no data type **string** in C; nor is **string** a reserved word of the grammar. Internally, C compilers represent strings as arrays of characters terminated by a **NULL** character. As a result, string literals in C have a data type of *array of characters*. (Refer to the section on arrays later in this appendix.)

Symbolic Constants

Symbolic constants are a feature of the preprocessor. A statement of the form

```
#define SYMBOLIC_NAME REPLACEMENT_VALUE
```

directs the preprocessor to replace all unquoted occurrences of the string `SYMBOLIC_NAME` with `REPLACEMENT_VALUE`. Refer to the symbol, `NO_OF_ELEMENTS`, as it appears in Listing B.1 for an example.

`const` Qualifier

C also provides a **const** qualifier that may be applied to variable declarations. A statement of the form

```
const double PI = 3.1459;
```

signifies to the compiler that the variable `PI` cannot be modified. As a result, you must initialize all **const** variables when you declare them.

B.3 DECLARATIONS

Identifier Names

A C identifier (i.e., the name of a variable, function, or label) is a sequence of one or more letters, digits, and underscores. An identifier name must begin with a letter or the underscore; the first 31 characters are significant.

Declaration Syntax

Variable declarations have the general form

$$type \; identifier\_name \; [\; = \; initial\_value \;] \; ;$$

where *type* represents a data type and *identifier_name* is a valid C identifier name. Optionally, you may also initialize variables using values expressed as compile-time constants. Listing B.1 contains several variable declarations; we also provide some additional examples below:

```
int i = 15;        /* Signed Int          */
signed int j;      /* Signed Int          */
short k = 0, m;    /* Signed Short        */
unsigned n;        /* Unsigned Int        */
float f;           /* Float               */
long double x;     /* Extended Precision  */
```

Arrays

C allows programmers to create arrays using statements of the general form

$$type\ array\_name[\ const\_expr\ ];$$

where *type* represents the data type specified for each element of the array, *array_name* is a valid C identifier name, and *const_expr* represents a compile-time constant expression that specifies the size of (i.e., number of elements in) the array. The variable, **data[]**, in Listing B.1, is an example of an array declaration in C.

We reference individual array elements by their *offset* rather than their *index*. Thus, valid element references for an array declared as

```
int a[ 10 ];
```

are from **0** to **9**. There are several examples of array references in Listing B.1.

We may create multidimensional arrays simply by adding additional sets of brackets:

```
int three_dim[3][7][9];
```

The preceding statement creates a three-dimensional array. C compilers ensure that memory allocation for arrays is contiguous. (Refer to the discussion of pointers later in this appendix.)

Structures

C programmers can create aggregate data types called **struct**s. For example, the statement

```
struct emp {
        int id;
        char name[10];
};
```

declares a **struct** with a tag (i.e., name) of **emp**. This structure has two *members:* an integer variable named **id**, and a character array named **name[]**.

We can declare instances of a **struct** using statements such as

```
struct emp x;
```

We can reference individual structure members using the dot (.) operator, as in

```
x.id = 1024;
```

We can also declare and reference arrays of structures:

```
struct emp managers[ 10 ];
         .
         .
         .
managers[i].id = 1024;
```

B.4 OPERATOR SET

Unary

Unary operators require one operand. C has several, including the following:

—	Unary minus (negation) operator
!	Logical *Not* operator
~	Bitwise *Not* operator
*	Indirection operator (see below)
&	Address operator (see below)
++	Increment operator
——	Decrement operator.

We can use both the increment and decrement operators can be used in either *prefix* (e.g., **++i**) or *postfix* (e.g., **i++**) form. The position of the operator is significant. When used in prefix form, the interpretation is *increment then evaluate;* when used in postfix form the interpretation is *evaluate then increment*. For example, consider the following two code fragments:

```
i = 10;              i = 10;
x = ++i;             x = i++;


   (1)                  (2)
```

In both cases, the result contained in **i** is **11**. However, in case 1, **x** is set to **11**; in case 2, **x** is set to **10**. The **for** loop of Listing B.1 contains an example of the increment operator.

Binary

Binary operators require two operands. Let's begin with the basic arithmetic set:

+	Addition operator
−	Subtraction operator
*	Multiplication operator
/	Division operator
%	Modulus operator (integer remainder).

In Listing B.1, we use a binary addition operator (+) in the body of the **while** loop.

The relational operators include

<	Less than operator
<=	Less than or equal operator
>	Greater than operator
>=	Greater than or equal operator
==	Equality operator
!=	Inequality operator.

Expressions that employ relational operators evaluate to either the integer value **1** (signifying true), or the integer value **0** (signifying false). (See the section on conditional expressions later in this appendix.) Several examples of relational operators appear in Listing B.1.

The logical operators include

&&   Logical *And* operator
|| Logical *Or* operator
!   Logical *Not* operator.

You can use the logical operators to create complex expressions. For example, the statement

```
if( a > b  && c < d )
    do something();
```

asserts two conditions before invoking the function
`do_something()`.

C is often referred to as a high-level, low-level language. One reason for the latter half of the appellation is the bitwise operator set:

&   Bitwise *And* operator
| Bitwise *Inclusive-or* operator
∧   Bitwise *Exclusive-or* operator
<<   Left shift operator
>>   Right shift operator.

These operators can only be applied to integer-based operands.

Ternary

C has one ternary operator, also called the *conditional operator*. Its syntax is

$$expr_1 \ ? \ expr_2 : expr_3$$

We evaluate the entire expression beginning with $expr_1$: If $expr_1$ evaluates to true (see the discussion on expression evaluation later), then we evaluate $expr_2$; otherwise, we evaluate $expr_3$. For example, we could determine the smaller of two values using the following statement:

```
min_val = a < b ? a : b;
```

We use the conditional operator in the definition of the macro, **MAX**, in Listing B.1.

Assignment Operators

The basic assignment operator in C is the equal sign (=). (PASCAL programmers please take note.) C also provides a set of compound assignment operators, which take the form

$$expr \quad <binary\ operator> = \quad expression$$

These operators combine a binary expression with an assignment. For example, if we want to increment a variable by some value other than 1, say 10, we could write

```
i += 10;
```

B.5   EXPRESSIONS AND STATEMENTS

Comments

C comments begin with the unquoted character sequence **/*** and terminate with the unquoted sequence ***/**. Comments in C do not nest.

Expressions

A primary expression in C includes identifiers, constants, strings, and nested expressions enclosed within parentheses.

Conditional Expressions

In C, the interpretation of any conditional expression (e.g., **if(condition)**) can be stated simply: Zero is *false*, non-zero is *true*. C programmers tend to rely heavily on this construct and write expressions such as

```
if( i % 2 )
    do_something();
```

which will invoke the function **do_something()** only when **i** contains an odd value.

This can also lead to interesting results when combined—erroneously—with the simple assignment operator (=). For example, given the assignments

```
i  =  10;
j  =  11;
```

the expression

```
if( i = j )            /* ERROR: assignment NOT
equality */
    do_something();
```

will evaluate to true because:

1. We are *assigning* i to j, not comparing their values.
2. The result of an assignment statement is the value being assigned (in this case 11).
3. The result of the expression (11) is non-zero.

However, when used correctly, this construct can add power and expressiveness to our C programs. For example, consider the following code fragment:

```
while( (a[i++] = getchar()) != '\n' );
```

In it, we

1. Perform an I/O operation.
2. Assign the result to an array element.
3. Increment an index variable.
4. Perform a relational comparison.

Note that all of this processing occurs within the conditional expression of a **while** loop.

Statements

In C, statements are terminated with a semicolon (;). Readers familiar with some other languages—most notably PASCAL—should take note. In C, the semicolon is a statement *terminator*, not a statement *separator*.

Compound Statements

A *compound statement* (sometimes called a *block*) is a series of one or more statements enclosed within braces:

```
{
        statement_1;
        statement_2;
                .
                .
                .
        statement_n;
}
```

You may use a compound statement wherever a single statement is valid.

B.6   CONTROL FLOW

The if Statement

The basic form of the **if** statement is

```
if( condition )
    statement;
```

You may add an optional *else* clause:

```
if( condition )
    true_statement;
else
    false_statement;
```

Unless you explicitly use braces, C associates an **else** with the closest preceding **if**. In the following example,

```
if( condition1 )
    if( condition2 )
        statement1;
else
    statement2;
```

the compiler associates the **else** with the inner **if**, not the outer one. If that is not your intention, you must use braces:

```
if( cond1 )
{
    if( cond2 )
        statement1;
}
else
    statement2;
```

The switch Statement

C's **switch** statement is a multiway branch:

```
switch( expr )
{
    case const_expr:
        statements;
    case const_expr:
        statements;
    default:
        statements;
}
```

The value of **expr**—which must evaluate to an integer (or character)—is compared against the case labels. If there is a match, execution begins with the first statement associated with the label. If there is no match, execution begins at the optional **default** label (if there is one). It is important to note that **case**s fall through. That is, regardless of the entry point, execution continues through to the end of the **switch** unless a **break** statement (discussed later) is encountered. In the latter case, execution resumes with the statement following the **switch**.

The while Loop

The syntax for the **while** loop is

```
while( condition )
    statement;
```

Execution continues as long as **condition** evaluates to true (i.e., non-zero).

The do-while Loop

The **do-while** loop has the form

```
do
     statement;
while( condition );
```

Like the **while** loop, this loop continues to iterate while its control expression is true. However, this construct guarantees at least one iteration because it has its condition test positioned at the end.

The for Loop

The syntax of a **for** loop is as follows:

```
for( expr1; expr2; expr3 )
     statement;
```

expr1 is the loop initialization statement; it is executed once, just prior to the loop's first iteration. **expr2** is the loop conditional statement; the loop will continue to iterate while the condition remains true. **expr3** is the loop increment statement; it is executed after each iteration of the loop body. The semicolons are the only symbols required between the parentheses. The preceding **for** loop is equivalent to the following **while** loop:

```
expr1;
while( expr2 )
{
     statement;
     expr3;
}
```

Loop Termination and Continuation

The keyword statement **break** may be used within the body of a loop or switch. If executed, it causes program execution to pass to the statement following its enclosing construct.

The keyword statement **continue** may be used only within the body of a loop. If executed, it immediately causes program execution to begin the next iteration of the innermost enclosing loop.

B.7   POINTERS

The C declaration for a pointer is

> *data_type   *ptr_name;*

where *data_type* determines the type of object at which *ptr_name* may point. For example, we can define a pointer to integer as

```
int *iptr;
```

Note that **iptr** does not hold integer values; rather, it can hold the addresses of other integer variables.

The statement

```
iptr = &i;
```

assigns the address of **i** to **iptr**. That is, we say that **iptr** points at **i**, and that we can access the contents of **i** *indirectly* through **iptr**. The symbol **&** is a *unary* operator that yields the address of its operand.

Once assigned, we can use a pointer to modify the contents of the memory cell at which it points. Assuming all of the preceding declarations and assignments, the statement

```
*iptr = 6;
```

is equivalent to the assignment

```
i = 6;
```

The * operator *dereferences* the pointer **iptr**; thus, we access **i** *indirectly* via the pointer. Pointer dereferencing is dynamic. That is, the cell at which a pointer is pointing, at the time of dereferencing, is the one that is modified.

B.8   THE C PREPROCESSOR

C's preprocessor is a separate program—automatically invoked by the compiler—that does just what its name implies: processes C source files before passing the modified source code on to the compiler. It has several important features.

Symbolic Constants

Symbolic constants are defined as follows:

```
#define MAX_SCORES 10
```

A statement of this form causes the preprocessor to replace all un-quoted occurrences of the string **MAX_SCORES** with the string **10**. For example, consider the following code fragment:

```
#define     MAX_SCORES      10

main()
{
     int  i;
     int  total[ MAX_SCORES ];
          .
          .
          .
     if( i >= MAX_SCORES )
          .
          .
          .

}
```

After preprocessing, the following statements would be presented to the compiler:

```
main()
{
     int  i;
     int  total[ 10 ];


          .
          .
          .
     if( i >= 10 )
          .
          .
          .

}
```

Macros with Arguments

Symbolic constants may also accept arguments. For example, consider the following definition:

```
#define SQUARE(x)    ((x)*(x))
```

The expansion of **SQUARE** is now dependent on its use. If we code

```
z = SQUARE(y);
```

the preprocessor will expand it to

```
z = ((y)*(y));
```

Note that **x** serves as a place holder. That is, whatever argument we place in the **x** position will appear wherever **x** appears in the expansion.

Include Files

Another widely used feature of the preprocessor is the file inclusion facility. The following preprocessor directive:

```
#include        "defs.h"
```

directs the preprocessor to replace the **#include** statement with the entire contents of the file **defs.h**. The **include**d file may contain any valid C and preprocessor statements, including nested **#include**'s.

There is another form of the **#include** directive:

```
#include        ⟨filename⟩
```

The angle brackets direct the preprocessor to search a predetermined location for one of several system-supplied header files. The exact location is system dependent, and the files contain definitions of a global nature.

EXERCISES

1. What effect, if any, would changing the position of the increment operator from prefix to postfix have on each of the following statements?

   a. **++i;**

```
b. for( i = 0; i < 10; ++i )
        a[i] = i;
c. j = ++i;
```

2. Given the following macro definition from Listing B.1,

```
#define MAX(A, B)    ( (A) > (B) ? (A) : (B) )
```

what is the value of all variables after executing the following statements?

```
int a, b, c;

a = 20;
b = 20;
c = MAX( a++, b );
```

3. What value is assigned to c after executing the following assignment statement?

```
int a, b, c;

a = 20;
b = 10;
c = a < b;
```

4. How many times, if any, will the following loop execute?

```
int a, b, c;

i = -5;
while( i )
        do_something();
```

Suggested Readings

Adelson-Velskii, G.M., and Landis, E.M. "An Algorithm for the Organization of Information," *Dokl. Akad. Nauk SSSR*, Mat., 146(2):263–66, 1962.

Aho, A., and Corasick, M.J. "Efficient String Matching: An Aid to Bibliographic Search," *Communications of the ACM*, 18:333–40, 1975.

Aho, A., Hopcroft, J., and Ullman, J. *Data Structures and Algorithms*, Reading, Mass.: Addison-Wesley, 1983.

Aho, A., Hopcroft, J., and Ullman, J. *The Design and Analysis of Computer Algorithms*, Reading, Mass.: Addison-Wesley, 1974.

Aho, A., and Ullman, J. *Principles of Compiler Design*, Reading, Mass.: Addison-Wesley, 1977.

Amble, O., and Knuth, D.E. "Ordered Hash Tables," *Comp. J.*, 18:135–42, 1975.

Augenstein, M., and Tenenbaum, A. "A Lesson in Recursion and Structured Programming," *SIGCSE Bulletin*, 8(1):17–23, February 1976.

Augenstein, M., and Tenenbaum, A. "Approaches to Based Storage in PL/I," *SIGCSE Bulletin*, 9(1):145–50, February 1977.

Auslander, M.A., and Strong, H.R. "Systematic Recursion Removal," *Communications of the ACM*, 21(2), February 1978.

Baeza-Yates, R. "Some Average Measures in M-ary Search Trees," *Information Processing Letters*, 25(6):375–81, July 1987.

Bays, C. "A Note on When to Chain Overflow Items Within a Direct-Access Table," *Communications of the ACM*, 16(1), January 1973.

Bellman, R. *Dynamic Programming*, Princeton, N.J.: Princeton University Press, 1957.

Bender, E., Praeger, C., and Wormald, N. "Optimal Worst Case Trees," *Acta Informatica*, 24(4):475–89, August 1987.

Bentley, J. "Programming Pearls," *Communications of the ACM*, August 1983.

Bentley, J. "Programming Pearls: Thanks Heaps," *Communications of the ACM*, 28(3):245–50, March 1985.

Bentley, J. "Programming Pearls: How to Sort," *Communications of the ACM*, 27(4):287–91, April 1984.

Bentley, J. *Writing Efficient Programs*, Englewood Cliffs, N.J.: Prentice-Hall, 1982.

Berge, C. *Theory of Graphs and Its Applications*, Mass.: Methuen, 1962.

Berry, R., and Meekings, B. "A Style Analysis of C Programs," *Communications of the ACM*, 28(1):80–88, January 1985.

Berztiss, A.T. *Data Structures, Theory and Practice (2d ed.)*, New York: Academic, 1977.

Bird, R.S. "Notes on Recursion Elimination," *Communications of the ACM*, 20(6):434, June 1977.

Bird, R.S. "Improving Programs by the Introduction of Recursion," *Communications of the ACM*, 20(11), November 1977.

Bitner, J.R., and Reingold, E.M. "Backtrack Programming Techniques," *Communications of the ACM*, 18:651–56, 1975.

Blum, M., Floyd, R.W., Pratt, V., Rivest, R.L., and Tarjan, R.E. "Time Bounds for Selection," *J. Comput. Syst. Sci.*, 7:448–61, 1973.

Boothroyd, J. "Algorithm 201 (Shellsort)," *Communications of the ACM*, 6:445, 1963.

Borodin, A., and Munro, I. *Computational Complexity of Algebraic and Numeric Problems*, New York: American Elsevier, 1975.

Bowman, C.F. "Backtracking," *Dr. Dobbs Journal of Software Tools*, August 1987.

Bowman, C.F. "Pattern Matching Using Finite State Machines," *Dr. Dobbs Journal of Software Tools*, October 1987.

Bowman, C.F. "Objectifying X-Classes, Widgets, and Objects." *Object Magazine*, July/ August 1993.

Boyer, R.S., and Moore, J.S. "A Fast String Searching Algorithm," *Communications of the ACM*, 20(10):762–72, 1977.

Brainerd, W.S., and Landweber, L.H. *Theory of Computation*, New York: Wiley, 1974.

Brown, P.J., "Programming and Documenting Software Projects," *ACM Comput. Surv.*, 6(4), December 1974.

Bruno, J., and Coffman, E.G., "Nearly Optimal Binary Search Trees," *Proc. IFIP Congr.* 71, North-Holland, Amsterdam, 1972, pp. 99–103.

Burge, W.H. "A Correspondence Between Two Sorting Methods," *IBM Research Report RC 6395*, IBM Thomas J. Watson Research Center, Yorktown Heights, N.Y., 1977.

Carlsson, S. "A Variant of Heapsort with Almost Optimal Number of Comparisons," *Information Processing Letters*, 24(4):247–50, March 1987.

Chang, H., and Iyengar, S. "Efficient Algorithms to Globally Balance a Binary Search Tree," *Communications of the ACM*, 27(7):695–702, July 1984.

Cheriton, D., and Tarjan, R. "Finding Minimum Spanning Trees," *SIAM Journal on Computing*, 5(4):724–42, December 1976.

Cichelli, R., "Minimal Perfect Hash Functions Made Simple," *Communications of the ACM*, 23(1):17–19, January 1980.

Cook, S.A., and Reckhow, R.A., "Time-Bounded Random Access Machines," *Journal of Computer and System Sciences*, 7:354–75, 1973.

Cranston, B., and Thomas, R. "A Simplified Recombination Scheme for the Fibonacci Buddy System," *Communications of the ACM*, 18(6), June 1975.

Deo, N. *Graph Theory with Applications to Engineering and Computer Science*, Englewood Cliffs, N.J.: Prentice-Hall, 1974.

Dijkstra, E. "A Note on Two Problems in Connexion with Graphs," *Numerische Mathematik*, 1:269–71, 1959.

Dijkstra, E. "Notes on Structured Programming," in *Structured Programming*, New York: Academic, 1972.

Dobosiewicz, W. "Optimal Binary Search Trees," *International Journal of Computer Mathematics*, 19(2):135–51, 1986.

Earley, J. "Toward an Understanding of Data Structures," *Communications of the ACM*, 14(10):617–27, October 1971.

Elson, M. *Data Structures*, Palo Alto, Calif.: Science Research, 1975.

Elspas, B., Levitt, K.N., Waldinger, R.J., and Waksman, A. "An assessment of techniques for proving program correctness," *ACM Computing Surveys*, 4(2):97–147, 1972.

Er, M. "Efficient Generation of Binary Trees from Inorder-Postorder Sequences," *Information Sciences*, 40(2):175–81, 1986.

Esakov, J., and Weiss, T. *Data Structures: An Advanced Approach Using C*, Englewood Cliffs, N.J.: Prentice-Hall, 1989.

Even, S. *Graph Algorithms*, Potomac, Md.: Computer Science, 1978.

Fischer, M.J. "Efficiency of Equivalence Algorithms." In R.E. Miller and J.W. Thatcher (eds.), *Complexity of Computer Computations*, pp. 153–67. New York: Plenum Press, 1972.

Fischer, M.J., and Meyer, A.R. "Boolean matrix multiplication and transitive closure." *Conference Record, IEEE 12th Annual Symposium on Switching and Automata Theory*, pp. 129–31, 1971.

Fishman, G.S. *Concepts and Methods in Discrete Event Digital Simulation*, New York: Wiley, 1973.

Flajolet, P., and Prodinger, H. "Level Number Sequences for Trees," *Discrete Mathematics*, 65(2):149–56, June 1987.

Flores, I. *Computer Sorting*, Englewood Cliffs, N.J.: Prentice-Hall, 1969.

Flores, I. *Data Structure and Management*, Englewood Cliffs, N.J.: Prentice-Hall, 1970.

Floyd, R. "Algorithm 97: Shortest Path," *Communications of the ACM*, 5(6):345.

Floyd, R. "Algorithm 245 (Treesort3)," *Communications of the ACM*, (7):701, 1964.

Floyd, R., and Rivest, R.L. "Algorithm 489 (Select)," *Communications of the ACM*, 18(3):173, March 1975.

Floyd, R., and Rivest, R.L. "Expected Time Bounds for Selection," *Communications of the ACM*, 18(3), March 1975.

Ford, L.R., and Fulkerson, D.R. *Flows in Networks*, Princeton, N.J.: Princeton University Press, 1972.

Foster, C.C. "A Generalization of AVL Trees," *Communications of the ACM*, 16(8), August 1973.

Frederickson, G. "Data Structures for On-Line Updating of Minimum Spanning Trees, with Applications," *SIAM Journal on Computing*, 14(4):781–98, November 1985.

Frederickson, G. "Fast Algorithms for Shortest Paths in Planar Graphs with Applications," *SIAM Journal on Computing*, 16(6):1004–22, December 1987.

Frederickson, G. "Implicit Data Structures for Weighted Elements," *Information and Control*, 66(1–2):61–82, July–August 1985.

Gajewska, H., and Tarjan, R. "Deques with Heap Order," *Information Processing Letters*, 22(4):197–200, April 1986.

Gabow, H.N. "Two Algorithms for Generating Weighted Spanning Trees in Order," *SIAM Journal on Computing*, 6(1):139–150, 1977.

Galil, Z. "Real-time algorithms for string-matching and palindrome recognition," *Proceedings of the Eighth Annual ACM Symposium on Theory of Computing*, pp. 161–173, 1976.

Garey, M.R., Graham, R.L., and Ullman, J.D. "Worst-case analysis of memory allocation algorithms," *Proceedings of the Fourth Annual ACM Symposium on Theory of Computing*, pp. 143–150, 1972.

Garey, M.R., and Johnson, D.S. "The complexity of near-optimal graph coloring," *Journal of the ACM*, 23(1):43–49, 1976.

Garey, M.R., Johnson, D.S., and Stockmeyer, L. "Some simplified $\mathcal{NP}$-complete problems," *Proceedings of the Sixth Annual ACM Symposium on Theory of Computing*, pp. 47–63, 1974.

Gerasch, T. "An Insertion Algorithm for a Minimal Internal Path Length Binary Search Tree," *Communications of the ACM*, 31(5):579–85, May 1988.

Glaser, H. "Lazy Garbage Collection," *Software Practice and Experience*, 17(1):1–4, January 1987.

Goller, N. "Hybrid Data Structure Defined by Indirection," *Computer Journal*, 28(1):44–53, February 1985.

Golomb, S.W., and Baumert, L.D. "Backtrack Programming," *Journal of the ACM*, 12:516, 1965.

Gonnet, G., and Munro, J. "Heaps on Heaps," *SIAM Journal on Computing*, 15(4):964–71, November 1986.

Good, I.J. "A Five-Year Plan for Automatic Chess," In E. Dale and D. Michie (eds.), *Machine Intelligence*, Volume 2, pp. 89–118. New York: American Elsevier, 1968.

Goodman, S.E. and Hedetniemi, S.T. *Introduction to the Design and Analysis of Algorithms*, New York: McGraw-Hill, 1977.

Gordon, G. *System Simulation*, Englewood Cliffs, N.J.: Prentice-Hall, 1969.

Gotlieb, C., and Gotlieb, L. *Data Types and Data Structures*, Englewood Cliffs, N.J.: Prentice-Hall, 1978.

Graham, R.L. "Bounds on multiprocessing timing anomalies," *SIAM Journal of Applied Math*, 17(2):416–29, 1969.

Gries, D. *Compiler Construction for Digital Computers*, New York: Wiley, 1971.

Hancock, L., and Krieger, M. *The C Primer*, New York: McGraw-Hill, 1982.

Hantler, S.L., and King, J.C. "An Introduction to Proving the Correctness of Programs," *ACM Computing Surveys*, 8(3):331–53.

Harary, F. *Graph Theory*, Reading, Mass.: Addison-Wesley, 1969.

Harbison, S., and Steele, G. *C: A Reference Manual (2nd ed.)*, Englewood Cliffs, N.J.: Prentice-Hall, 1987.

Harrison, M.C. *Data Structures and Programming*, Glenview, Ill.: Scott Foresman, 1973.

Hinds, J. "An Algorithm for Locating Adjacent Storage Blocks in the Buddy System," *Communications of the ACM*, 18(4), April, 1975.

Hirschberg, D.S. "A Class of Dynamic Memory Allocation Algorithms," *Communications of the ACM*, 16(10):615–18, October 1973.

Hirschberg, D.S. "An Insertion Technique for One-Sided Height-Balanced Trees," *Communications of the ACM*, 19(8), August 1976.

Hoare, C.A.R. "Quicksort," *Comput. J.*, 5:10–15, 1962.

Hopcroft, J.E., and Tarjan, R.E. "Dividing a graph into triconnected components," *SIAM Journal on Computing*, 2(3):135–57, 1973.

Hopcroft, J.E., and Tarjan, R.E. "Efficient Algorithms for Graph Manipulation," *Communications of the ACM*, 16(6):372–78, 1973.

Hopcroft, J.E., and Ullman, J.D. *Formal Languages and Their Relation to Automata*, Reading, Mass.: Addison-Wesley, 1969.

Hopcroft, J.E., and Ullman, J.D. "Set merging algorithms," *SIAM Journal on Computing*, 2(4):294–303, 1973.

Horowitz, E., and Sahni, S. "Computing partitions with applications to the knapsack problem," *Journal of the ACM*, 21(2):277–92, 1974.

Horowitz, E., and Sahni, S. *Fundamentals of Data Structures*, Woodland Hills, Calif.: Computer Science Press, 1976.

Horowitz, E., and Sahni, S. *Algorithms: Design and Analysis*, Potomac, Md.: Computer Science, 1977.

Huang, B., and Langston, M. "Practical In-place Merging," *Communications of the ACM*, 31(3):348–52, March 1988.

Huang, J.C. "An Approach to Program Testing," *ACM Comput. Surv.*, 7(3), September 1975.

Huffman, D. "A Method for the Construction of Minimum Redundancy Codes," *Proc. IRE*, 40, 1952.

Hughes, J.K., and Michton, J.I. *A Structured Approach to Programming*, Englewood Cliffs, N.J.: Prentice-Hall, 1977.

Iyenger, S., and Chang, H. "Efficient Algorithms to Create and Mantain Balanced and Threaded Binary Search Trees," *Software Practice and Experience*, 15(10):925–42, October 1985.

Jalote, P. "Synthesizing Implementations of Abstract Data Types from Axiomatic Specifications," *Software Practice and Experience*, 17(11):847–58, November 1987.

Johnson, D.S. "Fast allocation algorithms," *Proceedings of the Thirteenth Annual Symposium on Switching and Automata Theory*, pp. 144–54, 1972.

Johnson, D.S. "Worst-case behavior of graph coloring algorithms," *Proceedings of the Fifth Southeastern Conference on Combinatorics, Graph Theory, and Computing*, pp. 513–28. Winnipeg, Canada: Utilitas Mathematica Publishing, 1974.

Kelley, A., and Pohl, I. *A Book on C (2d ed.)*, Benjamin Cummings, 1990.

Kernighan, B., and Ritchie, D. *The C Programming Language (2nd ed.)*, Englewood Cliffs, NJ: Prentice-Hall, 1988.

Kernighan, B., and Plauger, R. *Software Tools*, Reading, Mass.: Addison-Wesley, 1976.

Kernighan, B., and Plauger, P.J. *The Elements of Programming Style*, New York: McGraw-Hill, 1970.

Kernighan, B., and Plauger, R. *The Elements of Programming Style (2nd ed.)*, New York: McGraw-Hill, 1978.

Kernighan, B., and Plauger, P.J. "Programming Style: Examples and Counter Examples," *ACM Comput. Surv.*, 6(4), December 1974.

Kernighan, B., and Ritchie, D. *The C Programming Language (2nd ed.)*, Englewood Cliffs, N.J.: Prentice-Hall Software Series, 1988.

Knowlton, K. "A Fast Storage Allocator," *Communications of the ACM*, 8(10), October 1965.

Knuth, D. "Optimum Binary Search Trees," *Acta Informatica*, 1:14–25, 1971.

Knuth, D. *The Art of Computer Programming, Volume I: Fundamental Algorithms (2nd ed.)*, Reading, Mass.: Addison-Wesley, 1973.

Knuth, D. *The Art of Computer Programming, Volume III: Sorting and Searching*, Reading, Mass.: Addison-Wesley, 1973.

Knuth, D. "Structured Programming with Goto Statements," *ACM Comput. Surv.*, 6(4):261, December 1974.

Knuth, D. *Fundamental Algorithms (2d ed)*, Reading, Mass.: Addison-Wesley, 1973.

Knuth, D. *Sorting and Searching*, Reading, Mass.: Addison-Wesley, 1973.

Knuth, D. "Big Omicron and Big Omega and Big Theta." *SIGACT News*, 8(2):18–24, 1976.

Knuth, D. "The Complexity of Songs," *SIGACT News*, 9(2):17–24, 1977.

Kosaraju, S.R. "Insertions and Deletions in One-Sided Height Balanced Trees," *Communications of the ACM*, 21(3), March, 1978.

Kruse, R. *Data Structures and Program Design (2nd ed.)*, Englewood Cliffs, NJ: Prentice-Hall, 1987.

Larson, P. "Dynamic Hash Tables," *Communications of the ACM*, 31(4):446–57, April 1988.

Ledgard, H., with Tauer, J. *C with Excellence*, Indianapolis, Ind.: Hayden Books, 1987.

Lewis, T.G., and Smith, M.Z. *Applying Data Structures*, Boston: Houghton Mifflin, 1976.

Lockyer, K.G. *An Introduction to Critical Data Analysis*, London: Pitman, 1964.

Lockyer, K.G. *Critical Path Analysis: Problems and Solutions*, London: Pitman, 1966.

Lodi, E., and Luccio, F. "Split Sequence Hash Search," *Information Processing Letters*, 20(3):131–36, April 1985.

Lum, U.Y. "General Performance Analysis of Key-to-Address Transformation Methods using an Abstract File Concept," *Communications of the ACM*, 16(10):603, October 1973.

Lum, U.Y., and Yuen, P.S.T. "Additional Results on Key-to-Address Transform Techniques: A Fundamental Performance Study on Large Existing Formatted Files," *Communications of the ACM*, 15(11):996, November 1972.

Lum, U.Y., Yuen, P.S.T., and Dodd, M. "Key-to-Address Transform Techniques: A Fundamental Performance Study on Large Existing Formatted Files," *Communications of the ACM*, 14:228, 1971.

Maekinen, E. "On the Rotation Distance of Binary Trees," *Information Processing Letters*, 26(5):271–72, January 1988.

Manna, Z., and Shamir, A. "The Optimal Approach to Recursive Programs," *Communications of the ACM*, 20(11), November 1977.

Martin, J. *Data Types and Data Structures*, Englewood Cliffs, NJ: Prentice-Hall, 1986.

Maurer, H.A., and Williams, M.R. *A Collection of Programming Problems and Techniques*, Englewood Cliffs, N.J.: Prentice-Hall, 1972.

Maurer, H.A. *Data Structures and Programming Techniques*, Englewood Cliffs, N.J.: Prentice-Hall, 1977.

Maurer, W., and Lewis, T. "Hash Table Methods," *Comput. Surv.*, 7(1):5–19, March 1975.

McCabe, J. "On Serial Files with Relocatable Records," *Oper. Res.*, 12:609–18, 1965.

Merritt, S. "An Inverted Taxonomy of Sorting Algorithms," *Communications of the ACM*, 28(1):96–99, January 1985.

Millspaugh, A. *Business Programming in C*, The Dryden Press, 1993.

Moffat, A., and Takaoka, T. "An All-Pairs Shortest Path Algorithm with Expected Time $O(n^2 \log n)$," *SIAM Journal on Computing*, 16(6):1023–31, December 1987.

Morgan, C. "Data Refinement by Miracles," *Information Processing Letters*, 26(5):243–46, January 1988.

Morris, R. "Scatter Storage Techniques," *Communications of the ACM*, 11(1):38–44, January 1968.

Morris, J.H., Jr., and Pratt, V.R. "A Linear Pattern-Matching Algorithm." *Tech. Rep.*, 40. University of California, Berkeley, 1970.

Motzkin, D. "Meansort," *Communications of the ACM*, 26(4):250–51, April 1983.

Nielson, N.R. "Dynamic Memory Allocation in Computer Simulation," *Communications of the ACM*, 20(11), November 1977.

Nievergelt, J., and Farrar, J.C. "What machines can and cannot do." *ACM Computing Surveys*, 4(2):81–96, 1972.

Nievergelt, J., and Reingold, E.M. "Binary Search Trees of Bounded Balance," *SIAM Journal on Computing*, 2:33, 1973.

Nievergelt, J., and Wong, C.K. "On Binary Search Trees," *Proc. IFIP Congr. 71*, North-Holland, Amsterdam, 1972, pp. 91–98.

Nijenhuis, A., and Wilf, H.S. *Combinatorial Algorithms*, New York: Academic, 1975.

Nilsson, N. *Problem-Solving Methods in Artificial Intelligence*, New York: McGraw-Hill, 1971.

Nipkow, T. "Non-Deterministic Data Types: Models and Implementations," *Acta Informatica*, 22(6):629–61, March 1986.

Ore, O. *Theory of Graphs*, vol. 38: Providence, R.I.: American Mathematical Society, 1962.

Ore, O. *Graphs and Their Uses*, New York: Random House, Syracuse, N.Y.: Singer, 1963.

Page, E.S., and Wilson, L.B. *Information Representation and Manipulation in a Computer*, London: Cambridge, 1973.

Pagli, L. "Self-Adjusting Hash Tables," *Information Processing Letters*, 21(1):23–25, July 1985.

Peterson, J.L., and Norman, T.A. "Buddy Systems," *Communications of the ACM*, 20(6), June 1977.

Pohl, I. "A Sorting Problem and its Complexity," *Communications of the ACM*, 15(6), June 1972.

Powell, M. "Strongly Typed User Interfaces in an Abstract Data Store," *Software Practice and Experience*, 17(4):241–66, April 1987.

Pratt, T.W. *Programming Languages: Design and Implementation*, Englewood Cliffs, N.J.: Prentice-Hall, 1975.

Prim, R. "Shortest Connection Networks and Some Generalizations," *Bell System Technical Journal*, 36:1389–1401, 1957.

Purdom, P.W., and Stigler, S.M. "Statistical Properties of the Buddy System," *Communications of the ACM*, 17(4), October 1970.

Purdum, J., Leslie, T., and Stegemoller, A. *C Programmer's Library*, Que Corporation, 1984.

Rabin, M.O. "Complexity of Computations," *Communications of the ACM*, 20(9):625–33, 1977.

Reingold, E.M. "On the Optimality of Some Set Merging Algorithms," *Journal of the ACM*, 19(4):649–59, 1972.

Reingold, E.M., Nievergelt, J., and Deo, N. *Combinatorial Algorithms: Theory and Practice*, Englewood Cliffs, N.J.: Prentice-Hall, 1977.

Rich, R.P. *Internal Sorting Methods Illustrated with PL/I Programs*, Englewood Cliffs, N.J.: Prentice-Hall, 1972.

Rivest, R.L., and Knuth, D.E. "Bibliography 26: Computer Sorting," *Comput. Rev.*, 13:283, 1972.

Roberts, Fred S. *Discrete Mathematical Models*, Englewood Cliffs, N.J.: Prentice-Hall, 1976.

Roberts, Fred S. *Applied Combinatorics*, Englewood Cliffs, N.J.: Prentice-Hall, 1984.

Sager, T. "A Polynomial Time Generator for Minimal Perfect Hash Functions," *Communications of the ACM*, 28(5):523–32, May 1985.

Sahni, S.K. "Approximate Algorithms for the 0/1 Knapsack Problem," *Journal of the ACM*, 22(1):115–24, 1975.

Sahni, S.K. "Algorithms for Scheduling Independent Tasks," *Journal of the ACM*, 23(1):116–27, 1976.

Sahni, S.K., and Gonzalez, T. "𝒫-Complete Approximation Problems," *Journal of the ACM*, 23(3):555–65, 1976.

Savage, J.E. *The Complexity of Computing*, New York: Wiley, 1976.

Schorr, H., and Waite, W.M. "An Efficient Machine-Independent Procedure for Garbage Collection in Various List Structures," *Communications of the ACM*, 10(8):501–506, August 1967.

Sedgewick, R. "Quicksort," *Report no. STAN-CS-75-492*, Department of Computer Science, Stanford, Calif., May 1975.

Sedgewick, R. "Permutation Generation Methods," *ACM Comput. Surv.*, 9(2):137, June 1977.

Sedgewick, R. "Quicksort with Equal Keys," *SIAM Journal on Computing* 6(2):240–267, 1977.

Sedgewick, R. *Algorithms*, Reading, Mass.: Addison-Wesley, 1983.

Shell, D.L. "A High Speed Sorting Procedure," *Communications of the ACM*, 2(7), July 1959.

Shen, K.K., and Peterson, J.L. "A Weighted Buddy Method for Dynamic Storage Allocation," *Communications of the ACM*, 17(10):558–62, October 1974.

Shore, J. "On the External Storage Fragmentation Produced by First-Fit and Best-Fit Allocation Strategies," *Communications of the ACM*, 18(8):433, August 1975.

Shore, J. Anomalous Behavior of the Fifty-Percent Rule in Dynamic Memory Allocation," *Communications of the ACM*, 20(11), November 1977.

Sleater, D., and Tarjan, R. "Biased Search Trees," *SIAM Journal on Computing*, 14(3):545–68, August 1985.

Sleator, D., and Tarjan, R. "Self-Adjusting Heaps," *SIAM Journal on Computing*, 15(1):52–69, February 1986.

Sprugnoli, R. "Perfect Hashing Functions: A Single Probe Retrieving Method for Static Sets," *Communications of the ACM*, 20(11), November 1977.

Stanat, D.F., and McAllister, D.F. *Discrete Mathematics in Computer Science*, Englewood Cliffs, N.J.: Prentice-Hall, 1977.

Stephenson, C.J. "A Method for Constructing Binary Search Trees by Making Insertions at the Root," *IBM Research Report RC 6298*, IBM Thomas J. Watson Research Center, Yorktown Heights, N.Y., 1976.

Stout, Q., and Warren, B. "Tree Rebalancing in Optimal Time and Space," *Communications of the ACM*, 29(9):902–908, September 1986.

Stroustrup, B. *The C++ Programming Language*, Reading, Mass.: Addison-Wesley, 1986.

Tarjan, R.E. "Depth-First Search and Linear Graph Algorithms," *SIAM Journal on Computing,* 1(2):146–60, 1972.

Tarjan, R.E. "On the Efficiency of a Good but Not Linear Set Union Algorithm," *Journal of the ACM,* 22(2):215–25, 1975.

Tarjan, R.E. *Data Structures and Network Algorithms,* SIAM, 1983.

Tarjan, R.E. "Algorithm Design," *Communications of the ACM,* 30(3):204–12, March 1987.

Tenenbaum, A. "Simulations of Dynamic Sequential Search Algorithms," *Communications of the ACM,* 21(9), September 1978.

Tenenbaum, A., and Widder, E. "A Comparison of First-Fit Allocation Strategies," *Proc. ACM 78,* December 1978.

Tenenbaum, A., and Augenstein, M. *Data Structures Using Pascal (2nd ed.),* Englewood Cliffs, N.J.: Prentice-Hall, 1986.

Touretsky, D.S. *LISP, A Gentle Introduction to Symbolic Computation,* New York: Harper & Row, 1984.

Tremblay, J.P., and Sorenson, P.G. *An Introduction to Data Structures with Applications,* New York: McGraw-Hill, 1976.

Tsakalidis, A. "AVL Trees for Localized Search," *Information and Control,* 67(1–3):173–94, October–December 1985.

Tucker, A. *Applied Combinatorics,* New York: Wiley, 1980.

Van Emden, M.H. "Increasing Efficiency of Quicksort," *Communications of the ACM,* 13:563–67, 1970.

Van Tassel, D. *Program Style, Design, Efficiency, Debugging, and Testing (2nd. ed.),* Englewood Cliffs, N.J.: Prentice-Hall, 1978.

Vuillemin, J. "A Unifying Look at Data Structures," *Communications of the ACM,* 23(4):229–39, April 1980.

Walker, W.A., and Gotlieb, C.C. "A Top Down Algorithm for Constructing Nearly Optimal Leixcographic Trees," in R. Read (ed.), *Graph Theory and Computing,* New York: Academic, 1972.

Wegner, P. "Modifications of Aho and Ullman's correctness proof of Warshall's algorithm," *SIGACT News,* 6(1):32–35, 1974.

Weinberg, G. *The Psychology of Computer Programming,* New York: Van Nostrand, 1971.

Wickelgren, W.A. *How to Solve Problems: Elements of a Theory of Problems and Problem Solving,* San Francisco: Freeman, 1974.

Williams, J. "Algorithm 232 (Heapsort)," *Communications of the ACM,* 7(6):347–48, June 1964.

Wirth, N., "Program Development by Stepwise Refinement," *Communications of the ACM,* 14(4):221–27, April 1971.

Wirth, N. *Systematic Programming: An Introduction,* Englewood Cliffs, N.J.: Prentice-Hall, 1973.

Wirth, N. "On the Composition of Well-Structured Programs," *ACM Comput. Surv.,* 6(4), December 1974.

Wirth, N. *Algorithms + Data Structures = Programs,* Englewood Cliffs, N.J.: Prentice-Hall, 1976.

Wood, D. "The Towers of Brahma and Hanoi Revisited," *Journal of Recreational Mathematics*, 14:17–24, (1981–2).

Yao, A.C. "On the average behavior of set merging algorithms," *Proceedings of the Eighth Annual ACM Symposium on Theory of Computing*, pp. 192–95, 1976.

Yourdon, E. *Techniques of Program Structure and Design*, Englewood Cliffs, N.J.: Prentice-Hall, 1975.

Index